D1484009

BITTERSWEET

The Story of the Heath Candy Co.

By
Richard J. Heath
with Ray Elliott

Tales
Urbana, Illinois

To my parents
Skiv and Madeline Heath

INTRODUCTION

It was announced through the national media in January 1989 that Leaf, Inc., a Finnish conglomerate, had purchased the remaining 51 percent of the family-owned stock of the Heath candy company, one of the nation's best-known candy and ice cream companies. With that purchase, Leaf became sole owner of the company L.S. Heath and his two oldest sons, Bayard and Everett, had started in a little ice cream parlor and confectionery on the west side of the courthouse square in Robinson, Illinois, in 1914.

A picture in the *Robinson Daily News* showed John J. Morris Jr., the chief executive officer of the Heath company and the founder's grandson, giving the key to James A. Hanlon, the new president of Leaf, Inc., and, ironically, a former Heath executive, in a ceremony to mark the end of the Heath family's involvement in the company—the end of a seventy-five-year story.

Morris, the only family member still actively involved with the company when it failed to stave off Leaf's takeover bid, left the company and, with his mother, Mary Morris, and aunt, Ruby Dowling, majority owners of the stock, took the thirty-five million dollars from the proceeds of the sale and opened a venture capital firm on the east side of the courthouse square in the center of Robinson soon after the sale was final. Chairman of the board and principal of the venture capital company, then called Bay-Mor Investments, Inc., Morris said he formed "the Heath investment partnership pool" to help bankroll relatively small companies in need of capital to assist them in avoiding what happened to the Heath company and to spur economic development in "America's heartland."

What happened to the Heath company happens to most family-owned businesses (and roughly 95 percent of all businesses in the United States are family-owned) sooner or later. They go out of business or are taken over by another company. Family-owned businesses are reported to have an average life span of only twenty-four years. Most that don't make it nearly as long as the Heath company have similar problems: Does George Jr. or cousin James take over as CEO? Does a disagreement between John and his sister, Carol, affect a major business decision? Does Kenneth have an equal position even though he doesn't have the same business know-how as that of his relatives? What happens when the family business talent and interest thins out and a non-family administrator comes on board? How do quality non-family employees stay on with the prospect of future advancement amid family squabbling? And how well are individual, as well as corporate, finances handled and maintained?

The Heath company had all of these problems and more. They were compounded by intense jealousies, meddling spouses, changing values and plain, old-fashioned greed.

In the aftermath of the company's stormy history, Morris enlisted the aid of three former Heath personnel to assist in the venture capital endeavor. Former president Ronald K. Bailey Sr. became the venture capital firm's president and chief executive officer. His son, Ronald Jr., became the firm's chief financial officer, and Marcia Elder became the firm's secretary. Located far from the financial centers of the eastern megalopolis, Chicago and California, Bay-Mor became a small-town venture capital firm with a tenth of the money most people in the business consider necessary for survival.

Despite Morris' intentions and the firm's high-sounding goals, things didn't go as well as expected from the beginning. Bailey Sr. retired at the age of fifty in December 1990. "I got sick of hearing the same old story," he said. "'If we only had the capital, we could make it.' Everybody is undercapitalized." Bailey Jr. left the firm and opened his own accounting firm. Morris changed the name of Bay-Mor, Inc., to Heath Investment Capital, Inc., and built a lavish new office near the local country club.

While location and limited finances may make things difficult for the firm, Robinson, where the Heath family developed the internationally known Heath English Toffee Bar, has been the site of other survival or success stories. Robinson is where author James Jones wrote much of *From Here to Eternity*, one of the best-remembered World War II novels. And Robinson is where Richard J. "Dick" Heath promoted a Professional Golf Association (PGA) tournament in the smallest town ever to host one.

Dick Heath is the son of one of the Heath company founders. When his father, Everett, died in 1951 and Dick had just turned twenty years old, he became a member of the Heath company board of directors. After graduating from the University of Illinois and serving a two-year hitch in the U.S. Army, he became a full-time employee of the Heath company and served as vice president and treasurer until he left the company in 1969 after an internal struggle that left the family divided and headed directly for the Leaf buyout years later.

This is the story of the Heath family that Dick heard, observed and experienced from his early recollections to the end of the family business in 1989 with the passing of that key and that can be ascertained from material in the public record. Other family members undoubtedly have a different version. Dick's grandfather, Lawrence Seymour (L.S.), told his version in a book published privately just before his death in 1956. That book has supplied much of the early family history and perspective in what follows. Bayard Sr., Dick's uncle, started to write his version but died before he finished it. Other family members have talked about writing their versions. No one has to date.

This version is the story of the Heath family business, from the early realization of one man's dream to the later crumbling of that dream's legacy. Most people can identify with aspects of this story in their own lives, whether they have been involved in running a family business or have just been part of a family. All the petty jealousies, the driving ambitions and the family infighting are familiar to people everywhere.

It is, of course, the story of the struggles encountered in the everyday running of a major business and how a family that seemingly started out so close came unraveled. But most of all, it is the story of the timing and luck it takes for a family business to go as far and stay in business as long as did L.S. Heath and Sons, Inc.

— RAY ELLIOTT
DECEMBER 1994

1

Five-year-old Dick Heath watched his father get up from the supper table and walk slowly toward the coat rack just inside the front door of the two-story frame house. Everett Heath, or Skiv as nearly everyone called him, was a stocky man of forty whose slicked-back hair had been white for nearly ten years. He was one of four brothers who, together with their father, owned and operated the family business as a partnership called L.S. Heath and Sons.

"Get your coat on, son," Skiv said as he put an arm into the sleeve of his overcoat. "It's time to go."

The time was twenty minutes 'til six on a Sunday evening in the early fall of 1936. A hot, dry summer that had scorched the Midwest and made sleeping a sweaty, fitful nightmare had abruptly given way to fall.

Furnaces kicked on and stoves were fired up to warm the sitting rooms and protect against the window-rattling wind. "The Jack Benny Show" came on the radio at six o'clock. Families everywhere with radios gathered around to listen.

His father stood by the door, waiting for Dick to get his coat. The boy walked reluctantly towards the door, dragging his feet as he went. He couldn't imagine anything worse than going out with his father on Sunday evening to collect money for overdue home-delivery milk bills, especially when it was warm inside and his mother and sister got to listen to the radio.

But his father said that was what was expected of the Heath men. They had to make enough money for company expenses and have enough left over to keep the company going and the families together.

Skiv hated for Sunday evening to roll around, too, because he sympathized with those who owed the company money. It was the middle of the Depression, and people had a reason for not paying on time. "Ready for this, son?" Skiv said, parking the car in front of the first house, taking his account book and getting out of the car.

"Why don't we stay home with Mother and Joan?" Dick asked as they walked through the yard on narrow planks to the front door of a small bungalow with one step leading up to the small porch. "I don't like to go out with you when it's so cold."

"I don't like to go out at all," Skiv said and knocked on the door. "But somebody has to collect these past-due accounts or we'd be out of business."

A yellow porch light came on, and a woman with a small baby slung over her hip and one arm wrapped around the baby opened the door. She peered out into the night. "Oh, hello, Mr. Heath," she said. "I couldn't think who'd be knockin' on my door this time of evenin'."

"I've come about the milk bill, ma'am, uh, it's $8.45 now," Skiv said, turning the account book so the woman could see how far she was behind. "Can you pay me tonight?"

The woman stared intently at the book for a full minute. Skiv stood patiently, started to say something but changed his mind. "I was going to pay the driver, Mr. Heath," the woman said, a slight whine in her voice. "But I just had to pay my heat bill. You know there ain't no work now that cold weather's here. What can I do? I need heat, and I need milk for the little ones. If it was just me an' Jim, I wouldn't mind doin' without milk."

"Can you give me anything on the bill tonight?" Skiv asked.

"Not tonight. You know I would if I could. Honest, Mr. Heath."

Looking behind the woman and inside the house, Dick saw a man sitting quietly in the dimly lighted living room, two other children huddled close to him. The man kept his eyes lowered but appeared to be listening intently.

"You just pay me when you can," Skiv said. "Just remember, though, we've got to pay our bills, too."

"Thank you, Mr. Heath. Maybe Jim'll find work soon. You doin' any hirin' at Heath's?"

"Not right now, ma'am."

"You keep Jim in mind if you do, Mr. Heath. Ain't right for a man not to have work so he can take care of his family."

"That's right," Skiv said in agreement and smiled. "We appreciate your business."

The rest of the night was a repeat of that first encounter in one way or another. Sometimes Skiv collected money; sometimes he didn't. Wherever they went, the two heard about how hard it was to make ends meet. But whether he collected the bill or didn't get a cent, Skiv always smiled and thanked everybody for doing business with the Heaths. These Sunday evening collections with his father were Dick's early introduction to the world of business.

It was only the year before that he had first gotten involved in a company function. It had started with an argument between his father and mother. The company sponsored a women's softball team, and Skiv wanted to take him to the

Robinson park where the Heath team was playing one evening.

"Hell, no, you're not taking him down there," Madeline said, raising her voice and glaring at Skiv. "He could get hurt."

"He could get hurt here, Madeline," Skiv said. "He could—"

"You're not taking him."

"I'm not only taking him," Skiv said defiantly, "but he's going to be the batboy. The girls want him."

Dick was bewildered. He didn't know why his parents were shouting at each other. He didn't know what a batboy was. But the next thing he knew, he was at the softball game. And he was the batboy. One of the young women took him aside and explained what he was to do. Skiv was talking to the rest of the team as they rejoined the group, Dick dragging a bat behind him.

"I guaranteed Madeline that the kid wouldn't get hurt," Skiv said to the team. "Don't get me in trouble, girls."

The women laughed and took the field. Dick looked around in the twilight of the summer evening as the ball game was about to start. Players were chattering back and forth at each other. Spectators were scattered along both baselines and behind the chicken-wire screen, shouting words of encouragement to both teams. A feeling of excitement surged through Dick as he had never felt before.

He ran and got bats as he had been told, although he forgot one once when the lanky first baseman hit a towering fly ball down the right-field line and sprinted around the bases, little puffs of dirt kicking up from her shoes with each stride, only to have the umpire signal it foul. Dick's eyes were still on the woman when she jogged back to the plate and picked up her own bat.

Each time the team was at bat, he kept one eye on the batter and the other eye on the rest of the team as he paraded up and down in front of them. He knew he loved them; he just couldn't figure out which one he loved most. To him, they were all lovely and adorable. He only stood as high as the bottom on their shorts and almost went out of sight when he was in the pack of them. They always tousled his hair or had a pleasant word for him as he moved along.

"You girls be careful to see that little Dickie doesn't get run over," the family patriarch L.S. Heath called out from behind the fence. He was a five-foot-six-inches tall, spry, balding man of sixty-five years who watched over his grandson with the same sense of pride and responsibility that he did his company and the rest of his family.

After the game, everybody told Dick he had done a great job. He'd had the time of his life. The attention, the excitement, the adrenaline rushing through his body had all felt good. Then a fight broke out. Everybody crowded out by third base, hollering and screaming. One of the players grabbed him and took him to his father's 1931 Ford Coupe. Dick didn't know what to think for a while, but he saw his father laughing when he got to the car.

"Those girls sure got riled up," Skiv said. "Thought things were going to get out of control there for a minute. Dad told 'em if they didn't break it up right then, he'd fire the lot of them. That stopped it. What did you think of the ball game, son?"

"It was great. Can I come again?"

"We'll see what your mother says. She may tan the both of us. But can't that Ione Syveston really whip that ball in there underhanded? Isn't she some pitcher?"

"She's great, Dad. They're all great," Dick said, thinking about the evening. It would have been even better if his father would have given him some money. Skiv was tight with money, though, so there was no pay for his work. But Dick knew that evening that he was going to work for the company some day and that he would move up in the company. He had heard about working for the company before that, but he didn't understand how much he would like it until the softball game.

With his realization, he remembered a time a year or so earlier when the family was eating supper one evening. The telephone rang, and his father got up to answer it. "It's probably that somebody's dry ice has melted with a five-gallon can of ice cream," he said as he picked up the receiver.

While Skiv talked, Dick crawled up and bit him on the leg to get his attention. Skiv was preoccupied with the conversation and apparently didn't see his son, but by reflex kicked him part-way across the room. Dick bounced off the wall, wailing; Madeline stood in the center of the room, screaming at Skiv.

"Look what you've done," she said, lifting Dick in her arms and laying his head on her shoulder. "There, there. Mother has you now. Everything's all right. How could you kick your son like that, you bastard?"

"If he grows up some day and works at the plant," Skiv said as he hung up the telephone, "he'll get kicked a damn sight harder than that."

"I hope he never has to work at the plant," Madeline said. "You've changed. You've all changed since you sold the store and moved out to the plant. I don't want him to be like that. I don't — "

"Where else is he going to work in these times? He's darn lucky to have a family that has a plant for him to work in."

That was the end of the conversation. Skiv was a tough man, living in rough times. He was preparing his son for the business world. If Dick fouled up in those early years, Skiv would yank his ears. What Skiv said was the law. No questions asked. Dick learned discipline. His sister, Joan, on the other hand, could have set the house on fire and Skiv wouldn't have said a word to her. The Heath men went into the business; the Heath women took care of the house and the family.

L.S., or Father Heath as most of the family called him, saw that the family and the business ran that way. He knew what was happening in each of his children's lives and their families, and, in his own way, was generous to them all. He never forgot any of his grandchildren's birthdays and was there to give Dick the initial J to go with the name Richard at his birth. L.S. thought the boy should at least have an initial.

On Dick's seventh birthday, he was playing in the front yard with two friends when he saw L.S. drive his Model T Ford sedan up to the house, stop and get out.

"Happy birthday, Dickie," he said, removing his wallet from the breast pocket of his suit and taking a bill from it. "I wanted to give you five dollars for your birthday."

"Thank you, Father Heath," Dick said, taking the money. "That's very kind of you."

The old man saw Dick's friends watching and a frown crossed his face. "You boys come here," he said, opening his wallet again. "Here is five dollars for each of you. You have a birthday, too, and it would be bad manners for me to give Dickie that money in front of you and not give you any."

He was driving away before either boy recovered enough to do more than mumble thanks. Dick felt a pride swell in him at the kind of man his grandfather was and the way he had made the boys feel. As the Model T rounded the corner, one of the boys said, "Geez, I never had a five-dollar bill before."

Time was that L.S. Heath wouldn't have had five cents to give the boys, never mind five dollars. He often thought about those days.

2

The Heath family moved west in the early 1800s and settled just across the Wabash River and a few miles up river from Vincennes, Indiana. Rennick, the oldest of ten Heath children, was born in Virginia in 1804. Near where the family settled, he squatted on a piece of land and built an inn from native white oak in 1826. Known as the Heath Inn, it was a stage-coach stop on the road from Vincennes to Palestine, Bellair, Greenup and points north and west. The inn had two twenty-square-foot rooms, each with a large native stone fireplace, and two smaller rooms on the east end that were used as bedrooms.

Abraham Lincoln stopped at the inn late one afternoon in 1830 on the way to his family's new home in Illinois. He visited with Rennick for a few minutes, then took the family a mile and a half north on the bank of a small stream called Doe Run Creek. The two men met again in Springfield in 1832 when the Black Hawk War broke out. Both volunteered for service and, with Lincoln's recommendation, Rennick received a commission as a captain.

It wasn't until after he returned from the war that he got around to filing for 78.25 acres under the Homestead Movement. That was in 1833. As the pioneers continued moving west, a settlement grew up around the inn and became known as Heathsville. Many of Rennick's family continued to live in the area. His youngest brother and the youngest of the family, Milton, was born there in 1829 and lived nearby his whole life.

Milton remained unmarried until well into his forties when he married Clomana Ann Cowden, a widow with two children. Her parents, William and Sarah Waldrop, were early pioneers in Crawford County who lived near Palestine, one of the oldest towns in Illinois and an early military fort. Before Illinois became a state in 1818, Fort LaMotte was located on the site of Palestine as a defense against the Indians for the early settlers. The fort was built about the time of the War of 1812.

Crawford County, named after a Revolutionary War soldier and U.S. senator from Georgia, General W.H. Crawford, was organized in 1816 at a legislative session of the Illinois Territory and carved out of what had previously been part of Edwards County. In making Crawford County the eleventh county organized in the territory, the act of the Legislature fixed the county boundary by saying, "Beginning at the north of the Embarras River, and running with said river to the intersection of said line dividing township three and four, north of range eleven west of the second principal meridian; then due north until it strikes the line of upper Canada then to the line that separates this township from Indiana, thence south to the place of beginning, shall constitute a separate county called Crawford, and the seat of justice shall be the house of Edward N. Cullom, until it shall be permanently established."

Cullom bought the land where the fort had stood, and Palestine was laid out from part of this purchase. With statehood for Illinois and the expansion of the westward movement, Palestine was given an important role in the settlement of the state. A United States Land Office was opened there in May 1820 and continued until August 1855. Pioneers passed through the area to purchase or enter land on which they planned to settle. Augustus C. French, Illinois' ninth governor (1846-52) and the first to be reelected, came to Palestine from New Hampshire in 1839 and began his political career as a receiver in the land office and served in the tenth and eleventh general assemblies before being elected governor.

After the death of Clomana Cowden's husband, she took her oldest child, Rose, to live with the Waldrops near Palestine and kept John at home. Some time later, Milton and Clomana were married and lived in the log cabin on the bank of Buck Creek south of Heathsville. The couple had a daughter of their own, Margaret, who was born just after the end of the Civil War. Then on November 29, 1869, Lawrence Seymour Heath, the boy who would become the Heath family patriarch, was born in the cabin. His father was nearly fifty years old at the time.

Eighteen months later, Milton traded for forty acres of land just across the Lawrence County line and built a hewn-log house for his family. He covered the logs with clapboards thirty inches long and split out of white oak. A small ravine divided the land in half. About five acres of it was cleared for cultivation, and the rest stood in timber. It was difficult to scratch out a living on the place. To help feed the family and keep the farm going, Milton sold small sewing machines. When he had the time and needed the money, he'd tuck one of them under his arm and leave on horseback to sell it.

Early in his life, he had kept a store and planned to keep one again. Holding his small son on his lap one day, Milton pointed from the north door of the house to a white sycamore tree. "See that tree?" he asked. "I'm going to build a store out of that tree for you."

He never lived long enough to build the store, though. In fact, he had hardly established the farm when he died on November 19, 1872, ten days before his son's third birthday. Just before Milton died, the family gathered around his death bed. Realizing the desperate situation he was leaving his family with, he tried to do what he could.

"There's some poplar boards up in the loft," he said to Clomana. "You get somebody to make my coffin from them. That'll save you some."

After he died, Clomana asked one of their good neighbors if he would make the coffin.

"Guess I could," Sam Pinkstaff said. "But Milton Heath was too good a man to be buried that way. If I have to, I'll pay for the coffin myself."

That proved to be unnecessary. Clomana made arrangements with the undertaker to trade a little white calf for the coffin and the funeral bill. The family watched the coffin lowered into the ground and the grave filled, then rode home in a two-horse wagon. Alone at home after the funeral with her three children, ages three, six and nine, Clomana stood with her back to the fireplace, warming herself against the fall chill and said, "Oh, Lord, what will we do now?"

Providing for the family was left to her and nine-year-old John. Work was scarce since most farm families did their own work. Clomana took in washing and ironing from a neighbor family when they needed help. She also made quilts for the family for which she was paid a dollar per spool of thread. She bought yarn and knitted mittens and socks for fifty cents a pair.

Later, she managed to acquire a team of horses and an old wagon to haul wood. John helped her cut cord wood and haul it to the grist mill in Russellville three miles to the south.

As he grew older, L.S. helped in any way he could. The first money he earned was fifty cents, two twenty-five-cent pieces, for picking and shelling a two-bushel sack of hickory nuts. He thought highly of the money and how he earned it but hadn't had it long when he almost lost it. One of the boys who attended his school could stand on his head. This impressed the other boys. L.S. wanted to be able to perform the feat and practiced privately by the side of a straw stack. The money fell out of his pocket. He discovered that it was gone and returned to the straw stack, moving the straw around until he found the two missing quarters.

A psychological low point in the family's fight for survival came one morning when L.S. was about seven years old. Everyone got up and found nothing except cornmeal to eat. They were accustomed to making do with what was available, so Clomana made mush and was going to try to fry some for breakfast. But the lid of the stove was cracked, and all the wood they had was either green or wet. She tried to start a fire but was never able to do more than get a brown spot the size of a dime to appear on the wood.

Even later, when the boys were able to find work, things happened that caused emotional setbacks for the family. John, then fifteen, got a job shucking corn for a neighborhood farmer named Uncle Frank Curry. Although L.S. was only nine, he went along to help. On the way to the field early one morning, Jack Bryant from Russellville hailed them.

"I got some bad news, boys," Bryant said. "Rose's boy, Harry, got scalded bad this mornin'."

Harry was their nephew, the one-year-old, first-born son of their sister Rose. She had grown up and married a Cummins and lived nearby. The boys returned home immediately to get their mother and sister Margaret and rushed through the morning to be by the young family's side. When they arrived at the Cummins house, Rose was in a state of shock. The child had been playing on the floor when a pot of boiling coffee had been accidently knocked off the sloping hearth of the stove and splashed all over his curly, blond hair, head and face. His eyes were swollen shut from crying and the boiling coffee, his face scarlet red, pieces of his skin dropping off haphazardly from the scalded areas and his small fingers digging away at the pain when he'd somehow pry them loose from his father's hands. The doctor could do nothing much to help. The family waited in agony until the boy finally died in the middle of the afternoon.

Clomana Heath hadn't been able to attend school and get an education in her youth. Like parents everywhere, she wanted her children to have what she hadn't had the opportunity to secure. So she wanted her kids to go to school. That wasn't possible very long for John, who dropped out of school at twelve to help support the family and allow the younger children to attend.

Even buying books was nearly impossible. Most of the time the children were able to get books from the older children in the district. While he attended rural schools, L.S. had only two books of his own. One was *Harvey's Grammar*. He had needed it when school started but he had no money. Then he trapped a mink one day, stretched and tanned the hide and sold it for eighty cents—the price of the book.

John scolded him for the way he spent the money. "You should've bought something of some use," he said. "An education will never 'mount to a damn."

L.S. bought another book he needed, *McGuffey's Reader*, for $1.60. He earned the money for this book by shucking corn in the mud for forty cents a day. John couldn't understand doing back-breaking work from sunup to sunset for four days and then spending the money for a book. The only other book L.S. ever owned as a child was a small dictionary he earned as a premium by selling visiting cards to his neighbors.

Finding the money or the means to buy clothing was equally difficult for the family. Somehow they'd scrape together enough so L.S. could have one pair of boots a year. His toes would stick out through the front by spring. The boots doubled as skates in the winter when he'd have round-headed tacks put on to fill the soles of the boots, allowing him to skate and save shoe leather at the same time.

Clomana made most of the family's clothing. She would take the wool from sheep to a neighbor woman who would card it, spin it and weave it into a cloth called jeans. The cloth was boiled in a copperas solution to produce a greenish color or boiled with the bark of a dogwood sapling to make a reddish color. This latter method was also used to make ink. It worked well to practice penmanship, but it faded out in a few days and virtually disappeared.

So the family made do. That was quite evident with a pair of britches Clomana made for L.S. one time. She only had half enough of the jeans material of the greenish color for a pair. For the other half, she traded a high chair to another neighbor woman. All the woman had, however, was jeans of the reddish color. The finished product was green in the front and red in the back. While the britches were of different colors, they wore as well as any and caused L.S. no problems because they were slightly unusual.

One pair of britches his mother made him, however, caused L.S. a great deal of humiliation. They were two inches above his boot tops at the time. Either he had outgrown the britches or they had shrunk. His mother would console him when she made a pair too small or he had outgrown them by telling him they would stretch. If she had made them too large, she would tell him they would "draw up." Regardless, he had to wear the britches or wear nothing.

Two young men in dark suits visited the school one day when the young woman teacher called his class up to recite. As the students walked across the floor, L.S. heard the two men laughing at his britches sticking up over his boots. The teacher fought back a smile. His face flushed beet red and shame crashed down on him like a falling star streaking downward and out of the sky.

The strain of Clomana's responsibility to feed and clothe the family and her desire to keep the younger children in school often caused her to talk about her desperate situation and what would happen to them. "I don't know how we're going to make it," she would say. "Looks like I'm going to have to send you to the poor house."

L.S. didn't know what or where the poor house was, but his vivid imagination filled his head with frightful thoughts. As things turned out, the family stayed together and somehow made it by making do with what was available. It cost only a nickel for a lamp chimney to brighten the blaze of the coal oil lamp and provide light for L.S. to study by. But it was a nickel the family needed elsewhere. So the young boy studied by the dim, chimneyless lamp as the smoke drifted upward and escaped through the cracks in the loft and clapboard roof.

Life wasn't pleasant. But despite the hard times, L.S. had a desire to learn and thought about school and education from an early age. What enjoyment he got out of life came from simple things like getting a new lead pencil that cost a penny without an eraser or six new slate pencils that cost a nickel. Receiving a slate that scholars, as students were called in those days, used instead of paper tablets and cost from fifteen to twenty-five cents, according to their size, was also a pleasure.

Real, if only temporary, pleasure came from getting a store-bought ruler for drawing straight lines rather than the usual homemade ones. A girl from his school whose family traded in Vincennes had the first ruler he had ever seen with the company's ad on it. He wanted one like it from the first time he saw the girl at school with it but never thought it would be possible.

School closed at the end of the term, and he forgot about the ruler. Then one day he was walking by the school and saw a window pane was out. He went to the window to look in and saw the ruler on the window sill. Contrary to his mother's teachings to him about the value and necessity of honesty, L.S. took the ruler. For a few days, he kept it hid from his mother. Unable to keep it hidden any longer, he finally slipped the ruler from his hiding place and took it with him when he visited a man splitting rails not far away. The man borrowed the ruler under the pretense of measuring something and refused to give it back.

"I lost this ruler awhile back," the man said, sticking it in his hip pocket. "I been wonderin' what became of it."

L.S. tried protesting but finally gave up and returned

home. He was still filled with guilt when school began in the fall. When he saw the girl, he would look away and avoid her eyes. The feeling was so strong that he only disregarded his mother's teachings once more as he was growing up. That time he and some other boys slipped into a neighbor's watermelon patch and were picking a plump, ripe watermelon when the owner discovered them. He chased the barefooted boys through a burr patch. They hollered out in pain, hopped lamely, but kept going until they got away from the owner.

3

As the young Heath grew older, he began to realize that like the bird that spends almost its entire existence searching for food, the family spent its entire waking hours searching for food and clothing. Family members could think of little else and found satisfaction in meeting their barest needs. Much of their food came from wild game and fruits. Without a rifle or shotgun of any kind, the game was restricted to what the family dog would catch, usually a rabbit, or tree for them in a hollow log. Then someone would twist a forked stick around the rabbit's leg and pull the rabbit out of the hole and grab it.

Rabbits will not defend themselves. One day L.S. reached in a hole to grab a rabbit and instead saw a groundhog, which will defend itself. L.S. was able to withdraw his hand and move quickly away from the tree without being injured. But he was frightened and was more cautious afterwards.

Wild fruits were plentiful but limited to a few varieties. Grapes and blackberries were most abundant. Clomana preserved the grapes by filling a glazed jar and then covering them with sorghum molasses. She canned the blackberries and sealed the lids on with sealing wax.

With only five acres of tillable land out of the forty acres, little was left over after feeding the team. When John was older, the family would sometimes rent ground from a neighbor. Not only was that ground usually the least productive available, but the boys had only a breaking plow and a double shovel to get the crops planted. Nor was the equipment they had in the best condition. If the harness broke, they mended it with hickory bark pealed from a sapling.

From the time L.S. began shucking corn when he was nine years old, he was more and more expected to help the family make a living. He and his sister were given the job of cutting corn stalks each spring so the ground could be prepared for a new crop. They chopped off the stalks with hoes, then gathered the stalks in their arms and piled them in stacks to be burned. The stacks were usually burned at night with everyone standing nearby watching the flames shoot toward the sky.

After the ground had been prepared for planting and the rows were laid off with a small turning plow, John dropped three grains of corn to the hill by hand every three and a half feet or so. L.S. followed along with a hoe and covered the seed corn. He also learned to drop corn, and at twelve years old he became good enough that he was hired to plant corn for neighbors. For this work he received fifteen cents a day, working from sunup to sundown with an hour out for dinner or about fourteen hours of work a day.

When the corn was up in the family patch and ready for cultivation, John used a double shovel and plowed up one side of the corn and then back down the other side. Since there was no fender to protect the young corn plants, many were covered with dirt. The young L.S. followed John and uncovered the plants the plow had covered.

Much of the family's time was spent raising and harvesting the crops. But in the summer of 1881, the chinch bug (a small black and white bug that destroys grain and grass) consumed the countryside and nobody raised anything. The family had ten acres of good-looking corn that summer. After the wheat in an adjoining field was cut, the chinch bugs moved to the corn fields with such force that they ate the corn in only a few days. Each stalk was covered with the bugs.

Like many other children of the period, L.S. was sick much of the time. Malaria caused the family the most sickness. In addition to malaria and the normal childhood diseases, L.S. had typhoid and pneumonia and was bothered by stomach trouble. Clomana never expected him to live past childhood. Undernourishment and the general living conditions almost certainly guaranteed he wouldn't live a long life.

The land around the family cabin was swampy and contributed to the unhealthy conditions. Mosquitoes, flies, rats, mice, muskrats, opossums, raccoons, minks, polecats, rabbits, squirrels, turtles, snakes, lizards, frogs, toads, salamanders, birds and a host of other insects surrounded them in abundance.

Of the lot, the malaria-carrying mosquito made life for the family more miserable than anything else. Just as the sun would slip over the horizon and darkness settled over the clearing around the cabin, the mosquitoes invaded in full force. Window and door screens were unheard of, and mosquito netting was unknown. Smoke was the only defense against the invading army. Clomana burned dry chips in an old baking oven, placing it in the center of the cabin where it would fill every corner of the cabin with the smoky fumes.

Regardless of the heat in the hottest of the summer months, the doors were closed at night. Smoke filtered up through the cracks in the loft and the roof and drove the mosquitoes out into the night, allowing the family to sleep. Those same cracks let the rain drip steadily in during a storm, making it necessary to move beds in search of a dry spot to avoid getting soaked.

Cold weather brought other problems. Near evening one cloudy afternoon in late winter, after it had been raining all day and Clomana and John were away, L.S. and Margaret were huddled together in front of the fire trying to keep warm. Without warning, the chimney came tumbling down. Bricks, fire and ashes narrowly missed hitting and seriously injuring them. Both children were badly scared and stood staring out the gaping hole in the cabin when the older members of the family returned home some time later.

Spring and warm weather were still weeks away. A makeshift cover was placed over the hole that had been the chimney. The cook stove was used for heating and cooking for the rest of the winter but couldn't provide the amount of heat generated by the fireplace. After the ground settled in the spring, and the family had survived the winter, a bricklayer from Russellville built a new chimney.

These were the roughest times. But a mother's love and the family closeness pulled them through whatever the difficulty. Whippoorwills and other sounds of the night from the surrounding dense woods and thick underbrush reminded them of their loneliness and alienation on long nights. Most often their clock would not be working to let them know how long before daylight. In the daytime, they guessed the time of day by the shadow of a tree or the post on the porch, but at night they just guessed.

Because of this meager and lonely existence and his mother's encouragement, young L.S. developed a strong desire to learn. At the age of eight, he competed for a reward of merit to be presented to the student who had received the most merit marks during the school year. He was sick on March 16, 1878, and wasn't able to attend the last day of school. But Margaret brought the diploma home to him. Winning the award increased his thirst for knowledge and boosted his ambition to excel as a student.

Reading a book was a rare privilege, and L.S. looked forward to it when he had the opportunity. The first book he ever read was a biography of Frank and Jesse James, well-known, former Confederate soldiers who never stopped fighting when the Civil War ended and were still at large. Because of his Virginia roots and the romantic portrayal of the James brothers, L.S. thought they and Cole Younger, another famous outlaw who rode with them, were heroes.

During his early years, L.S. also read John Bunyan's *Pilgrim's Progress*. An allegory of the Christian way by the early Puritan, the story shows man's progress through life to heaven or hell. The young Heath enjoyed the book a great deal and thought extensively about the implications.

He also read the story of a bashful young man named John Flutter and thought it was quite humorous. *Peck's Bad Boy*, a popular novel of the time with the proverbial bad boy as the hero, found its way on his reading list because it was available. The only other book available to him was a history of the Civil War in the United States. He read the book several times and became somewhat of an expert on the war. Conversations with his Uncle Rennick broadened his perspective about the war and local participation in it and familiarized him with the early history of Illinois from a first-hand account.

Harvesting the crops and the fall work were finished in time for the beginning of the five months of school. The term began the first week of October and let out early enough in

March to prepare for spring planting. Money to complete the planting was hard to come by.

When L.S. was eleven years old, the teacher gave him the job of building a fire in the stove each morning and sweeping and dusting the school room. He was paid five cents a day, twenty-five cents a week. Except for the last four days of school, he was paid by the week. At the close of the school term, the teacher gave him a silver dollar that John used to buy seed corn for spring planting.

At the age of thirteen, L.S. took a job shucking corn with John on October 12 and was unable to attend school until the job was finished. They finished on December 23, and L.S. went back to school the next day, just in time to receive a treat of a nickel's worth of stick candy from the teacher with the rest of the students. The treat wasn't required, but the students often banded together and locked the teacher out if he didn't treat them to the candy.

Corn shucking paid the boys two cents a bushel. Together they could shuck about fifty bushels a day on a good day. A good day meant they had no problems and were in the field at sunup and worked until it was almost dark. At this time of the year, the corn was often covered with frost or snow. The two had no gloves and used a homemade shucking peg to snap the ear of corn out of the shuck and off the stalk. Their hands chapped, then broke open and bled. To help alleviate the pain, they filled the cracks with tallow each morning.

Despite the pain, hardship and being away from school for more than two months, this particular job of shucking corn was one of the highlights of the young Heath's boyhood. Clomana took some of the money and bought enough cotton flannel to make him two pairs of underwear, the first he had ever worn. Before he had only worn a coat, a shirt and some britches.

He wore these homemade clothes until he was seventeen years old. Then he got an overcoat called a shoddy because it was made from reclaimed wool fibers. He paid four dollars for the coat. About the same time he got his first store-boughten suit and white collar. The collar was made of paper and had to be replaced frequently because perspiration stained it. For a dime, he was able to buy one of the new celluloid collars that would last up to a year. They would yellow after a few months of wear but were worn as long as they kept their shape.

Work was scarce and wages were low throughout the Wabash River Valley area. Like many young men looking for work from that part of the country in the next seventy-five years, John decided to "go north" to find a job. In the spring of 1883, he went to Douglas County and found a job on a farm for twenty-three dollars a month, room, board and washing included. He worked from April until August, and the family thought it would have enough money to comfortably get through the winter. But John came home with only a few dollars in his pockets. All he had to show for four months of work was that few dollars and a twelve-dollar suit of used clothes.

The young L.S. was particularly disappointed in John because he was such a hard worker. Nevertheless, he couldn't save money, spending whatever came his way. On the other hand, L.S. was just the opposite and had learned to save from a story in *McGuffy's Reader*. In the story, a boy named Ben found a piece of whipcord, wound it up and put it in his pocket. His friends teased him about saving everything.

Some time later, Ben took part in a bow and arrow shooting contest. Ben was a good marksman, and the other boys feared he would win the prize. But when the string on his bow broke, the boys were delighted and thought that was the end of the contest for Ben. Their delight was shortened, however, as they watched him take the piece of whipcord from his pocket.

"If there isn't that everlasting whipcord," one boy said. "I'll learn a lesson from this."

That lesson and Benjamin Franklin's adage, "A fool and his money are soon parted," had a lifelong influence on the young Heath. He learned to save but never became what he called stingy. He thought he was more like the farmer who fell in the cistern. Hearing his calls for help, his wife went to his rescue. But he had pulled the rope in with him so she could do nothing to get him out of the cistern.

"I'll ring the dinner bell and call the hands in from the field for dinner," she said.

"What time is it?" the farmer, an economical man, asked.

"Eleven o'clock," the wife said.

"Never mind," he said. "I'll just swim around in here until the men come in to dinner."

While John was working up north during the spring and summer of 1883, thirteen-year-old L.S. used the team to plant the five-acre patch in corn and tend it. The seventy-five bushels of corn he raised was used as feed for the family and the team that winter. The two brothers shucked that corn, too. Then in January, John got married. He and his bride lived with the family and helped out there until he was able to rent fifty acres with a log cabin three miles away.

John continued to help with the family and was soon able

to buy the new place at a tax sale. The land was poor, and the attorney's fees in the lawsuit that was filed in which he had to defend his tax-deed title was about all the land was worth.

During the first farming season, L.S. helped John with the work. Clomana would get the boy up early for breakfast. He would then walk the three miles to John's farm and begin work at sunup. Both of them would work until sunset, and L.S. would walk home.

While helping John on both places and contributing to the family in that way, L.S. was able to get extra work at wheat harvest and corn shucking time and still stay in school. At sixteen and although he weighed only about 110 pounds, he was able to do any kind of farm work. Pluck and determination, rather than physical strength, made this possible.

Along about this time, he proved just how much pluck and determination he had by cutting wheat. A cradle was often used for this job. But a dropper, similar to a mowing machine, with wooden fingers attached behind the sickle was more often used. The driver's foot elevated these fingers to hold the wheat. He would drop the carrier fingers into the ground when he thought he had enough wheat. The wheat stubble would hold the wheat while the carrier slid out from under it.

Picking the wheat up in his arms, the binder would take enough straw in his hand to make a band and tie the wheat in bundles. Three men were needed to bind the wheat after one dropper. Other men followed to shock or gather these bundles together. Then the bundles were stacked butts down to make a standard-sized shock. A cap to keep the shock from getting wet was formed with two bundles. Because threshing machines were scarce, the wheat had to be stacked carefully to protect it from the weather until the machine was available.

Stacking wheat was considered an art, and few men could do it well enough to protect it from the weather.

During this period, the local stacking expert got sick just as the rather large crop turned ripe. L.S. wanted to learn a variety of tasks and had carefully watched the stacking process. He approached the farmer when it became evident that there was no one to do the job.

"I can stack the wheat," the boy told the farmer confidently.

"Why you're only a button," the farmer said, laughing.

"I'm sixteen," he said. "And I know I can do the job. I've been watching how it's done, and I know I can do it. Just let me try. You don't have anybody else. If I don't know what I'm doing, you'll be able to tell right away."

The farmer reluctantly let him try. To everyone's surprise, L.S. did a good job. From then on, he had more work than he wanted.

Another craft he learned about the same time that wasn't as much hard work but equally difficult was how to cut hair, or shingle hair as it was called. People who had a knack for cutting hair were even more scarce that those who could stack wheat. The closest barber was in Vincennes, Indiana, more than twenty miles away. When a boy's hair got too long and needed cutting, his mother would put a crock over his head and trim his hair around the edge of the crock. That was done twice a year.

John decided he could cut hair and practiced on his younger brother, demonstrating little talent or skill. To get the hair even, John would simply keep cutting until he cut down to the scalp in several places. By the time he quit, he would be laughing at his handy work.

"You look like a speckled pup," he would say and laugh.

To avoid the look John's haircuts gave him, L.S. started cutting hair and learned quickly to do it well. Because he was good at it and because he never charged anyone, he cut sixteen heads of hair on a Sunday in the summer of 1885. Like learning to stack wheat well, he always had plenty of work as a barber and soon regretted learning to cut hair.

But it was his desire to know things and do things well that prepared him for life. Not only did he want to do things, but he wanted to do them better than anyone else. From this early experience, L.S. learned to believe the adage, "If you would have a thing well done, do it yourself."

A story about the farmer and the lark had developed this belief early in young Heath's life. The farmer and his son looked at a wheat field where the lark had built her nest to determine when the wheat was ripe. It appeared to be ripe, and they decided to cut the next day if the neighbors would help.

The young birds were frightened and wanted to move immediately. But their mother assured them there was no cause for alarm because the wheat wouldn't be cut the next day. When the next day came, the father and son came and talked about the neighbors helping the following day. Again, the mother bird told her young that the wheat would not be cut the next day.

After the neighbors didn't show up the next day, the farmer told his son they would cut the wheat themselves. This time the old bird told her chicks that it was necessary for them to move: The farmers were going to cut the wheat themselves and not depend on others.

Even though he knew that in many cases a person can't do things alone and do without help, L.S. Heath preferred to do things for himself and would never ask anyone else to do something for him that he could do for himself. At the same time he developed this self-reliance and thought it was a virtue, he found a great deal of pleasure in doing things for other people.

Margaret Heath married Henry Draper when she was nineteen years old and lived a short distance from her family. She died at the same age, eleven days after giving birth to a daughter, Nellie. L.S. was devastated. Only three years in age separated him and Margaret, and they had been constant companions in their lonely surroundings since he could remember.

On the morning of her death, L.S. was on his way to Birds, seven miles away, to see about a job as a clerk in a store and stopped in to see his sister. Margaret was alone with the baby and near death at the time. Not realizing that, L.S. went on his way.

The storekeeper didn't need any help, and L.S. headed back home immediately. It was late afternoon when he got back to his sister's home. By this time, Clomana was there to care for Margaret, whose condition had worsened rapidly since morning.

While Clomana continued to do what she could for her daughter, L.S. hurried the three miles to John's place to bring him to gather around Margaret's deathbed. Clomana was standing at the door crying softly when her two sons arrived.

"Margaret has passed away," she said.

The family buried Margaret in the old cemetery at Russellville and marked her grave with a small tombstone Clomana bought for ten dollars. Henry Draper and his parents soon moved to Paoli, Indiana, with the baby, Nellie. She was ill for much of her young life and died at the age of six. The Heath side of the family only saw her once in the interim.

A year after Margaret's death, in the fall of 1886 when L.S. was seventeen years old, he and his mother went to live with John. Up until that time, L.S. had gone to school at Hazel Dell in the northeastern corner of Lawrence County, Illinois. After the move, he attended Canaan School in the southeastern corner of Crawford County. Always a good and conscientious student, he did well there and passed the County Superintendent's examination at the county seat in Robinson for a teacher's certificate in April 1887.

The night before the examination, his uncle took him on horseback to stay with an aunt four miles northeast of Robinson. Early the next morning, they returned to Robinson where he was reluctant to enter the room where the examination was being given because he didn't have suitable clothes. The hat he wore was in a dilapidated condition. It was shaped something like an ice cream cone and resembled the dunce cap the old-time school teachers used for disciplinary purposes. Before entering the room, he removed the hat and then dropped it behind a small table at the rear of the room. After the examination was over, he grabbed the hat and hurried out the door.

In those days, the minimum age for teachers was eighteen. Although L.S. had passed the examination to teach, he was only seventeen and couldn't yet teach. So he kept working on the farm until September 1887 when he entered Central Normal College at Danville, Indiana, to further his education. The term was for only ten weeks. He was able to finance the term by selling a three-year-old mare he had acquired as a colt for work he had done for a farmer who was unable to pay. The colt had developed into a beautiful sorrel mare and a fine saddle horse that brought a top price of fifty dollars. From money saved during the summer, he had bought a ten-dollar suit. Tuition was eight dollars, and room and board was two dollars a week.

It was difficult for him to leave home. Other than staying with a relative, he had never slept away from home before. But he was so happy about the opportunity and had much encouragement from a friend, George W. Lackey, who was a senior at the Danville school, that he got the courage to leave. Since L.S. lived fifteen miles from the train station, he stayed all night with George. His father took the two boys to Vincennes in a two-horse wagon. At school, George found a room for L.S. to rent and took care of him like a younger brother.

His mother was still living with John when L.S. left for school. But shortly after he left, she went back to the old house and lived alone in the woods, half a mile from the nearest neighbor. That worried L.S., and he watched the mail closely for a letter from her. There wasn't much time to worry, however. He was kept busy from the moment school opened. Like the rest of the students at the college, he was required to keep notebooks, which he took home after the term was over. One student lost his trunk and felt that he had lost a year's worth of education.

The pace was fast, but capable teachers served as an inspiration to the students. L.S. came away with a desire to succeed in life. One incident had a more profound influence on his subsequent life than anything else he remembered. A graduate of the college named J.E. Sherrill who had a successful book publishing business in Indianapolis addressed the students at chapel one morning. He told the students that "keeping everlastingly at it will bring success." L.S. wrote that in the flyleaf of his algebra book and followed the motto from that day on.

School ended on November 10, 1887. He left for home the following day, taking a train to Paris, Illinois, then making a connection for Flat Rock and home. The train to Paris was late, and he had to take a later train south and arrived at eleven p.m. The rest of the family had expected him ten hours earlier and went back home. He walked the seven miles to the old house in the woods, arriving at one a.m. with $1.40 left from the fifty dollars after paying tuition, books, room and board, postage and train fare.

Upon his return from college, he worked on the farm until he found his first teaching job for a five-month winter term in 1888-89 at Union School in the northeastern part of Lawrence County. The pay was thirty dollars a month. As a young man, L.S. was more than adequate as a teacher, but he was weak as a disciplinarian. Maintaining order in the classroom was the greatest recommendation for teaching at a country school in those days. He was successful enough that he was hired for a two-month spring term at Canaan, his old school in Crawford County, and for the winter term of 1889-90 at Higgins School, the district bordering Canaan on the west.

At the end of March and the end of the winter term, he went back to school in Danville, Indiana, and remained there until July 25. Believing that he did not intend to return to Higgins, the board of directors had hired another teacher. At the time, there was a vacancy at Taylor School about three miles southwest of Flat Rock. L.S. went to apply for the position in a borrowed horse and buggy.

"You'd have a hard time keepin' these boys in line here," one of the board members said, eyeing L.S.'s small stature and youth. "Discipline is a big problem for any teacher."

Not doubting the man's word but believing he could handle the situation as he was learning from experience, L.S. set about persuading the board to hire him. Because of the seriousness of the problem, the board was skeptical.

"Last winter," another board member said, "the boys cut a hole in the ice over in that slough yonder and stuck the teacher's head in the water."

"Look at that hole in the map there," another one said. "A big old boy threw a quarter of a brick through the window at the teacher. Just missed his head and tore a hole in the map."

"What you say is undoubtedly true," L.S. said. "But I'd like to have a chance to tackle the problem and see what I can do. Give me that chance and if I fail, I'll resign at the end of the first month and forfeit my salary."

That apparently persuaded the board. The directors hired him for a four-month term at thirty-five dollars a month. L.S. soon found out that the board had not exaggerated the discipline problem. It was touch and go regarding whether he would survive for the first few weeks. Finally, L.S. whirled toward one of the bigger boys who had tried to trip him as he walked down the aisle between desks, grabbed him by the ear and virtually dragged him to the corner at the front of the class. The boy's arms flailed wildly in an attempt to break free.

"Now you stand there facing the corner until you learn how to behave," L.S. said, releasing the ear, grabbing the boy's arm and guiding him into the corner. "Understand?"

"Yes, sir," the boy said, holding his ear and rubbing it gingerly.

After he demonstrated that he could control the students, L.S. earned their respect and was able to ease up and make friends with the boys who had made the problems. He finished the year out feeling that he had been successful and thinking he would have the position for the following year.

Just after the term was over, the board from the Higgins School offered him a six-month contract at $42.50 a month to return to that school. Before accepting, L.S. advised the Taylor district board of the offer and it matched the Higgins offer. He accepted and taught there another year before becoming the principal at the Oblong School in the fall of 1892.

While he was teaching at Taylor, L.S. met and fell in love with "the prettiest girl" he had ever seen. Her name was Clara Ellen Frye. When he took the principalship, he didn't want to leave her behind and married her before moving to Oblong. The next year they moved to Robinson, where L.S. had accepted the principal's position at Robinson High School. He was twenty-three years old.

That fall, Bayard Emerson, the couple's first child, was born. The baby was fine, but Clara, not quite nineteen years old at the time, developed uremic poisoning and nearly died. She recovered, however, and later gave birth to three more boys and two girls. L.S. loved poetry and named his children after poets. Besides Bayard, Everett Edward was born in Effingham in 1896; Ruby Ethel was born in Robinson in 1898; Virgil "Pete" Dwight was born in Effingham in 1900; Vernon Lawrence was born in Edinburg in 1908; and Mary Ellen was born in Robinson in 1915.

As Clara lay hovering between life and death after Bayard's birth, the family doctor, A.G. Meserve, attended her regularly.

One of her friends and neighbors had just given birth to a girl a few days earlier. A day or so after Bayard's birth, the friend came by while the doctor was there.

"Why, Clara," the friend said, "you look bad. I never thought you'd look this bad."

Dr. Meserve looked at her sharply but waited until they were out of Clara's hearing before he spoke. "Of course she looks bad," he said. "She's a very sick young woman. But even if she does look bad, you didn't have a damn bit of business telling her she did. That won't help her one iota."

The neighbor was taken aback. "Well, I never," she said and stormed out of the house. She did speak more kindly to Clara after that, however, and nursed Bayard along with her own daughter while Clara recovered.

For most of the next fifteen years, L.S. taught school, served as principal or attended a college or university. He declined to return to Robinson High School in the fall of 1894 because of "the unsatisfactory teaching conditions" there. In addition to teaching eight classes daily, he was responsible for the discipline of the entire student body. Also entering into the decision was his desire to return to college. He entered Austin College in Effingham that fall and graduated in two years because of the credits he had gained at Central Normal.

Before moving to Effingham, though, L.S. took the bar examination in August. He had read law at the Parker and Crowley law office in Robinson and wanted to practice law. Although he was licensed to practice law in November, he stayed on at Austin because he had a growing family and was financially unable "to go through a starving period in establishing a practice."

By the time he graduated from Austin, L.S. had two sons.

He accepted the principalship of the East Side School in Centralia, Illinois, for the 1896-97 academic year. That position turned out to be no more desirable than had the one in Robinson. So he was easily persuaded by friends to return to Robinson in June and enter the primary race for superintendent of schools of Crawford County. The primary election was scheduled for February 28, 1898.

With very little money to support his family, let alone finance the primary campaign, L.S. borrowed the money for expenses and signed a note for six months to buy a horse to use in campaigning. When he lost the primary, he was relieved because he was out of money and had no idea how he would support his family, which would soon include another child, between the primary and the general election or finance another campaign had he won.

Shortly after the primary, L.S. sold the horse for a thirty-two-dollar note. He immediately discounted the note and sold it for twenty-four dollars and applied that to a grocery bill, leaving him with still more debts and no money until he could get a teaching position in the fall. Fortunately, the family did have meat. Just after returning to Robinson, L.S purchased two shoats to fatten and butcher in the fall. To feed the hogs, he helped a farmer cut wood under the hot August sun and was paid in corn. Although L.S. had never butchered hogs, he had seen it done and got along well enough to keep the family in meat all winter. But there was little else, and he didn't know what he was going to do for money.

His problems were soon solved. Just a little more than a month after the primary election, the president of Austin College walked up the sidewalk early one Sunday morning. L.S. was puzzled to see him but met him at the door and invited him in to hear that the professor of Latin and Greek at the college was seriously ill.

"I'm sorry to hear that," the young Heath said.

"Well, I am, too," the president said. "But until he recovers, I'd like you to take his place."

Hardly able to contain himself because of his good fortune but saddened because of the professor's condition, L.S. quickly accepted the offer of fifteen weeks employment.

"Be ready to leave this afternoon," the president said. "You will accompany me and begin classes in the morning."

The professor died before the end of the term, and L.S. was offered the position permanently. During his summer vacation, he taught at Crawford County Normal School and Teachers Institute. He continued that in subsequent summers and remained at Austin until August 1900 when he resigned and enrolled at the University of Illinois.

By this time, he had a wife, four children and his mother to support. Teaching summer school enabled him to finance the time at Illinois, and he had enough credits to graduate in a year. After graduating in June, he prepared for the state superintendent's examination for a teacher's life certificate. He took and passed the four-day exam in August, although he was nearly exhausted because he had been teaching or studying without interruption since he had started teaching at Austin College more than two years earlier. He weighed 103.5 pounds the day he finished the examination.

After graduation from the University of Illinois, L.S. became principal of Township High School in Edinburg, Illinois, then went back to Austin for a year. The Edinburg Board of Education met his terms for four hundred dollars more than it had ever paid to get him to return in the fall of 1903.

He remained in the principal's position, and the Heath family lived in Edinburg until January 1908 when L.S. was offered the chair of mathematics and physics at Carthage College in Carthage, Illinois. Finishing the year, he had been assured that he would be reappointed the following year.

That summer, however, he went back to Robinson, with the fifth child now, to see the oil boom and "saw the streets of Robinson were filled with people from the oil fields of Pennsylvania, West Virginia and other states" who had swarmed to the area when oil was discovered. He decided to move the family home "to cast (his) fortune with the boom" and bought a house with the four hundred dollars he had saved from teaching, securing the rest of the needed twenty-four hundred dollars in first and second mortgages and loans.

The second day he was back in town he went to work for the city council doing engineering work until the regular engineer returned. For the next six years, L.S. worked as a surveyor, sold some insurance and real estate and rented the "three upstairs rooms (in the family home) to workers in the oil field." Using folding beds, the family occupied the four downstairs rooms of the house.

Like most of the places L.S. had rented in previous years, the house he bought had land available for a good-sized garden and a place to keep chickens, a hog or two and a cow. From the time they were old enough, the two Heath boys had worked in the garden, taken care of the animals and helped contribute to the support of the family in any way possible. As always, the Heaths sold the surplus milk to their neighbors at a nickel a quart. Because of the demand for milk created by the oil boom in Robinson, L.S. bought two cows. Clara and Bayard did the milking at five a.m. and six p.m., and Bayard and Skiv delivered the milk to customers twice daily.

"My job," the elder Heath said, "is to keep the books and handle the money."

That aspect of his role in the family became more apparent as his place as the Heath family patriarch developed and spread throughout the community. Henry Wilkin, the Crawford County circuit clerk, owned an eighty-acre pasture on the south edge of Robinson that he rented out to other people with cows at a dollar a month per cow for a six-month period each year. He employed L.S. to manage the pasture and collect the rent in exchange for free rent for his two cows.

While the family lived in Edinburg, L.S. spent much of his summer months surveying farm ground with limited drainage so tile could be laid to make the land productive. He had plenty of work at six dollars a ten-hour day because much of the land required drainage tile. Bayard grew up working as his rod carrier for two dollars a day. The son had been trained to know what his father was doing and to do exactly what his father wanted him to do.

For the first few months after returning to Robinson, L.S. worked at first one job and then another. In early November, the Tidewater Pipe Line Company contracted him to establish the right-of-way for a pipe line to be run from Stoy, Illinois, to Bradford, Pennsylvania, in the northern part of the state.

Company engineers and surveyors had originally established the right-of-way but delay in starting laying the pipe line had resulted in many of the wooden stakes being destroyed. L.S. reluctantly accepted the job until Tidewater could get its own surveyors back on the job. His mother, who had long lived with the family, was seriously ill and not expected to recover. So L.S., with Bayard helping, worked at reestablishing the right-of-way until they crossed the Wabash River and had the line headed toward Terre Haute, Indiana, returning home to help care for Clomana Heath each night.

Shortly after moving into Indiana, L.S. resigned to stay closer to Robinson. Clomana died in January.

Before his mother died, however, L.S. was back in Robinson just before Christmas without any regular income or prospects of any kind until spring when he could get plenty of engineering and surveying jobs. Robinson postmaster Edward Baker was a longtime friend of L.S.'s and offered him a position that just opened up as assistant postmaster at one hundred dollars a month. Bayard was hired as the janitor at one hundred dollars a year.

The elder Heath stayed at the post office for nearly nine years. Despite his desire to break away from a salaried job, the circumstances dictated that he remain at the post office. The five Heath children were growing, and Mary was born during this period. Working together, the family provided a comfortable living for each other.

Skiv earned a dollar a day at Norris Brothers Machine Shop during the summer months. The third son, Pete, was the local distributor for *The Saturday Evening Post* and *Ladies Home Journal.* After he graduated from high school in June 1910, Bayard went to work as a clerk at the Globe Dry Goods store on the Robinson Square for five dollars a week. He worked from seven a.m. until nine p.m. Monday through Friday and until midnight on Saturday with only an hour off for dinner and an hour off for supper.

A few months later, a grocery store owner offered Bayard $7.50 a week to go to work for him. His boss at Globe promptly matched the offer, and Bayard stayed until the following October when shoe store owner O.G. Olwin offered him ten dollars a week to go to work in the shoe store. Bayard gave two weeks notice in October 1911 and started selling shoes. Beginning with Olwin's father, John, the Olwin family had years of successful experience in the retail business. Two other Olwin boys and a son-in-law operated retail stores in Robinson. In 1912, one of the boys, B.G. Olwin, bought a confectionery and ice cream parlor on the east side of the Robinson Square. He bought the store from some native Greeks, hired a French candy and ice cream maker named Maurice Jonquet to handle that end of the business and moved it to the west side of the Square in 1913.

Things were coming together for the Heath family by this time. Skiv graduated from high school in 1913 and began working as a salesman in the Boom Store on the Square. The younger kids at home took over the jobs Bayard and Skiv had long held. Pooling income and assuming as much responsibility for individual needs as they were able made it possible for L.S. to pay off the mortgage on the family home in early 1914 and breathe a sigh of relief.

Meanwhile, B.G. Olwin and his wife were growing tired of working fifteen to sixteen hours a day in the confectionery and ice cream parlor seven days a week and decided to put the business up for sale.

4

With Bayard and Skiv already working on the Square and L.S. not far away, the Heath family was a prime prospect for Olwin to approach about selling the confectionery. Friends advised L.S. not to buy the place.

"It'll take a lot of Coca-Colas to even pay the sixty dollars a month rent," one friend told him, strongly advising against the purchase.

Determined to start a family business in Robinson to keep the family together and employed, L.S. ignored the advice and bought the confectionery, soda fountain and ice cream parlor for three thousand dollars. This time he mortgaged the family home for sixteen hundred dollars and the store for the rest, closing the deal on January 7, 1914.

L.S. appreciated others' concern and knew that it was not always best to disregard the advice of friends. When it came down to the bottom line, however, he thought it was usually best for everyone to decide matters for himself.

"If a person depends much on the thinking of others," he often said, "he eventually forms a habit of doing so. One must know his own limitations and make his own decisions in matters of importance."

His instincts were correct. The confectionery was success-ful from the start. For nearly eighteen years, the Heath Broth-ers store was a popular hangout for people of all ages. Friends and neighbors enjoyed visiting and loafing at the store. It was sports central for the area. Results of football and basketball games were posted in the window. Next door to the store was a tavern called The Lobby, that had a ticker tape on which the current baseball scores came across the wire so the scores could be posted by the innings.

The confectionery, operated by Bayard and Skiv, sold soda fountain items, cigars, tobacco, sandwiches, ice cream and candies. But it was the candies that were emphasized from the beginning.

"This is the open season for candy," a December 18, 1914, ad flier read. "No license is needed, no hunting necessary. Just come to HEATH BROS. CONFECTIONERY, No. 11, West Side Square, where there is kept on hands at all times a fresh supply of those wonderful delicious HOMEMADE CANDIES in variety to suit every taste.

"When mention is made of home-made candy, most people think only of peanut brittle, taffy and fudge. We want to correct this impression, and we can best do so by enumerating some of the things we make. Here they are. ..."

The ad named at least thirty-four varieties and included a complete line of homemade candies much like a later-day Fannie Mae brand—peanut brittle, fudge, caramels, taffy, mints, bonbons, nougats, creams and pudding. But there was no Heath toffee. That was to come later.

World War I had been going on almost from the time the store opened. When the United States finally entered the war, it wasn't long until the Heath brothers went to the Army. During their absence, the rest of the family operated the business. The Frenchman, Maurice Jonquet, had stayed on when the new owners took over and made both the candy and ice cream. He worked for the business until some time after Bayard and Skiv returned from the service.

Before the war, Bayard had married Elizabeth Rice from Mount Carmel, Illinois. The business was doing so well that it stayed open from seven a.m. until midnight, seven days a week. Since Bayard was married, he wanted the earlier shift from seven a.m. to four p.m. Skiv took the four p.m. to midnight shift. Both men, only eighteen and twenty years old when the store opened as Heath Brothers, quickly established their separate identities as businessmen.

"Bayard," everybody said, "can slice a piece of ham so thin you can see through it. If you want a piece of ham, go in after four. Skiv will give you more for your money."

Even sister Ruby would wait until after four. "Skiv might not charge me for a cherry Coke," she said. "Bayard always gets the nickel."

During those early years, the Heath brothers, continuing the tradition of the former owner through their own initiative and with Jonquet's help, maintained and improved the quality of the candy they sold. The advertising proclaimed that the candies were not only of the "finest flavors" and "pure and wholesome," but that the "highest quality of ingredients enter into their manufacture."

"In buying candy for the children, don't think just any kind will do," the early ad said. "Just remember that children hold about the same views concerning 'tolerably good' candies as you do a 'tolerably good' egg."

All the candies were made in the back of the store in a rather dreary room. The candy was cooked in small copper kettles, heated by a gas flame and then poured out on a marble slab to cool and cut. After each variety was ready, it was displayed in the candy case at the front of the store and sold in bulk form. Most of the same candies and ice creams continued to be made after Jonquet left, and the confectionery continued to prosper.

All along, the elder Heath pursued his entrepreneurial bent and continued building the family business. As a result of the initial success of the confectionery in the first year, he built a small ice cream factory on South Jackson Street in Robinson on what would later house the Heath company. The building cost sixteen hundred dollars. Ice cream was first made there on April 9, 1915, to supply wholesale accounts and the confectionery. But with no home freezers and another ice cream company in town, business was slow.

In the beginning, L.S. had only eleven wholesale accounts: five in Robinson, two in Palestine, two in Oblong, one in Hutsonville and one in Flat Rock. Dirt roads and a lack of demand for ice cream made him give serious thought to his business venture. At times, he almost wished he had heeded his friends and kept out of business. It was often difficult to pay the help and meet the obligations.

But by heeding J.E. Sherrill's advice from years before to keep "everlastingly at it," he succeeded far more than he ever expected. With the profits from the factory and the store, L.S. bought a one-third interest in the Robinson Title and Realty at No. 5 East Side Square in 1917.

Two years later, he began churning butter at the ice cream factory and business picked up. A year later, he bought out his competitor, the Model Ice Cream Company, and also bought the Robinson Bottling Works. The bottling company enabled him to put out forty cases of pop a day. That same year, he bought the rest of the title and realty company and ran it by himself until he sold it in 1921. The real estate, insurance and abstract business provided money to buy the factory. It was that increase and the resultant demands on his time that prompted him to sell the title and realty company.

Bayard and Skiv picked up where they left off when they returned from the war. But they had changed. Skiv had been in France and had been away from Robinson for nearly three years. After a later disagreement over how to manage the business, he sold his part of it to Bayard, moved to Indianapolis and operated a retail ice cream store for three years.

Most of the same candies and ice creams continued to be made during this time. Pete had graduated from high school in 1918. He had been helping with the family business for a while and went into the ice cream business with his father. Maurice Jonquet helped Bayard run the confectionery after Skiv left for Indianapolis.

Beth Heath gave birth to Bayard Jr., the first of the third generation, on February 8, 1920. The family business the boy's grandfather had worked so hard to put together had been a reality for a little more than six years. L.S. hadn't spent all the time and effort only to see Skiv leave the family and had no intention of letting his son stay in Indianapolis for long.

"You belong here with the family," L.S. told his son when he decided to leave and continued to tell him for the nearly three years he was gone. "You have no business over there trying to fight those big ice cream companies. We all have plenty of work to do here. There are plenty of girls here, too."

It wasn't an easy task, but L.S. finally persuaded Skiv to sell out and return to Robinson and join him and Pete in the L.S. Heath and Sons ice cream, creamery and bottling business and get involved in the confectionery again. When it came to getting what he wanted from the family, the elder Heath was as flexible as a post. He was as generous as they come, but he knew what he wanted and knew how to get it.

During the 1920s, the business continued to prosper and the Heath extended family continued to grow. Bayard and Beth's second child, Patricia, was born in 1924. Pete married Thelma Gisso of St. Louis in 1927. She was a school teacher in Hutsonville, a little river town on the Illinois side of the Wabash, nine miles northeast of Robinson. Their first son, Robert, was born on May 8, 1928, and a daughter, Joyce, was born on May 6, 1930.

Skiv stayed single until he was thirty-five years old. The day before his niece Joyce was born, he married Madeline Shanks, originally from Terre Haute, Indiana. Her mother had been unable to support two daughters after her policeman husband died. At fourteen, Madeline had been sent to Lawrenceville, Illinois, to work in a dress shop and finish high school. Eventually, she was transferred to Robinson and lived with Clarence and Marguerite Midkiff. The latter worked in the dress shop with Madeline.

By the late 1920s, Bayard had developed what eventually became the Heath English Toffee Bar. The recipe may have come from the French candy maker Maurice Jonquet. Although he was no longer around, he had been making candy in the store for years. The recipe may also have come from a candy called "trail toffee" made by some Greek candy makers in Champaign, Illinois. Many little confectioneries were scattered around the Midwest in the early part of the twentieth century. Salesmen traveled the country selling chocolate. The recipe may have come from one of them in exchange for buying chocolate from him. It was a simple recipe that evolved into the toffee bar after years of candy-making experience and experimentation.

Wherever the recipe came from, the candy was well received. It quickly became popular in and around Robinson. At the time, it was just one more item to be sold in an effort to make a living. Travelers took the bulk toffee home with them, and the dairy trucks began selling the candy to other retail stores. Bayard made some changes in flavor and texture to create a candy with the taste of the Heath English Toffee Bar, using "choice almonds, pure creamery butter, cane sugar and coating it with a high-grade chocolate."

For some time, the elder Heath had been urging Bayard and Skiv to sell the confectionery and create a family firm at the South Jackson Street location. L.S. wanted them there with "the idea of expanding wholesale candy sales." He and Bayard made a trip to Terre Haute early in 1931 to sell the owner of Gillis Drug Store bulk toffee from the confectionery. Gillis told them he was getting out of the bulk business because bars were the coming thing.

On the way home, L.S. again urged Bayard to sell the store and get into the wholesale business. "We can make a million dollars," he said.

At the time, L.S. Heath was a sixty-year-old man who had always said a man should educate himself for the first fifty years of his life, then decide what he wanted to do. And as a result of his childhood experiences, what he wanted more than anything else in the world was for his children to all be in business together. He believed that families staying together was the strength of success.

His first three children, Bayard, Skiv and Ruby, were very much like him. Pete went along with his father, and Vernon and Mary were not involved in the family business at the time. Informal negotiations continued throughout the summer and fall of 1931 with Bayard and Skiv at the confectionery and L.S. and Pete at the ice cream and bottling plant on South Jackson Street. Ruby helped her mother take care of the house and believed her work was every bit as important as what her father and brothers were doing. The family increased again when Skiv and Madeline became parents for the first time when a son, Richard J., was born on May 21, 1931. Six months later in November of that year, the elder Heath realized his dream when Bayard and Skiv sold the confectionery to George A. Connett and moved the candy-making equipment to the family business on South Jackson Street.

The first Heath bars were made on December 31, 1931, at the height of the Depression and nearly eighteen years after the Heath brothers opened the store on the Robinson Square. Candy bars at the time were about four ounces and sold for a nickel. The Heath bar was only an ounce and sold for the same price. Most everyone in the candy business thought it would never sell because it was too small. But even then it was a favorite to those who tried it.

5

L.S. Heath won a major victory by getting Bayard and Skiv to sell the confectionery and join Pete and him in 1931 in the new partnership composed of the four. The country was in the Depression and money was scarce. But more importantly, it eliminated the possibility that Bayard and Skiv would go their own direction with the Heath candy bar.

Getting the family together in business, all under one roof, was L.S.'s way of taking care of his family and getting the help he needed to realize his dreams. He thought his way was fair to everybody. Bayard didn't like the idea at all, and although he felt very strongly that it wasn't the thing to do, he went along with it to keep peace in the family. Skiv cared about the welfare of the family, particularly in Pete's case. Pete had always had a drinking problem. That was no secret. Thelma had called Skiv many times to get Pete home or half-way straightened out.

Thinking it would be best for Pete, Skiv wanted his brother to be in the family business; however, Skiv had a problem with his father's interference in the candy end of the business. L.S., who was the mayor of Robinson at the time and more interested in the dairy end, basically agreed to stay out of the candy division to get what he wanted.

It was agreed, then, that Bayard would handle the candy office, Skiv would oversee the candy production, L.S. would run the dairy and bottling operation and Pete would assist him and be responsible for the trucks. Each of the four partners would take an equal draw of forty dollars a week. This was good pay but not excessive. Profits of the company were needed to stay in business.

Fresh milk products were added to the ice cream and butter business making it a full-fledged dairy. The production plant for the Heath bar was really only an improved extension of how the candy was made at the confectionery. The candy was still cooked in individual copper kettles, heated by a gas flame, spread out on a marble slab to cool, cut into bars with a knife and hand-dipped in a special Nestle Peter's blend of chocolate. Now, however, each bar was hand-wrapped and put into boxes of thirty and sold for a nickel a bar retail. Little automation was possible, and production was limited. But for the first time, people were employed solely to make the Heath English Toffee Bar. About fifty employees worked throughout the plant at the time.

For several years, Heath toffee had been sold by the pound in bulk form from the ice cream trucks. The Heath bar was now sold as a candy bar on the dairy trucks which were going into more and more counties around the Robinson area. It was soon decided to reduce the number of bars in a box from thirty to twenty-four and sell the box for eighty cents to a retailer. The retailers then sold the box of twenty-four bars for $1.20 to the public.

The first wholesale jobber for the Heath bar was E.J. Braum and Co. in Evansville, Indiana. L.S. was in Evansville on business one day in the spring of 1932. On the way to his meeting, he stopped by the Braum company and took one of the four boxes of Heath bars he had brought with him in to sell.

At sixty-two years of age and only five feet, six inches tall, L.S. looked like an elderly gentleman and didn't cut an imposing figure. He looked more like an aging scholar than the head of an up-and-coming candy company. He introduced himself and stated his business.

"No candy bar on the market has the quality of the Heath bar," he said, holding one of the small bars out for inspection. "Other candy makers might match it, but they won't make it any more pure."

"It is rather small," the sales manager said. "I don't think we could sell it."

"Yes, it is small," L.S. said, spreading his arms and bringing attention to his own small stature. "You'll have no trouble selling it once people taste it. Only the purest of ingredients are used in making the Heath bar. It is a blend of choice almonds, cane sugar and creamery butter coated with Nestle's finest milk chocolate."

The Braum man turned the small bar in his hand and eyed the little man standling exactly before him. "How much do these sell for?" the manager asked, aware that other employees were watching him and the sales presentation.

"The price is eighty cents a box to you," L.S. said, indicating that twenty-four of the one-ounce bars were packed in the box. "You would sell the box wholesale for ninety-six cents. The retailer would sell them for a nickel each or $1.20 a box.

"Now if you pay the account within ten days, you'll receive a 2 percent discount, making your cost 78.6 cents a box on larger orders. If you'll buy this box to try and sell but don't have any luck, I'll come down and pick up the box or the bars that don't sell."

Until then, the manager was hesitating. "Well, that sounds like a good idea," he said. "It doesn't sound like we'd have much to lose. Leave the box, and we'll see if we can sell it."

Handing him the box and thanking him, L.S. left the company and went on to his business meeting. On the way out of town, he decided to stop by Braum's before going back to Robinson. The manager and several employees looked up and smiled as he walked through the door.

"Do you have any more of those Heath English Toffee Bars with you, Mr. Heath?" the manager asked before L.S. had a chance to say anything. "I think we can sell some."

"Why, yes, I do," L.S. said. "I have three more boxes."

"We'll take them. The box you left earlier didn't make it out the door and were gone in less than an hour after you were."

L.S. looked puzzled.

"The employees ate them. They ate every last one of them. So I think we can sell them. You were right: All you have to do is try one. It was delicious—tasted just like homemade candy."

With the sale of those four boxes that afternoon, the Heath bar became a commercial seller to a wholesale jobber. Sales continued to be made in that way. At that point in 1932, the company had very few ways to generate sales and production.

Madeline Heath gave birth to her second child, Joan, on Skiv's birthday, November 5, 1932, and the first three sons' families were complete. But the Depression was still hanging on. Although the dairy was increasing sales through home delivery, the company couldn't always collect the bills because so many people were out of work.

Partly because of that situation and partly because L.S. was keeping the books anyway, he decided he would make out the income tax returns. He wasn't an accountant and believed that only cash could be counted. That was the bottom line to him. As far as he was concerned, if the bank balance wasn't higher at the end of the year than it was at the beginning of the year, there was no profit to report. He didn't consider accounts receivable, inventory, equipment or the change in net worth part of the profit.

"If we go out of business, who would buy anything?" he asked. "If we went out of business, we'd have to junk the inventory and the equipment."

He reasoned that accounts receivable or notes on receivables were not a part of the net worth of a business. The way he looked at it was that if receivables were considered a part of the net worth and net worth was increased by $50,000 that year, the profit would be $50,000 and taxes would have to be paid on $50,000. But suppose $25,000 of that was accounts receivable?

"How do you know if you can collect the receivables?" he asked. "When you do, the proceeds will end up in the cash account. I'll consider it profit when it's collected, then pay the taxes. Daddamnit, the government shouldn't be paid before we are."

While the elder Heath's theory made sense to him, the Internal Revenue Service wouldn't buy his philosophy and came calling. He explained his position to the man from the IRS.

"You go and collect these milk bills, if you can," L.S. said indignantly. "I'll give you your share when you come back in with the money."

The government man shook his head and turned to Skiv, hoping to find a friendly face and someone to help persuade the old man to see it the government's way.

"Come with me some Sunday night," Skiv said. "That's when I go out collecting. Maybe you'll have more luck than I do."

"The book says this is the law," the IRS man said. "I —"

"Bring the book, too," Skiv said, interrupting. "I'd like to see how much you can collect with it."

The agent threw up his hands in frustration and went to talk to Bayard about the situation. He was more agreeable and knew the agent had had enough of L.S. and Skiv Heath.

"They don't make sense," the agent told Bayard, unable to see the point that selling milk in the middle of the Depression was almost like not selling it at all.

In the end, of course, the IRS won the argument. Everyone agreed that the books could no longer be kept nor the income taxes filed as L.S had been doing them. Bayard took over the bookkeeping operation and did it the way the IRS required from then on.

None of the first four Heath children had been able to go to college. With the family businesses doing well, however, Vernon went to the University of Illinois and graduated with a bachelor's degree in journalism in 1928 and a master's degree in political science in 1929. He later went to work as a reporter for the *Decatur Herald* in Decatur, Illinois. Soon afterwards, he married Beatrice Kane from Pinckneyville, Illinois, a town in the southern part of the state, and was happy to be a journalist. His father was proud, but he wanted his son back in Robinson with the family.

Ruby was still helping out at home. Mary, the last of the

Heaths' six children, had come late in their lives and was the baby of the family in more ways than one. She, like Ruby, had great natural talent in music. Both became accomplished concert pianists. Mary went to Julliard's School of Music in New York City. Nothing was too good for her. She came along at the right time, had it comfortable growing up, and when she was ready for college, her father had the money to send her wherever she wanted to go. Her life growing up was just the opposite of the rest of her brothers and sister.

But what the Heath family was trying to do, like most of America during this period, was survive. While it was the candy bar that really got things rolling, the Pepsi Cola franchise proved to be a good supplementary product for the Heath company. Pepsi was a relatively new soft drink out of the East that was selling franchises to bottle and sell its drinks. The franchise didn't cost much. And at the time, Pepsi had only one franchise bottler west of the Allegheny Mountains. That left nearly three states available. So the Heaths bought in and became the only Pepsi franchise in Illinois and only the second franchise bottler west of the Alleghenies.

With some used equipment, the company got into the soft drink business on a bigger scale and started competing with Coca-Cola. Coke had done well and had about all the market with its six-ounce, zesty little cola. If the family had had more money and a strong enough belief in the future of Pepsi, it could have had the other states. The family liked the idea, the product and the song. The song began something like this: "Pepsi Cola/hits the spot/a nickel buys you a lot" and finished "Twelve full ounces/twice as much for your nickel." But because of the few nickels the company had and the family's lack of confidence to go all out, the company took only six counties around Crawford County. The younger Heaths thought the company had a large territory for a relatively small risk.

L.S., though, wanted to develop the dairy instead of "some soft drink that contained 98 percent water."

"Money's tight," he said as he and his sons discussed buying the franchise. "People will not buy soft drinks when money gets tight. But they will always buy milk."

Regardless, the company was in the soft drink business, with a used bottler and a flat-bed truck. To protect this part of the business, the family also decided to get into the beer distributing business. Too many of the taverns wanted both, so it made sense to also sell beer—at least in Crawford County.

From the beginning, Pete decided he was going to be in charge of the soft drink division of the company. That was to be his baby. L.S. was concentrating on the dairy, his biggest love. The dairy trucks were spreading out to seven or eight counties. Nothing made L.S. happier than to sell a quart of pure, wholesome milk. He felt he was doing a real service to the community.

Skiv ran the trucks and the candy production. The company started picking up candy brokers who were paid 5 percent of what they sold. These brokers usually had only four or five non-competitive lines but more candy was needed. Slowly but surely, the company figured out better ways to produce the candy and increase production. It was essentially all hand operations with the bars still being hand dipped in the hot chocolate and hand wrapped and boxed.

Since the IRS had insisted that L.S. stay away from the books and income tax returns, Bayard mostly tended to the administration of the partnership and all of its endeavors. One of these endeavors was a retail store that was open seven days a week. Everyone put in long hours and kept working hard.

It was one of the least controversial periods in the company. The four partners kept their salaries mostly to what they needed to live on. They accumulated enough capital to have the business grow each year. How much they increased their net worth during the next five or six years had to do with the next family crisis.

By this time, Vernon was the night editor of the *Decatur Herald* and was doing well in the newspaper business. But L.S. wasn't satisfied with that. "I want Vernon back in the business," L.S.said to Skiv one day. "And I want you to help me get it done."

"Dad, he's happy up there," Skiv said. "Why don't you let 'im be? Besides, Bayard won't go for him being a partner at this point."

"You get it done. I don't care how you do it."

"I would love to have him, but—"

"Daddamnit, Everett! You heard me. I want him here. You get him here."

The elder Heath knew that if anyone could sell the other two brothers and Vernon, it would be Skiv. He was the only one the old man thought could handle Bayard for sure. To please his father and keep peace in the family, Skiv approached Bayard.

"Oh, the hell with what Dad wants," Bayard said without hesitation. "I've been expecting that. Vernon doesn't know crap about business. That will make two we've got to carry."

Bayard was referring to Pete, whom Skiv always defended. But the negotiations continued until a compromise was finally worked out. Bayard insisted upon full market value for the interest in the partnership; Skiv agreed, provided

Vernon didn't have to have any money up front and had plenty of time to pay the full amount. Both agreed and decided to determine the net worth of the partnership and divide it by five for what it would cost Vernon to quit his job and return to the family business.

"We have it figured out, Dad," Skiv told L.S., who had stayed out of the negotiations. "Vernon will have to pay thirty-nine thousand dollars to become a full partner. He can pay it over a period of time out of his draw."

"That sounds fair," L.S. said. "What does Pete say about it?"

Pete didn't think much of the deal. Because the money was coming gradually from a salary draw and providing no immediate influx of capital into the business yet bringing another family member to support, he saw no benefit to it. The money Vernon had to pay to become a partner was hardly a number to get excited about since it wasn't going to be in the bank. But Pete liked Vernon better than he did Bayard, and Pete wasn't about to raise hell with L.S. or Skiv.

"He'll go along with what I say," Skiv said.

"Good," L.S. said. "You go up to Decatur and sell Vernon on the idea then."

So Skiv went to Decatur to see Vernon. That's all that was needed. He offered some resistance but soon gave in to his big brother's argument.

"I went to college to go into the newspaper business, Skiv," Vernon said, protesting the proposition. "I'm the night editor and like what I'm doing. I have no desire to do anything else—certainly not get into the pop and candy business. And certainly not for thirty-nine thousand dollars. That's more money than I'd make in ten years as a journalist."

"That's the point, Vernon," Skiv said. "You won't make any money as a journalist unless you own the damn paper. We need you with the family where we own the business and can all make good money. If it were up to me, I'd let you in for a lot less to get you back home just because you're my brother. But Bayard insisted that you buy in at the fair market value. Which is thirty-nine thousand dollars."

"That's highway robbery," Vernon said. "You might as well put a gun to my head and put me down the road."

As a father, L.S. knew his sons. And he knew Vernon would holler about the thirty-nine thousand dollars. Yet he had no doubt that Skiv's persuasive powers would prevail as they did. Vernon came, but he complained about it often. His contempt for Bayard, because he had insisted on the value of the interest in the partnership, was intense and ongoing.

Vernon was, however, a weak man both physically and emotionally. He was like a duck out of water in the Heath business. In another environment, he might have been fine. But in the Heath company, he was absolutely out of synch, even though it wasn't what you knew or how much ability you had that counted:It was having the right last name that counted with the family patriarch.

To their six children, L.S. and Clara Heath were Dad and Mother; to their sons' wives and the grandchildren they were Father and Mother Heath; to everyone else, they were Mr. and Mrs. Heath. And only one man was Mr. Heath. That's what he was throughout his lifetime, even after Bayard, Skiv, Pete and Vernon were called by their first names by the employees.

Even by this time, Milton Heath would undoubtedly have been proud of the dynasty his son had created. L.S. pretty much controlled the family. Despite intense disagreements, his sons were still with the company, married and hadn't killed or maimed each other. The women in the family had personalities just as diverse and as complicated as their husbands.

Clara Heath was a small, browbeaten woman who did everything her husband told her to do. She bore him six kids, took care of the house and was fairly pleasant to be around, if she liked you. The problem was that she didn't like her daughters-in-law, and they didn't like her and her ways.

Beth, Bayard's wife, and Clara Heath had many similar characteristics. Both could be shrews when they wanted to be; both had a hot temper and a quick, sharp tongue. Thelma, Pete's wife, also had a quick temper. But she was smart enough to stay out of the women's family politics of who had this, who had that and why she should have that. Bea, Vernon's wife, was much like him. She was so meek and quiet you hardly knew she was around, at least from outward appearances.

Madeline Heath was a beautiful woman who had been courted by Ray Luton, an up-and-coming Ohio Oil Company employee, at the same time Skiv was courting her. One day he said, "Madeline, I'm not going to fool around with this anymore. Either marry me now or let's forget it." She was as emotionally strong as Skiv but said yes because she loved him. While she didn't want any part of the family squabbling, she found it difficult to stay out of it. She was closest to Thelma, and their relationship grew closer over the years.

Of the six Heath offspring, Ruby probably had more of her father's bad personality traits. Just behind Skiv in age, she was a fairly large woman who was as selfish and greedy as they come. If she didn't get what she wanted when she wanted it, she would rant and rave and never let it be forgotten. Had she not been a Heath, nobody in the family would have cared about her one way or the other.

Her youngest sister, Mary, and the baby of the family, was just coming of age in the thirties. She was a likeable young woman with a good sense of humor who was fun to be around. Yet her appearance and demeanor could be deceiving, and she could be more devious and untrustworthy than anyone in the family when it came to getting what she wanted in life.

As the decade of the thirties moved along, the Heath women played rather minor roles in the development of the company. In those Depression-era years, they had an easier life than most of their neighbors and had only to worry about getting as much of the Heath pie as the next one. And as long as they were all living well and had more than most, there was really nothing to fight about.

6

In some ways, Robinson was unique among small towns in America during the thirties. People weren't rich, but with the Heath company, the pottery (a company that manufactured bathroom fixtures), the oil refinery and the oil fields in full production, most people got along fairly well. The refinery belonged to the Ohio Oil Company, headquartered in Findlay, Ohio, and was a leader in exploring and producing the rich oil fields in Crawford County and contiguous counties.

Many small farms were located in the rural area surrounding Robinson. Almost every farmer had a milk cow or two. And L.S. wanted to buy every available gallon of milk for the dairy. That helped the farmers, provided jobs and supplied fresh milk and other dairy products for area residents. Always with a soft spot in his heart for farmers, L.S. often loaned a hard-up one money so he could stay in business. The company bought four small farms for the going price of about fifty dollars an acre when the farms came up for sale.

Two banks survived the worst of the Depression after they combined assets with smaller banks. The Crawford County State Bank and the Second National Bank of Robinson stood tall on the north and east sides of the Square, respectively. Although Robinson was only a town of about five thousand residents, it had a country club located on the northeast side of town. Bayard and Skiv had become charter members in 1924.

All the while, the Heath company grew slowly until it employed nearly two hundred people. Still, the Heaths lived in modest homes, enjoyed frugal lifestyles and plowed the profits of the company back into the business as working capital.

That often caused arguments between husband and wife. Young Dick Heath overheard arguments between his parents from his earliest memory about the amount of money Skiv brought home.

"You hardly make enough money to feed us, let alone buy clothes and other things the children and I need," Madeline would say as the arguments heated up. "I'm sick and tired of living this way."

"You're sick and tired of it, Madeline?" Skiv would say, raising his voice. "We may not have much, but there are a hell of a lot of people who have a damn sight less. These are hard times. Everything will be better when we get those new kettles and conveyor belts. That will increase production and lower costs at the same time. Things are going pretty good, anyway."

"Sure they are. The kids wear their clothes until they are threadbare. Their shoes have holes in the soles, and their toes stick out the ends. I haven't had a new dress for so long I wouldn't know what one looked like. And if I did get one, Beth or Mary or Ruby or God only knows who would run to Mother Heath and say, 'Look at what Madeline got.' There's no money for anything, including your precious equipment."

To an extent, she was correct. While the Heaths made a good living at the time, there was very little left over for expansion and no money available to borrow for it. And as long as the Democrats were in power, the Heaths thought nothing would change.

Skiv's family lived in a small frame house, similar to what the other family members had. When Dick was five years old, he sat with his father listening to the radio for the election results between President Roosevelt and Alf Landon. Hearing that Roosevelt had won by a landslide, Skiv jumped to his feet and began yelling at Madeline.

"Start packing," he said. "We're going to move to Mexico. I can't stand four more years of FDR."

Of course, he did stand it. And the family stayed put in Robinson. When Roosevelt beat Wendell Wilkie in the 1940 election, Skiv was going to move the family to Canada. Yet in spite of all the problems, the families had many friends and provided a good life for their kids who had fun growing up in the years just before the Heath company really expanded.

One of Skiv's early friends, Charlie Dees, the county highway commissioner, played a major role in that expansion and growth of the company. Dees, from nearby Oblong, and Frank Reese, one of the early employees of the company, were Skiv's hunting buddies. Skiv loved to hunt quail, even though compared to Dees and Reese, he wasn't that good of a shot.

Many times the three of them would be out hunting together when a covey of quails flew, and the men all shot at the same time, not knowing who actually killed the bird or birds. More often than not it wasn't Skiv. Dees had a lot of respect for him, anyway; but what heightened that respect was one day when he knew Skiv had made the shot but never yelled that it was his bird. That modesty and sense of fair play probably led to a new and exciting chapter in the lives of all the families and certainly for the company.

"Bill Wyke and I were talkin' the other night about the oil field they're drillin' out over south of Newton, Skiv," Dees said one day in early 1940. "You're sort of a gambler, and we thought you might be interested in leasing a little patch of ground over there."

Wyke was one of Skiv's friends, too. Dees and Wyke, who owned and operated a gravel pit, had married sisters who owned some farm ground in Jasper County, south of Newton, about thirty-five miles southwest of Robinson. The land was right in the middle of one of the biggest oil fields in the state at the time. Gulf Oil Company and Pure Oil Company had leased virtually all the land in the field. Bell Brothers, a local company, had leased what the larger companies didn't get. All three companies had been hitting good producing wells.

"I don't know anything about the oil business, Charlie," Skiv said. "We make candy."

Dees laughed. "I know you do," he said. "But you don't have to know anything about the oil business. They've been making wells all over the place. All you have to have is a place to drill a well. And I have that for you."

"How's that?" Skiv asked, listening carefully.

"We were looking at our leases the other night," Dees said and chuckled before he continued. "We've got a little patch right in the middle of all this that somehow wasn't leased. Everybody overlooked it. If you want the lease and will drill a well, you can have it."

While Skiv didn't know much about the oil business, he was smart enough to know that it looked like a good opportunity to drill an oil well and make money—as good as he was ever likely to find. And he knew if there was a well there, it would provide necessary funds for the Heath company expansion and development.

Dees wanted to help a friend, but he also wanted a well

drilled on the farm. A land owner receives a one-eighth royalty off the top of any well produced on the property, without any financial risk.

"How much would it take to drill an oil well over there, Charlie?" Skiv asked.

"About five thousand dollars to drill it and equip it, if you hit a well that makes oil."

"Five thousand dollars?" Skiv said blankly. That was a lot of money. He knew the company didn't have five thousand dollars to gamble on drilling an oil well. Oil was selling at about $1.85 a barrel, and a good well would bring in much more than the original investment. But he also knew that there is no dead cinch in drilling and producing an oil well, no matter how good the site was. It was always a risky venture. Nevertheless, he wanted to take advantage of the opportunity. "How long do I have to give you an answer, Charlie?"

"How about a week?"

"Okay."

Skiv immediately took the proposition to the family. He got support from L.S. and Pete right away. Bayard was hesitant. He wasn't a gambler, but he was also smart enough to know about risks and rewards.

L.S. went to the Second National Bank of Robinson, where the company did its banking, and asked to borrow the money. The bank turned him down. That made the decision tougher because the company needed its working capital.

Finally, Skiv said, "I've got some friends who I could go to if we don't want to drill it."

The final decision belonged to L.S. And he wanted to drill the well. He looked at his other three sons when Skiv spoke and simply said, "We'll drill it."

They agreed. But it didn't set well with the wives. Their lives were improving as the company slowly grew, and the Depression was fading away to better times.

"What if it's a dry hole?" Madeline asked Skiv. "What next?"

"It won't be a dry hole. It'll make something."

"What does Bayard say?"

"He's for it."

"Do you have to, Skiv?"

"Yes, if we're ever going to be a real company."

"Why's that?"

"Because we could never accumulate enough capital to build a new candy plant. And without it, we'll always be limited."

"But we're making a nice living now. We'll always do that."

"I want us to do something more than just make 'a nice living.'"

"So what you're telling me is that to be successful the way you want to be, you have to gamble?"

"Isn't business all a gamble? Isn't life a gamble?"

"I guess so," Madeline said, resigned to the fact that the oil well was going to be drilled. She was comforted by the knowledge that the lease was only for enough acreage to drill one well.

The drilling rig moved in and drilling began in late July of 1940. For the first few days, nothing exciting happens at a well site except hard work. Two or three crews work around the clock getting the rig set up and the hole started. Few people besides the crew are around most of the time. Then as the depth where the formation that may have oil is getting close, the investors and other interested spectators start hanging around at all hours of the day and night.

Late one afternoon, the Heath family pulled up to its drilling site to see what was going to happen when the depth was reached and the well was expected to come in. It was hot and dusty, a powdery, light tan dust puffed up with each movement of tires and shoes while putting yet another layer on everything in sight. Nine-year-old Dick looked over at L.S.'s 1939 Ford sedan and saw his grandmother sitting in the front seat with a hat on, watching silently.

The rest of the family was gathered around an old trailer some 150 feet from the rig. At some 2,734 feet in the McClosky Sand formation, the crew had taken core samples. The whole area smelled like crude oil. Pump jacks were bobbing up and down at other well sites in all directions, pumping the raw crude into the huge tanks sitting near the wells.

Excitement and apprehension filled the air. Everybody stood around in groups, talking to one another, nervously keeping an eye on the rig or pacing back and forth. Nobody knew what was going to happen. Skiv and Charlie Dees had been in the dog house talking to the driller and were walking toward the group.

"Driller said there were some awful good shows (of oil) in the core samples," Skiv said to no one in particular and flashed a big toothy grin at them all. It had been twenty-six years since he and Bayard had opened the little confectionery on the Robinson Square.

At close to five o'clock someone said, "We'll know in a few minutes. Keep your fingers crossed."

There was a lot of activity at the well head, indicating that there was going to be a big show one way or the other. All eyes were glued to the hole. All at once a roar like that of a big freight train began building. The gas pressure was tremendous. Then there was a big bang and a blowing sound, and the oil started shooting high up in the derrick of the rig.

"We hit it," somebody yelled. "We hit a gusher."

Everybody was jumping up and down and screaming in the sultry heat of the late afternoon sun. Skiv and Pete walked towards the well and stuck their hands in the oil that was coating everything in the area and came back and rubbed it in L.S.'s thinning white hair until it was nearly black.

The drilling crew was covered with the thick, heavy crude oil from head to foot. Both the driller and the roughneck squinted through oil-splattered eyelids as they fought to shut down the spouting, shooting oil.

Even before the crew got the oil flow slowed down, the family patriarch called everybody together. L.S. wanted to give a speech.

"Now look here," he said, oil streaming down his forehead. "Listen here, listen here, listen to me, damn it. Be quiet. I want you to listen to me. Before any of you are going to start spending any of this money, we are going to build our new candy plant."

Clara Heath still sat silently in the car a few yards away as her husband spoke. He had made it plain and clear that the company would go ahead with plans to increase production now that the means were available. Foolish spending wouldn't be tolerated. The Heath men wanted a new plant, but they also wanted to benefit from the newfound wealth. Most everybody resented L.S.'s domineering control of the family and the business. Nobody but Skiv had the courage to challenge it at the moment.

"Well, I'll tell you what I'm going to do," Skiv said, "I'm goin' start smokin' big see-gars and goin' to Florida in the winter. That's for starters."

"You'll do no such thing," L.S. said sternly. "We're going to have that new plant. You boys have been talking about it for quite a spell, and that's what you're going to do. This well is going to make a lot of money and change things for us."

He was right about that. The well came in flowing twenty-seven hundred barrels a day and was the biggest well produced in Illinois at the time. It maintained that rate for several months and produced oil for years. And, of course, that kind of production brought the kind of money that couldn't help but change things.

Some of the proceeds went into Heath Enterprises, Inc. The company bought some real estate and a few buildings around Robinson, a result of L.S. not wanting the family money all in one place. The Heath Oil Company was also formed. It dabbled in other oil ventures occassionally but primarily funneled money into the main Heath company for the new plant which was completed in the early fall of 1941.

The newest, most modern and expensive building housed the dairy and bottling franchise. That was no surprise to anyone. The dairy was still the most important part of the company to L.S. The older building was remodeled slightly and more modern equipment was purchased to house and update the candy production, making it possible to increase production dramatically. L.S., Pete and Vernon had offices in the new dairy building. Bayard and Skiv had remodeled offices in the old building.

The two older brothers continued to run the candy business as they had from the inception. Bayard ran the administrative part and kept the books for the whole company. Skiv ran the candy production but oversaw all the milk can-pickup trucks, the Pepsi trucks and the dairy delivery trucks. He also got to the plant at five a.m. each morning to see that everything was in operation. At seven a.m., he would go down to the old confectionery store to have coffee with his old friends.

L.S. and Vernon ran the dairy. Although L.S. had wanted the new candy production equipment and plant, his heart was in the dairy business. There was never any question that he would rather sell a quart of milk than a Heath candy bar or a bottle of Pepsi Cola. And he never let anyone forget it.

Pete was in charge of the bottling operation which was housed in the same building as the candy production but run from a different office. The operation of the company resembled that of two or three separate companies.

Skiv didn't start smoking big cigars, and he had already spent three months of the previous winter in Florida. Dick had asthma and was so sick and weak that the doctor had told Skiv to get the boy out of the Midwestern climate or he could die. On borrowed money, Skiv and Madeline took Dick and Joan to Fort Lauderdale and rented a house on one of the canals. The kids went to school for a time, and the property owners tried to sell Skiv the old house and an acre of land for six thousand dollars. Madeline and the rest of the family talked him out of buying the place and keeping a home in Florida. When Dick recovered sufficiently to leave, they returned to Robinson.

But after the oil well was producing and the money was rolling in, Skiv did pay one thousand dollars for an acre lot across the old Marshall Road from the second hole of the golf course at the Crawford County Country Club. Skiv persuaded A.W. Allen, a wealthy doctor, to cut the acre out of a farm he owned. When Skiv spent another $17,500 to build a two-story, four-bedroom house with a large living room, hallway, den, dining room, kitchen, porch and attached two-car garage, everybody thought he was not showing good sense. The property was out on the northeast part of town, a mile or so from the Heath plant and a mile and a half from the center of town. Nobody could understand anyone building a house way out there next to the country club. Only a few homes were located out that way.

What caused the real furor in the family, though, was the concrete slab Skiv had laid in the backyard for a basketball court. Before it dried, Dick, for whom the court was built, wrote, "May 9, 1941," in the soft concrete. Bayard, Pete and Vernon had either built or bought nice, but smaller homes in the regular residential area of Robinson. The family thought Skiv was being too bold, showing an opulence that wasn't prudent. Most of the family raised hell behind his back. Even Clara Heath was upset over the house.

"Skiv's headstrong," L.S. said, not liking the situation but resigning himself to it. "Skiv's just being Skiv."

And perhaps he was. He had worked hard helping the family and the business get where they were, and he saw nothing wrong in enjoying the fruits of his labor and good fortune. The house was his pride and joy.

7

Just after the company expansion was completed and the new plant was in full operation, World War II broke out in the Pacific. Washington, D.C., lay nearly eight hundred miles east of Robinson. None of the family had ever been there; however, one day in the late spring of 1942, a man from Washington walked into the Heath company office and asked to see a Mr. Heath.

"Which Mr. Heath are you looking for, sir?" the receptionist asked. "There are several."

"The one who can sell me candy," the man said.

"Well, that would be Bayard or Skiv Heath. You can find them in the little office down the street. I'll call and see which one is available. May I tell them who's calling and who you represent?"

"Tell Mr. Heath I'm with the Department of the Army."

The Army had done some tests on candy to determine what would be best suited for supplying the troops. These tests had found that besides being good candy, because of the pure ingredients, the Heath bar had a relatively long shelf life. Based on the tests and needs, the Army placed its first order for $175,000 worth of Heath bars. That was a lot of nickel candy bars.

Coupled with the oil well, the huge order from the Army allowed the Heath company to catapult from a small regional company to a national company virtually overnight.

Skiv believed the war would be over in a few months, once the United States started flexing its muscle. But in the eighteen months between the oil well and the Army contract, an increasing number of young men were going off to military service and creating a labor shortage. More women and younger males took the jobs left behind.

Just after his eleventh birthday in the late spring of 1942, Dick Heath took his first job with the company other than his batboy days. The Army required that the government order be shipped in wooden cases with a waterproof liner in each case. Each corner of the cases had to be painted black with a green stripe around it. Dick's job was to paint the green stripe on the cases.

With the war effort in full swing, it wasn't long before everything seemed to be in short supply and had to be rationed. Even bottle caps were in short supply. The Heath company decided to recork the used bottle caps and reuse them. When the Pepsi drivers stocked the coolers and picked up the empties, they also picked up all the caps that had fallen into the slot of the coolers, put them in a cardboard box and brought them back to the plant to be sorted and recorked. That was Dick's second job with the company.

L.S. hired five other kids and Dick at a nickel an hour for the job. Dick's boyhood friends, Jack Chamblin and Bus Stevens, were among the boys hired. They sorted the various brands and different flavors into nearly twenty piles. When the caps were sorted, the boys chiseled out the cork, put in a new cork and ran the cap through a stamper.

"You boys are doing a fine job," L.S. said each time he came around to pay them.

The boys beamed but kept working, knowing that he would call for them or stop by at any time and might pay them an extra nickel for working so hard. They were already making an extra effort by looking hard for Vess bottle caps because the bottler paid extra for them.

"Here is one of those Vess caps you boys are looking for," L.S. said as he ran his fingers over a pile of caps, picked it out of the pile and handed it to Dick. "How many hours have you boys worked since I paid you last week?"

"Just about nine, Father Heath," Dick said standing erect in front of the elder Heath. "We've worked very hard, too, sir. We could get more caps sorted and stamped, if we had more. The drivers don't bring us enough to keep us at work all the time."

The truth was the boys worked as much as they wanted and could hardly wait to get their pay and run off to spend it on ice cream and candy. Further, the drivers kept them well supplied in bottle caps. L.S. looked around the huge pile of caps with a twinkle in his eyes while the other boys cast sideways glances at each other and dug through the piles.

"I'll see if I can't get the drivers to keep the bottle caps coming in with more regularity," L.S. said, smiling. "Busy boys are good boys. Come now, here's a fifty-cent piece for each of you."

The boys dropped their caps and scrambled to stand on line with Dick. As L.S. ambled in front of them, he dropped a shiny new silver Liberty Head half dollar in each of their outstretched hands.

"Thank you, sir," each boy said before the coin hardly touched his palm.

"You're welcome, young man," L.S. said to each one.

"Now get back to work, and I'll see you next week. Don't lose that money."

Before he was through the door, the boys were back at their piles of caps with the coin clutched tightly in their hands. After he was gone, they held the money up for closer inspection.

"Wow," Bus Stevens said. "Fifty cents. I can't wait to get up town. I want to get—"

Several excited voices talking at once drowned out what Stevens wanted. Each boy wanted something and wanted to talk about it. Jack Chamblin stood looking pensively at his coin.

"What are you going to do with yours, Jack?" Dick asked. "Are you—"

"Geez, Dick, I don't know. But why did you have to go and tell your grandpa that the drivers aren't bringing in enough bottle caps? There are plenty. Now he'll have 'em bring in a truck load, and we'll never get to play ball this summer."

"I just wanted him to know we were working hard," Dick said, a hurt feeling passing over him. "He gave us an extra nickel, didn't he?"

Practically everything was rationed during the war, including the butter, sugar, almonds and chocolate needed for the Heath bar. Because of the government contract, however, the Heath company was allowed all the ingredients it needed to make the candy. Some butter was being produced in the dairy, but it wasn't enough for the candy plant. So butter for the candy was shipped in with the sugar and almonds, and the dairy trucks supplied Heath customers all over the territory with butter.

The chocolate came from the Nestle company, which

produced a blend it called Peters that was perfect for use in making the Heath candy bar. Each fifty-pound block of Peters Blend broke down into ten-pound slabs so a man could open the box and put a slab at a time into the large metal cooking vats. Each vat held about two hundred pounds of chocolate which heated with a huge paddle that melted and circulated the chocolate. It was then pumped upstairs to the enrober, a machine that put a thick coat of chocolate around the toffee.

Totally modern, the new candy plant had been built on two floors. Upstairs, twenty to twenty-five copper kettles large enough to hold fifty gallons of cooking toffee lined each wall of a fairly large room. The kettles all sat on gas heaters. In a separate room, sugar was poured into the empty kettles that sat two to a cart. Once the kettles were filled with sugar, the carts were rolled to another room to get the fresh almonds which had just been run through a crusher.

Both the sugar and the almonds came in one hundred-pound bags. The chocolate, sugar and almonds were all shipped to the Heath plant in railroad cars. A spur of the New York Central Railroad had been built behind the plant where the cars were dropped off and positioned. Butter was shipped in by truck and stored in a cooler at an old warehouse nearby.

After the required amount of crushed almonds were added to the sugar, the cart and two kettles were pushed off to another room to add the butter. It was stored in a large metal vat that was heated and operated similarly to the chocolate vat. Sixty- to sixty-five-pound boxes of butter were dumped into each vat to be melted. The exact amount of butter was weighed out and added to each kettle. Finally, several pounds of toffee scraps from earlier batches were added to each new batch.

Then the kettles were wheeled to the gas heaters and

placed over them to cook. With all the heaters going at once, the heat in the cooking room was almost unbearable in the summer and barely tolerable in the winter. Each kettle of toffee was cooked for a specific number of minutes at a specific temperature, all the while being stirred with automatic mixers. Although the recipe, a closely guarded secret, specified the exact number of minutes the toffee was to be cooked, the head cook was so good at his job that he could look at the toffee and tell when it was done.

The rich, sweet smell of cooking toffee permeated the room and spread throughout the plant, seeping into every corner and lingering everywhere. When a batch of toffee was done, the mixing apparatus was lifted out of the kettle. A worker with a large, thick knife scraped the hot toffee from the mixer blade.

Then the finished kettles were loaded back on the carts and wheeled to another room containing two stainless steel slabs some eight feet wide by eighteen feet long. Each slab stood on legs and were recessed approximately a quarter of an inch from the outside edges. Two men with thick gloves grasped the handles on each side of the kettles and poured the bubbling toffee onto the slabs. Each slab had its own cooling apparatus to quickly lower the temperature of the toffee.

Another six men, each with a large, wide spatula, spread the runny toffee evenly over the slabs. When the toffee was spread, it looked like a giant sheet fitting evenly with the outside edge. The hot, pliable toffee cooled quickly and was right to cut in about three minutes.

Cutters came in two sizes. One was on a three-foot roll with a blade that was round like a wheel. Each wheel on the roll was three inches apart. This cutter was used to cut sideways (across the slab) on the eight-foot cut and had eight rolls of cutters with a handle on each side to roll it along like a giant roller used to roll out a pie crust. One man rolled it out to the middle of the slab, and a man on the other side pulled it to him. By doing this a couple of times, ribbons of toffee were cut three inches wide. This process was repeated all the way down the slab.

The other big cutter roller was eight feet long and had roller blades that were two inches wide. One man on each side would roll the cutter to the end and back again. By this time, there were many little toffee bars cut to size almost a quarter of an inch deep but not completely through to the slab.

With the toffee cooling all the time, the slab men cut the pliable candy into square-foot sheets and put them on sheet pans. These pans were placed on another cart and rolled to the enrobing room where the toffee was coated with chocolate and packaged on two assembly lines.

A shaker resembling a big tray was positioned at the beginning of the line. Two women stood on each side, breaking the large sheets by hand into individual bars. Since the toffee was already partially cut and hardened, the bars broke easily and were spread in lines on the shaker. Broken pieces were tossed on another tray to be recooked later.

The lines were larger that the bars and allowed a constant flow of them on the moving belt. Belts on each enrober had ten lines of bars within inches of each other. As the belts moved through a tunnel, hot chocolate squirted out jets and covered both the top and bottom of each bar. A woman on each side of the belt touched up the chocolate and inspected the bars when they left the enrobing tunnel.

Cooling rapidly, the finished Heath English Toffee Bar

moved on down the conveyor belt toward twelve wrapping machines at alternating spots on each side. A woman at each machine hand-fed the bars into the machine to be wrapped. When the wrapped bars came out, another woman with an ordinary spatula picked up the bars and put them into a box which held twenty-four bars. After the last bar was in place, the lid was closed, a sleeve wrapped around the box and it was thrown onto another conveyor belt.

The boxes moved along to a chute that carried them downstairs. There, two more women put twenty-four boxes in a cardboard box, sealed it with three-inch tape and stacked it, ready to be shipped. These boxes were called Item 576 — twenty-four nickel bars in each of the twenty-four boxes.

That was the procedure of making candy made possible by the oil well and was being used by the company when war broke out in December 1941. At that time, the company had only a few brokers handling its candy and could produce much more than it sold. Those brokers were paid as they had been when L.S. had first sold a wholesaler ten years earlier, 5 percent for the sale of each box of Heath English Toffee Bars. The brokers still paid eighty cents a box with a 2 percent discount on payment within ten days for larger orders and sold the nickel bars to retailers for ninety-six cents a box.

Without the new plant and increased production capabilities, the Heath company would never have been able to sign the government contract and introduce the Heath English Toffee Bar to millions of GIs around the world in World War II. That government contract was extremely important to the future of the company. The first order of $175,000 alone, not considering the value of the exposure, set the base of sales to come after the war. A picture of the government check was framed and hung in Bayard's office for years.

Not all was modern going into the war years, though. Since gas was rationed and trucks were hard to get, the retail milk route in Robinson was serviced by a horse pulling a milk wagon. Products were cooled with chunks of ice. Artie Cowden, foreman of the yard crew, took care of the two horses and housed them in stalls located at the back of the plant. Neighborhood kids got a big kick out of a driver in a horse and wagon delivering dairy products at a time when they thought the horse-and-buggy days were gone for good.

In 1941, with both the country and the Heath company poised for some of their finest hours, Mary Heath had gone to New York to study at the Juliard School of Music. Money was no longer an obstacle for members of the Heath family in pursuing their dreams. But Mary's dreams took another turn when she met John "Jack" Morris in Chicago.

He had graduated from the University of Minnesota and was in the stocks and bonds business in Chicago. Tall and ruggedly handsome, Jack was a great golfer who had once played on the U.S. Walker Cup team. After a brief courtship, he and Mary got married and planned to live in Chicago.

L.S. wouldn't hear of that. He was determined to keep his family around him and in the family business. With Mary's persuasive powers and his stubborn insistence, L.S. succeeded again. Jack was virtually coerced into moving to Robinson and joining the Heath company to handle shipping and purchasing for the candy division.

To further assure that Ruby would stay in Robinson, L.S. had built a home for her directly behind his own. That way she could also help take care of her mother. Later, Ruby married Bernard Dowling, a man from Kansas City who had been an

executive with General Motors. He had had a nervous breakdown and had to quit work. Although he was limited in what
he could do because of his illness, everybody liked him. L.S.
was particularly pleased with him because he readily agreed
to move to Robinson where he was given a job at the plant with
no assigned duties. Nobody cared. He never caused anyone a
problem.

All L.S. cared about regarding the family was that he had
them all gathered about him. With Ruby settled, the sly old
man had done it. He had them all together, what he had wanted
from the very beginning. Four of his offspring had left or
considered leaving, but he had solved that one way or another.
And what had started out with he and his wife and children
multiplied to many as their families grew. L.S. couldn't have
been happier with the way things were turning out.

Nor could he have been happier with the way his grandchildren were getting started in life. The oldest of them,
Bayard Jr., who had had a wild streak and had once run his car
through the front plate glass of a tavern on the Robinson
Square, had settled down and graduated from Duke University in the spring of 1941. He had met Patricia Reed, a coed
from Miami, at Duke, married her and moved back to Robinson
to work at the Heath plant after he graduated.

But World War II changed all of that. When the Japanese
bombed Pearl Harbor, Bayard Jr. volunteered and was sent to
Officer's Candidate School at Fort Knox, Kentucky. Jack
Morris was drafted. Both ended up in the European Theater,
Jack as a sergeant in General Mark Clark's Fifth Army and
Bayard as a captain in General George Patton's Third Army.

Bayard spent quite awhile in Louisiana before being
shipped to France with the Ninth Armored Division. When

General Patton turned his army to move in support of allied troops at the Battle of the Bulge near Bastogne, France, in December 1944, Bayard's unit was one of the first to arrive in the area. His company of eight tanks immediately ran into elements of a German Panzer division and took a beating. Since the Germans didn't know the allied strength at the time, the survivors were able to hold on through the night until more units of the Third Army arrived the next morning.

Because of the resulting confusion and the fact that his unit was technically knocked out of action, Bayard was listed as missing in action for eleven days. He ended up going all the way to the Elbe River and meeting the Russians.

During these war years, the next generation of Heaths were growing up in and with the business, just as Bayard Jr. and his sister, Joan, had before the war. Bob and Joyce, Pete's kids, were in high school. Dick and Joan were in grade school. John and Allan, Vernon's kids, were either in grade school or soon to be. John Jr. and Robert Morris, Mary's kids, were born after the war, completing the set of grandchildren L.S. counted on to keep the Heath company in the family.

Like every place in the country where the able-bodied men were in the service, Robinson had women, young men and old men available for the work force. Bayard Jr. had worked for the company during the summers, both in high school and college. By 1943, it was necessary for the Heath boys to work during school when they were needed. At twelve years old, Dick rode with Candy Schlosser or Joe Cox on the dairy trucks as their helper. Bob worked at the plant doing various jobs. Both boys continued to work throughout the war and developed a close relationship.

Dick, who was three years younger than Bob and had

looked up to his older cousin from the first time he could remember him. He didn't remember exactly when that was, but whenever it was he could remember telling his parents and hearing them say that Bob had a terrible temper. Thelma, his mother, had told them that Bob got so angry as a child that he would sometimes hit his head against the wall.

That temper rarely got in the way of the two cousin's relationship. While they grew closer as time passed, a rivalry between them developed regarding their athletic ability that they regarded as nothing more than the competitive spirits that grew from individual personalities and the Robinson-area athletic persona.

In 1942, the Robinson High School football team had been beaten by Palestine, a small town seven miles east of Robinson, in the first game of the season. One of Skiv's friends, Frank Reese, had played football at Notre Dame with the famous Four Horsemen under legendary Coach Knute Rockne. After graduating from Notre Dame, Reese served as a line coach for Hunk Anderson of the Chicago Bears and coached at North Carolina State. Later, he retired from coaching and worked as a cement salesman for Leigh Cement Company in Robinson. But he didn't lose interest in athletics or working with young athletes.

So after Robinson was beaten in that first game, Reese decided to help the team. He didn't want to interfere with Coach Harry Sockler, however, and started taking outstanding young athletes like Jack Kaley and other individual players and working with them in his back yard every Saturday morning. That was the start of the "golden years" of Robinson athletics. During this time, Robinson was a town of about five thousand people; and for the next ten years, more than half of them followed the team. Dick was only eleven years old when it started, and it was a great inspiration to him and also helped him frame a will to win.

On these teams in the war years were Kaley, Jim Brackett, Dave Steele, Mort Rich, Charlie Weck, Pro Combes, John Holloway, Frank Chamberlin, Doyle Dressback, Rex Sabastian and others. The football team, after that first loss in early fall 1942, went undefeated until a post-season game in 1947 when Bloom High School from the Chicago area won a 13-7 game in the mud at Robinson for the mythical state championship sponsored by the *Chicago Daily News*. That game drew more people as spectators than resided in Robinson at the time.

The basketball teams were almost as good. That winning attitude filtered down to the grade school team. Pro Combes, also a basketball star for the Robinson High School Fighting Maroons, often went to the grade school to work with the younger players. Dick and Jack Chamblin, close friends since Chamblin had moved from the oil fields of Texas in the late thirties, made the first team on a good basketball team as seventh graders.

Dick, tall and rangy, played center. And Chamblin, a little shorter but heavier and well developed, played guard with eighth graders Bus Stevens, Ed Wade, Don Simons, Marvin Smith, Harold Bennett and Jack Woodland, all good athletes. In the eighth grade, Dick and Chamblin teamed up with Lyle Daughtery, Joe Siler, Harold Meeks and others to go undefeated until the final game of the Grade School State Tournament when they lost to Anna. Observers thought both Dick and Chamblin were too old to be playing grade school basketball because of their size and ability.

In the spring of their eighth grade year, Coach Sockler

invited both boys out for spring high school football practice. This was to practice with a team that was unbeaten for three years. Chamblin, only thirteen years old, was such an exceptional football player that he made the starting lineup at fullback the next fall on another undefeated team. He made the all-state team by his senior year.

In addition to starting at fullback, Chamblin started at linebacker with Bob Heath, who was a senior and center on offense and made the All-Wabash Valley team.

Compared to his friend and cousin, Dick was an average football player. He was a starting end on the varsity team his junior and senior years and made the All-Wabash Valley team (composed of Terre Haute, Indiana, teams and several schools in Illinois) his senior year. Basketball was another story.

As a freshman, Dick started half the varsity games at forward; as a senior, Bob sat on the bench as a reserve guard. And despite their closeness and affection for each other, a jealousy in Bob and a rivalry in Dick developed that was always present afterwards, although neither of them seemed aware of the emotion for a long time or even knew it existed.

The entire Heath family enthusiastically supported the boys and the high school athletic program, attending most home games and many away ones. They were always eager to talk basketball with Dick. Perhaps L.S. was Dick's greatest fan. The elder Heath would show up at six p.m. for all the home games when Dick was in high school and claim a front-row seat.

Throughout both grade school and high school, the Robinson teams Dick played on did well in post-season play. In his high school career, the team advanced to the state tournament three times. He became the only player in school history to play on three state tournament teams and made the second team on the all-state squad his senior year. The year the team didn't reach the state, the team that won the state title beat Robinson in the sectional.

In golf, Dick shot his first par at the age of twelve. Both he and Bob were scratch golfers (no handicaps). But Dick won the Kentucky State Junior Amateur title two years in a row, which qualified him for the Nationals at Lincoln, Nebraska, and Peoria, Illinois, respectively. Gene Littler beat him in the semi-finals with Dick two strokes down with one hole to play. At the Nationals, they played match play, too—with Littler winning again.

In 1944, Dick and his sister, Joan, and Bob and his sister, Joyce, had gone to summer camp (boys and girls had separate camps) at St. John's Military Academy in Delafield, Wisconsin. Neil Armstrong and Bob Finnemore, two Oklahoma A&M football stars, and Bob Kurland, a seven-foot Oklahoma A&M basketball player, worked as camp counselors. Up until that time, Dick was closer to Joyce, who had told him about the birds and the bees on a bicycle ride when they were ten or eleven years old, than he was to his own sister or to Bob. At that camp, however, the boys learned to know each other better than they ever had in Robinson, and Dick grew to idolize Bob.

No more than they later realized or spoke about their jealousy or rivalry in athletics, neither did they talk about these feelings with respect to the company or the business. Both of them worked every summer at the plant. Over the four summers of their respective high school years, they worked at virtually every job available at the company and got to know the business. They worked just like the other employees and were paid the same wages. When they worked for Skiv, they were treated no differently than anyone else and were not allowed to fool around.

At age fourteen as a high school freshman-to-be, Dick had the city Pepsi Cola route in Robinson. Driver's licenses weren't required for the job. He drove a company truck with a deck body that required the driver to load and unload each empty and full case by hand.

Because of recent successes in high school athletics, the town was sports crazy. Dick wanted to put the Bubble-Up, one of the sodas bottled at the Heath plant, in Jim Rooney's grocery store. Rooney didn't want the drink because he didn't think it would sell. Dick persisted.

"Tell you what I'm agoin' do, Dickie," Rooney finally said. "I'll let you put the stuff in the store on one condition: If Robinson goes to the state tournament in basketball next spring, you have to promise to get me two tickets."

"I want the biggest display in the store," Dick said. Bubble-Up was his favorite drink, and he knew it would sell. "And I want it near the checkout counter."

"You've got a deal. But you'd better come up with the tickets."

Bubble-Up began selling wildly, and Dick became known as the Bubble-Up King. The basketball team made it to the state tournament. And Dick got the two tickets for Jim Rooney.

8

After the oil well had come in and money was no longer a problem for the family, L.S. became chairman of the board of the Second National Bank of Robinson. Bayard Sr. became chairman of the board of the Crawford County State Bank, the other bank in town. One day, the banks let them in the front door but wouldn't loan them the money to drill the oil well; the next day, after they hit the gusher, two Heaths end up chairmen of the boards.

It was these changes and different circumstances that dictated a restructuring of the company from a partnership consisting of the four Heath brothers and their father, all on an equal basis, to a family corporation. At the end of the war, thirty-one years after the store had opened on the Square, the tax rates had changed and Bayard was convinced the company should be incorporated.

So Bayard made arrangements for an insurance company in Indianapolis to take care of the details. Choosing not to set up a limited partnership, which would have protected the company liability from the five individual partners and avoided corporate taxes and dividend taxes on personal income, the insurance company representatives set up a corporation to enable them to sell key-man insurance policies of seventy-five thousand dollars each to the four brothers with the proceeds upon anyone's death going to the company.

Each partner agreed, or it couldn't have been done. That was the easy part. L.S., the intelligent, extremely well-educated little dictator, still determined to have his family all together no matter what, wanted Ruby and Mary to have an interest in the corporation. That took some doing. He needed Skiv's backing, as usual, to get the job done.

Bayard Sr. didn't like the idea from the outset and said so often. Neither of the sisters knew or cared anything about business, he said. Ruby's husband wasn't able to assume any responsibility because of his nervous breakdown but was already drawing a paycheck.

Mary's husband was still in the Army, but L.S. wanted him to come back to Robinson and take over purchasing and shipping in the candy division again. Bayard didn't mind that because Jack was competent and experienced, something Bayard had learned to respect in his brother-in-law. While the returning servicemen streamed into towns and cities across the country and the weeks and months passed quickly with the renewed optimism the victory of war had brought, the Heath family discussed its future. Skiv tried to explain it all to Madeline one evening at the kitchen table.

"We're going to incorporate the business, Madeline," Skiv said, pushing back from the table and fishing for a Chesterfield from the package in his shirt pocket. "The partnership is not going to work anymore from a tax standpoint."

"Is it just for taxes?" Madeline asked.

"No, I guess not. There are some other things involved. For one thing, Dad would like to give the girls an interest in the business."

"Oh, really. What do you think of that?"

"Well, I'd like to see my sisters have an income."

"What did they ever do to deserve it? Don't they have husbands to take care of them?"

"Yes, but they're Heaths. And Dad wants to give it out of his share."

"How would that work? Aren't you equal partners? I mean the five of you."

"Yeah. Up to this time, anyway. But we've agreed to give him a little more so he can give it to Ruby and Mary."

"So you're giving them some?"

"I guess you could say that."

"He hasn't done any more than anyone else, has he?"

"No, not really. But I'd like to see the girls get something. I care about them, too."

"I'll bet the others don't. I know Father Heath is asking you to sell the others on the idea."

"Probably."

"Skiv, I don't believe you. How could you let him get away with it?"

"Honey, he's my father. I know he's damn wrong, but I went along with him."

"He's nothing but a little Napoleon. He knows how to use you. When you know you're right, Skiv Heath, there's nobody in the world who could make you go against your principles."

"I don't want to talk about it. It's done and that's it."

"On this one, it could affect us all."

"No, it won't. They'd all be fair."

"Skiv, you live in a dream world when it comes to them. They would just as soon cut your throat as look at you."

"Now, Madeline."

"Oh, don't 'Now, Madeline' me. You know it's true. But it's your business, Skiv. It still doesn't make sense to me."

Whether it made sense was not a consideration for L.S. He wanted every member of the family treated equally. Competence or incompetence were unimportant to him in the matter. Having his family around him and well taken care of was important.

By this time, the candy division was far and away the main division of the company. And with Skiv and Bayard totally operating the candy plant, it continued to grow. Together, the dairy and the bottling division made some profit. Separately, a six-county Pepsi Cola operation hardly made a dent in the profit picture, and the dairy steadily lost money.

Part of the problem was that L.S., Pete and Vernon ran the dairy and bottling end of the business. But L.S. was the main problem. He loved the dairy business and would have every gallon of milk picked up that he could. What milk that couldn't be bottled in the new Pure Pak machines was made into cheddar cheese. If a farmer was having a hard time, all he had to do was come and see L.S. He would loan them money, sometimes taking only IOUs.

Even though his efforts at the dairy were not profitable, he knew the other divisions could give everybody something to do. He and Skiv were constantly bickering about the amount of capital that was being spent in the dairy. Bayard was even more outspoken about it. Despite the constant riff, the dairy stayed put, the family stayed together and the stock in the corporation stayed the way L.S. wished it to stay.

The way the corporation was set up when the company was incorporated in 1946 was with 12,800 shares, issued and outstanding, of common stock valued at one hundred dollars per share. Capitalization, then, was $1,280,000. That was the net worth of the partnership retained in the business after draws, salaries and income tax or assets minus liabilities, all approved beforehand by the IRS. The breakdown of stock before L.S. Heath made a split follows:

Lawrence S. Heath	3,200 shares
Bayard E. Heath Sr.	2,400 shares
Everett E. Heath	2,400 shares
Virgil D. Heath	2,400 shares
Vernon L. Heath	2,400 shares

L.S., who had promised his sons that if they went along with his desire to provide his daughters with an income, they would never have a say-so in the business, then transferred sixteen hundred shares, or eight hundred each, to Ruby Dowling and Mary Morris. That wasn't the whole story, either. There was one more wrinkle. His daughters' stock would be preferred stock with the same rights as common stock.

This decision was made and a six dollar-per-share dividend declared so Ruby and Mary would receive forty-eight hundred dollars annually. Bernard Dowling and Jack Morris were both on the payroll at the time, but they were not making as much as L.S. and his sons, who each were taking an annual salary of eighteen thousand dollars. With the dividends from the preferred stock, each of the six families had basically the same amount of income after the company was restructured and the corporation formed on January 1, 1946.

Other problems surfaced before and almost immediately after that date. Before the corporation was legal, a corporate name had to be chosen. Since the main business was the Heath candy bar and people referred to the company as the Heath candy company, the latter with an inc. tacked on seemed most logical for a national company—except that L.S. wanted something else. And he wanted the company's legal name to be L.S. Heath & Sons, Inc. Later market research showed that the name sounded more like a hardware store in Oblong to most people than like a national candy company.

But the names of many local companies across the country were memorials to the men who had succeeded in their greatest desire — starting a family business and surrounding themselves with their families all treated the same. This one was no different, particularly when that was what L.S. wanted.

Neither Skiv nor Bayard were pushovers. Both were tough as anyone when it came to business. While everyone knew Skiv's strength, his weakness to his father was also known. The two of them could argue, cuss each other, almost swing at each other, but Skiv would always go along with his father in the end. And L.S. knew that if he could sell Skiv on something, he would always get his way.

The company was named L.S. Heath & Sons, Inc.

Although L.S. was a dictator when it came to his family, he was also quite generous with everyone for his purposes. Even after the company became L.S. Heath & Sons, Inc., he continued manipulating the stock and tying family members to the company while distributing his stock among them. It made no difference to him that his daughters' husbands were getting paid and his daughters were receiving both stock and dividends. That is what he wanted.

"The girls will never run this business," he told his sons again after everything was in place. "As I told you, I want them to have an income. I think we all agree on that. And since you boys have plenty, I'm going to leave all my stock to the girls. Before I do that, however, I want to leave some to my grandchildren to always remember me."

Both Ruby and Mary were furious about the latter decision. That, of course, would cut into their stock. He didn't do it right away. But to the dismay of his daughters, he finally did nearly four years later.

Besides wanting to leave his grandchildren something to remember him by, he had no intention of letting the government come in and get a big chunk through inheritance tax when he died. He was seventy-seven years old when the company incorporated, and these plans were being made and carried out. At the time, he liked to go down to the Elks Club and have lunch with some of his contempories, Bill Bell and Alex McCandless, who had made fortunes in the oil business, A.W. Allen, a wealthy doctor who had opened a sanitarium bearing his name, and a host of others who liked to brag about how much they were worth. L.S. liked to brag, with a twinkle in his eyes, about how little he owned in his own name.

"I don't want the government to get a penny when I die," he would say shrilly and laugh.

But he didn't get around to giving the stock to his grandchildren until he was eighty years old. In the meantime, because of a lifetime gift deferment allowed by existing tax laws, three of the four Heath brothers gave their children stock in the Heath company in late 1948 or 1949. Those transactions follow:

Bayard Sr.	Bayard Jr., 325; Patricia, 325
Everett E.	Richard, 325; Joan, 325
Virgil D.	Robert, 325; Joyce, 325
Vernon L.	No stock was given to John and Allan

In 1950, L.S. got around to giving eight of his grandchildren fifty shares and two of his grandchildren one hundred shares out of his remaining sixteen hundred shares. Those gifts follow:

Bayard Sr.'s Children		Everett's Children	
Bayard Jr.	50	Richard	50
Patricia	50	Joan	50
Virgil's Children		Vernon's Children	
Robert	50	John	50
Joyce	50	Allan	50
Mary's Children			
John Jr.	100		
Robert	100		

Ruby had no children, so L.S. gave her husband, Bernard, fifty shares. Mary's husband, Jack Sr., also received fifty shares. No explanation was given about why the Morris boys were given an extra fifty shares each or why he decided to give his two sons-in-law any at all. But it didn't seem to matter. Nobody paid any attention. Even when he split his remaining nine hundred shares by giving 450 each to Ruby and Mary and literally owned no company stock in his name, the four sons' families still had more stock in each family than the daughters.

After all the stock shuffling ended in 1950, the families seemed pretty well set. Bayard Sr., Skiv, Pete and Vernon all had twenty-five hundred shares each among their families. Mary, her sons and husband had fifteen hundred shares among them, while Ruby and her husband had thirteen hundred for a combined total of twenty-eight hundred shares between the two families.

The major problem that was overlooked at the time of incorporation was what would happen if something happened to one of the sons. By incorporating, how the money draws were handled was automatically changed. As a partnership, the partners simply divided the profits and drew them out as they were needed. The corporation was entirely different because everybody took salaries and left the profits with the company. And what would happen, for example, if one of the partners died and his salary stopped? What could the family do as minority stockholders to get income?

Those questions were never addressed. Apparently, Frank Holmes, the insurance man from Indianapolis who helped set up the corporation was only interested in selling insurance. What could the seventy-five thousand dollars worth of key-man insurance owned by the corporation do for those who would need it in case of one of the Heath brothers' death? It wouldn't provide salaries. It couldn't buy the stock from the family for anywhere near the value. It couldn't do anything that any of them would personally have wanted in case of a tragedy. But then nobody foresaw any problems when the corporation was formed. Everybody thought it had been handled in the best interests of all.

9

Skiv Heath wanted his son to be a championship golfer, so he hired a golf pro named Red Wiley and paid him five hundred dollars to make the boy an accomplished golfer. That wasn't a difficult task. At fourteen and a freshman in high school, Dick was already a scratch golfer.

Both Dick and his cousin, Bob, were on the Robinson High School golf team. In March of 1946 when Dick was a freshman and Bob was a senior, they were playing at the State High School District Golf Tournament in Sullivan, Illinois. Because they wanted to get a good night's sleep and were going to be playing on sand greens, Bob had driven the two of them up to Sullivan on Friday night in preparation for the Saturday tournament.

Skiv was going to drive up early that morning to watch them play. He rose at his usual time of five a.m. to make the seventy-five-or-so-mile drive. As he walked down the stairs to the basement, he fell, landing at the bottom of the stairs on his head but breaking his fall with his left hand.

"Dumb son-of-a-bitch," he said, muttering to himself as he groped in the semi-darkness of the early morning for his glasses which lay a few feet away. "Wonder I didn't break my goddamn neck." He picked himself up and surveyed the damage. Damn hand feels like it's broken, he thought. And my head feels like somebody took a hammer to it.

Nevertheless, he drove to Sullivan through a half-rain, half-blowing snow to watch the boys play golf. They were on the course when he arrived.

"This is some weather to play golf in," he said, joking easily but holding his left hand in the palm of his right.

"What's wrong with your hand, Dad?" Dick asked before he went over to tee off.

"Nothing really, I don't think."

"Nothing? What are you holding it for then?"

"Oh, I hurt it a little this morning when I fell down the basement stairs. You go on and play golf. I'll be all right."

Both Bob and Dick later saw the swelling and could see that the hand was broken. After the tournament was over, Dick rode home with his father and insisted that he go to the doctor.

"Of course, I'm going to the doctor. But I wanted to watch you guys play golf. The way you played, though, I might as well have stayed home."

Father and son laughed. Dick had finished third, not bad for a freshman. Bob hadn't placed. But back in Robinson, Skiv went to the doctor, had the hand X-rayed and put in a cast. He didn't say anything about hitting his head in the fall.

Bayard Jr. returned from Europe after the war and declined to join the family business, deciding instead to enroll in law school at the University of Michigan where he graduated first in his class. During his years in law school, sons Wickliff and Peter, the first Heaths of the fourth generation, were born. After graduating and passing the bar exam, Bayard Jr., his wife, Pat, and two sons moved to Miami, Florida, and he became a junior partner in a well-established law firm. His first love had always been law.

Pat, Bayard Jr.'s sister, married Lou Keisling after meeting him at Indiana University. Lou was in the insurance business in Sacramento, California, and intended to stay there. He wasn't about to get caught up in the L.S. Heath web.

But Jack Morris Sr. returned from Europe after the war and went back to his old position in purchasing and shipping at the Heath plant. Bayard Sr. and Skiv welcomed him back and treated him like one of the family. Pete and Vernon, but especially Pete, were not so kind and often made cracks about how he got into the family business.

"Hell, he just married a Heath," Pete said, usually when he'd had a little too much bourbon. "He's just a hired hand."

"He's Mary's husband," L.S. said when he overheard. "You just take care of your end of the business and leave Jack alone. You'd be better off leaving that booze alone, too. I never saw anyone amount to a tinker's damn who drank as much as you do."

Family bickering hurt L.S. But the way the business was going would hurt him more. He was growing old, and the business was changing. The candy industry was growing all the time; the dairy was losing ground. He had put in the finest dairy equipment money could buy. Paper Pure Pak machines, expensive pieces of equipment, were purchased to bottle both quarts and half gallons. Everything had to be the finest available. Company trucks were picking up milk from six hundred farmers. If a farmer had two gallons of milk, a driver would go two miles out of the way to get it.

What hurt L.S. was that after taking care of Robinson and the area during the war, the major dairies with cardboard milk cartons and new refrigeration equipment could travel a long distance to dump their products on a market by cutting costs, and his customers would leave him for the competition. He learned the hard way that there is little product loyalty where price is concerned. Even Skiv got angry when he saw somebody buy a competitor's product. Losing a six-case order of candy didn't cause as much fuss as somebody buying one quart of Borden's milk.

A Grade A milk program was instituted where the farmers would receive a higher price for their milk if they had the proper equipment and their milk went into the carton instead of the cheese vat. But the Heath company still paid many farmers Grade A prices when their milk went into the surplus cheese vat.

The company also financed nearly $800,000 of equipment for dairy farmers, deducting payments from their milk checks for the loans. Hardly a day went by when some farmer wasn't in L.S.'s office. During the years just after the war, the company purchased four separate farms from financially strapped farmers.

Little else changed in the years immediately following the war. More members of the fourth generation of the family were born. After graduating from Robinson High School, Bob Heath enrolled at the University of Illinois in the College of Commerce to study management. He also enrolled and took ROTC for infantry service. His sister, Joyce, followed him to Illinois in the fall of 1948 and majored in Spanish. When he graduated in May 1950, Bob, like Bayard Jr., had no interest in joining the Heath company and took a job with Owens-Corning Fiberglass in Granville, Ohio. Perhaps with L.S. still in charge, his grandsons didn't want any part of the company and were strong enough to resist his efforts to get them to return to Robinson and the family business.

On the other hand, Dick had no doubt where he would end

up after college. And it became more apparent as time passed. By the time he was in high school, he had worked at about every job performed at the Heath plant. That included picking up one hundred-pound cans of raw milk from the farms, unloading sugar and chocolate from rail cars, shipping finished candy, driving his own Pepsi Cola route, working in a slab room in the candy kitchen, helping on dairy delivery trucks, packaging ice cream and cottage cheese, unloading supplies, casing Pepsi Cola and milk products and other miscellaneous jobs. He loved the business as much as he loved sports.

   With all the great high school teams in Robinson during the war and post-war years, he had a great deal to love. The school year of 1947-48 was undoubtedly the best of them all in both football and basketball. The same athletes (Rex Sabastian, Harry Hedden, Dick Loughery, Bob Allison, Marvin and Don Smith, Harold Bennett, Friday Chapman, Norm Lackey, Don Bailey, Ted Poland, Larry and Bob Marby, Don Simons, Vaughn and Don Kaley, Joe Siler, Harold Meeks, Lyle Dougherty, Norman Freeman, Melvin Goff, Bus Stevens and Jack Chamblin) played both sports. Dick played on both teams, too. In football, they were undefeated, beating two solid teams out of Terre Haute, Indiana, and the Big 12 champion, Champaign, Illinois.

   In basketball, they went undefeated in November and December, knocking off No. 1 Canton. They won the prestigious sixteen-team Centralia Holiday Tournament in Centralia, Illinois. Dick and Bus Stevens were selected for the all-tournament team. Jack Chamblin made the second team, and Dick was voted the tournament's Most Valuable Player. Neither the football team nor the basketball team lost a game from September through the last of January. They had a good shot at winning the state basketball championship but blew a big lead in the first round against Marshall High, a good Chicago team.

The Ohio Oil Company was building a hundred million-dollar addition to its refinery in Robinson during Dick's sophomore year of high school. Pritchard Construction Company was a sub-contractor to Bechtel Corporation, which had the contract for the job. The head of Pritchard was a man who had played college basketball at the University of West Virginia. After he moved his family to Robinson in January, he and his daughter, an eighteen-year-old senior, attended a basketball game between Robinson and Champaign.

Playing against Red Fletcher, Champaign's all-state center, Dick scored twenty-five points and played one of the best games of his career. After the game, the head of the construction company sent Dick a note to the locker room and asked him to drop by his house that night to meet him. It turned out to be more than just meeting the man. Although Dick was only a sophomore and the contractor's daughter was a senior, they started dating and continued until the family moved to a new job in New Jersey.

By this time, Dick still had a year of high school left. The young couple wrote each other every day and wanted to get married. Skiv and Madeline Heath were not about to let that happen.

"You're not even dry behind the ears, Dick," Skiv said. "You're still in high school."

"But if I could marry her, I could get the jump on the next generation since you took so long to marry Mom and get me here," Dick said. He didn't want to lose the petite, blue-eyed blonde whom he thought was the love of his life.

Skiv wasn't buying any part of it and began making plans for his son after high school. When Skiv made up his mind to get something, he was about as successful as his father.

"You're going to Duke and play basketball, son," he said, ending any talk of a premature marriage.

So in September 1949, Dick entered Duke University on a limited basketball scholarship. The young woman he began dating in his senior year of high school enrolled at the University of Illinois. By the following spring, they were very much in love. Although Dick had played on Duke's freshman basketball team, he soon realized that while he was an outstanding high school player he would never play much as the major college level and began thinking about transferring to Illinois.

Part of the reason was because of his girlfriend. But he also wanted to be closer to home because of his father's health, which had begun to wane after his fall. It was a slow, subtle change, but Madeline could see it more than anyone else. She thought it was from all the hours he worked and the pressure he felt to make things work.

With the dairy continuing to lose money and rising costs of the candy production, a solution had to be found to maintain the profit margin of the Heath candy bar that still sold for a nickel. Rather than raise the price of the bar or shirk on the quality of ingredients, a decision was made to shrink the weight in the one-ounce bar. Candy sales were increasing simply by adding more brokers. The company did nothing as far as promotion and advertising.

All the while, Skiv continued to get to the plant at five a.m. to see the trucks off and go to the old confectionery at seven a.m. for coffee with his friends. He always took a fifteen-minute nap at noon and never got home before six p.m. He oversaw the milk trucks that picked up the milk, the bottling trucks and the dairy trucks and totally ran the candy production plant with no interference from anybody. Without the title, he was the closest you could get to a general manager of the company.

On top of everything, Clara Heath, who had been senile for several years, died after a lingering illness. Shortly after, L.S., then just past eighty years of age, started seeing a woman in her mid-fifties who worked for Skiv as one of the two women packing twenty-four-count boxes of candy into shipping cases. One time in the middle of the afternoon when the two packers were the busiest, L.S. came by and got the woman to go off with him.

When Skiv came by a few minutes later, boxes of candy were already starting to pile up all over the place. The other woman was working furiously.

"What's going on here?" Skiv asked, visably upset.

"I can't handle all of these boxes by myself," the woman said, just as visably upset.

"Where's your helper?"

"Your dad came by here about twenty minutes ago and took her with him."

"What for?" Skiv asked, struggling to control his temper. "Where'd they go?"

The woman hesitated, looking at the boxes collecting on the floor and finally said, "Why don't you check at Mr. Heath's home?"

"I'll get you some help," Skiv said as he wheeled and strode out the door and toward his father's house a block away.

His step quickened as he got closer to the house and saw the car parked in front. He was aware of rumors of his father's philanderings, but this was the first time Skiv had ever come face to face with it. He bounded up the steps and through the door. Looking around quickly downstairs and seeing no one, he took the stairs leading upstairs two at a time. Before he reached the top step, he heard noise from his father's bedroom. By the time he got to the door, L.S. was sitting on the edge of the bed, groping for his trousers. The woman was pulling the covers over her head.

"What the hell?" Skiv said, stopping short and breathing hard from climbing the stairs so rapidly. "You old fool—"

"Goddamnit, Skiv, what are you doing here? You're supposed to be at the plant."

"So is she. And why the hell have you got her here in my mother's bed? Get her dressed and get her out of here. I'll wait for you downstairs."

When the woman came down a few minutes later, she avoided Skiv's glare and hurried out the door. Later, L.S. came down the stairs fully dressed and hollered at Skiv as he paced back and forth across the living room.

"Now see what you've done, Skiv," L.S. said, shouting shrilly. "You've gone and embarrassed the life out of that poor woman."

"That woman was supposed to be at work, not here screwing you in my mother's bed."

"That's enough, Everett. I won't hear any more of that talk. You mind your place."

A few minutes later, nothing settled and both men exhausted, Skiv stormed out the door. Neither of them mentioned the incident again, and the woman always cringed whenever she saw Skiv. He stared coldly at her, but he didn't fire her.

Dick could hardly keep a straight face when his father told him about the incident, but he listened attentively. The aspect that seemed to bother Skiv most and kept coming up over and over in the conversation was that it had happened in his mother's home.

"I suppose they were both wrong, Dad," Dick said. "But you've got to admit that he's a hell of a man for his age. I hope I'm that good of a man when I'm that old."

"Get out of here. You're as bad as he is."

In the summer of 1950, Skiv was not well and was failing more and more. The family and employees at the plant were concerned, yet he continued his grueling work schedule. Dick returned to Duke in the fall. Because of his father's condition, however, he knew he would never finish college there. And he didn't go out for basketball either.

Early on, he had pledged the Alpha Tau Omega fraternity as had his cousins, Bayard Jr. and Bob. His girlfriend at Illinois wore his fraternity pin. With both his father and his girlfriend on his mind, in January 1951, Dick transferred to the University of Illinois, slightly more than one hundred miles northwest of Robinson. The move solved only part of Dick's problems.

War broke out in Korea in June 1950, and Dick was subject to the draft. Bob, who was living in Granville, Ohio, and still in the management training program with Owens-Corning, had completed ROTC in college, was called up and was being trained as an infantry officer at Fort Benning, Georgia. He was later sent to Korea. Bayard Jr. was still in the Reserves and was called up to teach ROTC in Beloit, Wisconsin. Dick knew his time was coming.

"Why don't you get into the ROTC program?" one of his fraternity brothers asked Dick soon after he was enrolled at Illinois and settled in at the ATO house.

"I don't think I can. I've already had three semesters of college."

"Let me introduce you to the colonel in the Transportation Corps. You're a basketball player; he's a basketball nut. He'll get you in."

The colonel was a tall, angular man with close-cropped, graying hair who took great pride in his Transportation Corps' basketball team. Because of their mutual interest and what each could do for the other, the two hit it off immediately.

"You that Heath kid from Robinson that played up here in the state tournament a couple of years ago?" the colonel asked.

"Yes, sir, I am."

"You're some basketball player. Still play?"

"Yes, sir. I played for Duke's freshman team last year. My dad's health is not good, and I wanted to be closer to home. I doubt that I would have played much, anyway."

"Will you play for me?"

"Yes, sir. Be happy to."

"Good. You get signed up for the program. I'll sign the required waiver, and you can take ROTC I and II at the same time. Then you can make up the second semester by going an extra semester to school. How's that sound?"

It couldn't have sounded better to Dick. He was much closer to home in case his father took a sudden turn for the worse. His girlfriend lived in the Gamma Phi Beta sorority house a few blocks from him. And, of course, he no longer had to worry about the draft. Life looked pretty good.

Life was looking pretty good for his high school friend Jack Chamblin, too. After a great senior year in football and being selected to the all-state team as fullback, he was widely recruited by top football colleges around the country. He chose perennial powerhouse West Point, coached by the legendary Colonel Red Blake. Troubled with poor eyesight and unable to read the scoreboard from the field, Chamblin nevertheless passed the required physical.

He had ranked third academically in his high school graduating class and had no problems with the West Point curriculum. On a strong team ranked No. 1 in the country in pre-season polls, he was named to the offensive guard starting position. It was the fall of 1951, the beginning of his sophomore year.

Just as school started, the West Point scandal broke and fifty-one members of the Army football team were kicked out of the academy because of a violation of the honor code. A cadet was honor-bound not to cheat and to report anyone he knew to be cheating. Chamblin was one of the fifty-one who were expelled unceremoniously because he hadn't revealed to the authorities that cheating was occurring. A short time later, he was able to get to a phone and called Dick in Champaign to explain what had happened and what he wanted to do.

"I want to come to Illinois," Chamblin said, "and bring the whole goddamn team. The old man is pissed off and won't help me do anything."

"Get your ass out here. I'll get you a job at the house and see to it that you get a free ride for dues and room and board. No sweat there. In the meantime, I'll check into other things you need to know and let you know what I've found out when you get here."

The Big Ten conference head called an emergency meeting to discuss the ramifications of players from West Point transferring to Big Ten schools and imposed two years of ineligibility on any transfers. Jack Chamblin was the only player to transfer to Illinois. He received an athletic scholarship and was allowed to practice with the team during the two-year period.

Illinois played UCLA on September 29, 1951. Chamblin was all settled in at the ATO house and putting the West Point scandal behind him. Skiv and Madeline had driven up from Robinson for the kickoff. Dick had seen them before the game. They were going out to eat afterward and then drive back to Robinson.

"Why don't you stay up tonight?" Dick asked. "I'll go to breakfast with you in the morning."

"No, I want to get back home," Skiv said. "I rest better in my own bed."

Illinois defeated UCLA 27-13. Dick went out with his girlfriend for the evening. Shortly after midnight, he returned to the ATO house and went to bed in the open dorm. An hour later, Chamblin was at his bedside. "Wake up, Dick," he said, shaking his shoulder slightly. "It's your dad. We've got to go to Carle Clinic."

"Is it serious?" Dick asked, knowing it was.

"I don't know. Get dressed while I get the car. I'll drive."

Both young men were quiet during the five-minute ride to the hospital. They knew it was serious but didn't know what to expect. Madeline was in the examining room, visably shaken and ashen faced. The doctor, B. Smith Hopkins, who had seen Skiv several times before, stood at the door.

"Come in," he said. "I want to get this straight with everyone."

Skiv was sitting up on the examination table with a hospital gown around him. He said nothing as Dick walked through the door, but recognition flashed in his eyes.

"Let me explain this," Dr. Hopkins said. "He's had a stroke. I'm going to try something that may keep him from being paralyzed and save his life. I'm going to do a spinal injection to take off the pressure."

Dick's face was drained and matched the color of his mother. He wasn't in shock, but the doctor's words sailed over his head so quickly he wasn't sure what he had heard. But he fully understood the doctor's next words.

"It may kill him," he said. "He knows that but wants me to go ahead."

Thirty seconds after Dr. Hopkins gave him the spinal injection, Skiv Heath was dead. At the age of fifty-six, the real leader of the Heath family, the glue that held it together, was gone. The family and many employees and friends were virtually in shock. Everybody knew he was in poor health, but nobody thought he would be gone so soon.

His death affected everybody. Pete was never the same again. From that time on, he lost interest in the business and went to his office, going through the motions for whatever time he was there. Bayard Sr. was left without his right arm to run the candy operation. Vernon had lost his big brother he had depended upon almost his entire life. Both Ruby and Mary knew they had lost a brother who had truly cared for them.

L.S. knew what he had lost. Clara's death was a personal loss to him, but Skiv's death really shook him hard. More than any of his sons, L.S. depended upon him and saw him as an unselfish, loyal, generous man who would be sadly missed by the family, the company and the community.

"I've lost more than my son, Dick," L.S. said to his grandson. "I'm not sure what I'll do."

"I know," Dick said. "He was a giant. I'm not saying that because he was my dad, either. That's what people have been telling me over and over."

"I know, I know," L.S. said and shuffled off.

Of everyone close to Skiv, Madeline seemed initially strongest. She had seen her husband fail gradually from the time he'd fallen down the basement stairs more than five years earlier. None of the various doctors had accurately traced his health problems to the blow to his head, but Madeline had no doubt and marked the day as the beginning of his slow decline. She had steeled herself for the inevitable.

The plant was closed for the funeral. Several hundred employees, townspeople, out-of-town friends and business associates and family members filled the church and spilled out onto the street at the funeral. Longtime friend Leo Rappaport of Indianapolis gave the eulogy and said much of what people had already said or wanted to say but couldn't.

After the funeral, some of the family stopped by the house to be with Madeline and her children. Dick was in the back yard alone when Bayard Sr. came around and said he wanted to talk to him.

"People have to understand, Dick," Bayard said slowly, measuring his words, "that when someone dies, their income stops with them."

Things could have been different before the partnership transferred to a corporation. What Bayard was saying, Dick knew, was that the business couldn't afford to grow and pay dividends. The seventy-five thousand dollar key-man insurance belonged to the company and would be used its benefit.

"There's a possibility the company can pay Madeline Skiv's salary for two years," Bayard said, watching Dick carefully. "But that would be it. So I think your mother, Joan and you should sell me your stock. I can make arrangements to buy it."

Bayard's words hit Dick like a thunderbolt. He was stunned. And for a moment, he was speechless. Then he was infuriated but held his anger. His father was hardly in the ground.

"Bayard," Dick finally turned to him and said evenly, "you're the one who's dead. I'll get you out of that plant if it's the last thing I'll ever do. You'll see what I'll do to you."

Dick turned and quickly walked away, thinking of an idea about how to get rid of Bayard as he walked. When he saw his mother, he didn't tell her about Bayard's proposition. A couple days later, he finally did. "If L.S. thinks Dad was good at selling that bunch," he said, "wait until they really see a good one."

By then, he knew exactly how he was going to get rid of Bayard and wrote Bob a letter in Korea, telling him how he was going to accomplish the job in time. Dick knew that he shouldn't feel the way he did at twenty years old. But he did. What happened in the back yard that day of his father's funeral virtually ended his relationship with Bayard Heath Sr. for years. Never once, however, did Dick let it change his feelings for Bayard Jr., whom he had grown to love like a brother.

The night of the funeral, Dick got so drunk with his sister Joan and his cousins, Pat and Joyce, that he passed out. For the next three or four months, he was never himself in any way, and the fall of 1951 was miserable for him. His father's death, his mother's distraught condition after reality set in and his

Uncle Bayard's behavior all contributed to this.

Dick's girlfriend was kind and understanding to him after the funeral. He hardly spoke to her, simply telling her that he wanted his pin back. It would have been difficult for him to act more stupidly or callously, since he did care for her and had planned to marry her.

School wasn't high on his list of priorities, either. In three semesters at Duke, Dick had maintained a solid B average. At Illinois that fall, he flunked a management course and barely passed his other courses. He was in Robinson almost as much as he was in Champaign and couldn't study when he was at school. It wasn't until December that he started snapping out of his haze.

10

The original board of directors of L.S. Heath and Sons, Inc., had seven members—L.S., Bayard Sr., Skiv, Pete, Vernon, Ruby and Mary. Mary soon decided that she wanted her husband, Jack, to have her seat on the board. L.S. had gotten what he wanted: All his sons and daughters were in business with him and practically all were treated equally. This was the makeup of the board from the inception of the corporation on January 1, 1946, until Skiv's death on September 29, 1951. During those years, L.S. was the chairman of the board; Bayard Sr. was president and treasurer; Skiv and Pete were vice presidents; and Vernon was secretary.

A board of directors meeting was called in December, and Dick was invited to attend from Champaign. L.S. presided over the meeting and called it to order.

"Now that your dad is gone, Dick," L.S. said, officially starting the business, "we would like you to serve on the board."

After having taken corporation finance at Duke the year before and knowing that the Heath company was an Illinois corporation subject to cummulative voting to elect board members, Dick knew he could serve on the board whether any of them wanted him or didn't want him. He smiled.

"Thank you for the invitation," he said. "I appreciate it. But if you'll check your State of Illinois bylaws, you'll find I could elect myself or anyone else I choose. I represent as much stock as the other three major stockholders sitting in this room."

He wasn't trying to be smart or discourteous. It was a fact. Stockwise, he was no different than Skiv had been; however, some found that fact difficult to accept and showed that they did.

"The rest of the family will have to vote to have you as a member of the board, Dick," L.S. said. "That's the way it's done."

"It doesn't make any difference whether they do or they don't. I have enough stock among Mother, Joan and me to elect myself to the board."

So at the age of twenty, not yet a junior in college, and with the support of his mother and sister, Dick elected himself to the board of directors of L.S. Heath and Sons, Inc. He wanted to make his point. He knew it took cummulative voting for seven directors and 1,280 shares to elect a director on a seven-person board. L.S., Ruby and Mary did not have enough stock to elect all three of them to the board. Two of them, yes. Dick didn't say anything, though.

Everybody talked at once after he made his speech about electing himself. Bayard Sr. knew his explanation of the procedure and his interpretation of the law was correct. So did Jack Morris.

"He's right about that," Jack said quietly.

Jack probably knew about as much as anyone in the room about how a board was supposed to function. But he also knew that he was an in-law first and a member of the board of directors second. Sitting in the first board meeting after Skiv's death was a learning experience for everyone.

Up to this point, Dick had only known his relatives socially and casually. He had heard his father talk about the past, rarely criticizing anyone and only mentioning the arguments and disagreements. Now Dick was seeing a side to his family in a setting he hadn't seen before.

Most of the board members had previously looked at Dick as Skiv's kid. Now they were having to deal with him as an equal. They all knew how the board had functioned in the past. From what he'd learned in college, Dick knew how he thought a board was supposed to function.

What Dick saw at that first meeting was the real L.S. Heath and his family. He saw the dominance of L.S. and Bayard, the weakness of both Pete and Vernon, the quietness of Jack Morris and the selfishness and lack of knowledge of Ruby.

How in the hell did all these people ever get together in the first place, Dick wondered. And how can they all get along to run a major business? It was easy to see why Skiv's death was such a blow to them.

L.S. and Bayard conducted the meeting and made decisions as though no one else was present at the meeting. One of the biggest problems was Madeline and how to take care of her. Since the company had received seventy-five thousand dollars from the insurance, it was decided to pay her Skiv's salary for two years.

"That's only about forty thousand dollars," Dick said. "What about the rest of it? If Skiv had known he was going to die so soon after the partnership was changed to a corporation and things were going to end up like this, I don't think he would have agreed to the change."

"The premiums on the policy were paid by the company, Dick," Bayard said. "We don't have to give your mother anything. But we want to do that. Right now, we need working capital for the company to grow."

L.S. agreed and the others nodded their heads. Bayard elaborated on the need for outside shareholders to provide some of it. It wasn't until after Bayard Jr. came back to the company that a solution to make the stock divisions fair to everyone was worked out. His idea was to let everyone convert half of their common stock to preferred stock. This way everyone would be treated equally. And with everyone getting preferred stock, a six dollar-per-share dividend would also be paid to everyone.

When Bayard Jr. took the proposal over to Ruby's house to get her agreement, she didn't like the idea of everybody getting dividends. Madeline had been paid for two years, and Bayard Jr. thought the stock division was as fair as it could be under the original corporate charter. Ruby finally went along with the solution because everybody else had. But Bayard Jr. had a difficult time persuading her, and she never let him forget it.

"The bitch finally agreed to it," Bayard Jr. said to Dick later. "Our relationship will never be the same. But the hell with it. It was the only fair thing to do."

"That's the way to look at it," Dick said. That's what he liked about his cousin. Bayard Jr. would never compromise principles of right or wrong, no matter what. He was a leader in the family in that regard, Dick had no doubt.

With Dick's addition to the board, a new generation of the family had arrived on the scene. His appearance and comments at the meeting cast him in the role of a harbinger of sorts, announcing that the old ways were not always the best ways and wouldn't always be followed.

But first, Dick had to finish college. Bob had to survive Korea. And Bayard Jr. had to give up practicing law.

Since Skiv had been running the candy production besides all the other things he was doing at the time of his death, a big void was left. Much like his father in many respects, Bayard Sr. told his son that the family needed him to return to Robinson and the company to take over the candy plant.

Further, Bayard Sr. told his son, because he had a law degree, it was essential that he become involved in the overall administration of the company. With some hesitation and much regret, Bayard Jr. said goodbye to his law practice and joined his relatives at the plant.

Before Skiv's death, Bob had been shipped to Korea. He was a first lieutenant in the Second Infantry Division, assigned to a rifle company as a platoon leader. His relationship with Dick had grown close over the years. When it came time to leave, Dick gave his cousin a special lightweight .45 caliber automatic pistol to take with him.

The war had reached a stalemate with both sides dug in along the 38th Parallel while truce talks were being carried on. Platoons were assigned patrols every third night. One night the battalion commander ordered a frontal assault on a Chinese-held hill. Initially, they hit the wrong hill and alerted the whole area. The commander went ahead with the attack with the enemy ready and waiting.

Bob's thirty-nine-man platoon led the first company of the three-company assault force. More than half of his platoon was wiped out in the initial assault. A Chinese mortar, apparently full of cinders, hit Bob, wounding him severely. Conscious but bleeding badly, he directed the retreat until he passed out.

With Bob still bleeding but more dead than alive, his platoon sergeant threw him over his shoulder and carried him back to their lines. He was medevacked to a field hospital and sent on to a general hospital in Japan. When Bob was recovering, the division commander awarded him at his bedside with a Silver Star for his actions on the hill that night.

When he was able to be moved, Bob was flown back to the States to recuperate. Pete and Thelma, his parents, and Dick met him briefly at Scott Air Force Base near Belleville, Illinois. From there, he was flown to Battle Creek, Michigan, to be put back together.

His parents were shocked at his condition. He was pale and drawn, unable to walk and quiet. They hardly knew what to say. With Skiv's death just a few months earlier, it was almost more than Pete could take. Tears rolled unashamedly down his cheeks as he shook his hand and stepped back for Thelma to hug her son.

"Hey, hey," Bob said, somewhat embarrassed at the attention. "I'm getting along fine. I'll be back as good as new before you know it, even kicking Dick's butt all over the golf course."

"That'll be the day," Dick said. "How about right now? You're not leaving for a while yet."

Bob laughed weakly. "Not today," he said. "But you'd better get your clubs polished up."

After a while, he was able to travel and went to Champaign to visit Dick. Of course, he was unable to play golf. So they played checkers, a game Dick had learned to play very well from his old high school football coach Merle Crosby. While they played and for years afterwards, cinders from the mortars kept popping out of Bob's wounds onto the checker board.

"You make a helluva mess there, Cuz," Dick said the first time he saw the cinders. "What is that anyway?"

When Bob told him, Dick was taken aback and didn't know what to say at first. But he was acquainted with Bob's temper and knew that he wouldn't want any sympathy.

"I think it's some kind of trick because I'm beating your ass so consistently," Dick said. "You sure as hell don't get no extra kings for that mess. You don't get any strokes on the golf course, either."

"Fuck you. It's your move. Quit talking so much and play checkers."

Bob didn't tell Dick much about the night on the hill. After the initial silence when he first asked about it, he never mentioned it again unless Bob said something. He did say that he had had the .45 with him and that his sergeant later told him that the pistol and all the magazines he'd been carrying were empty.

After Bob got out of the hospital and was discharged from the army in 1952, he decided to go back to Robinson to join the company. While both he and Bayard Jr. were in the military, the company had paid them the difference between their Army pay and the six hundred dollars per month the company had been paying them. Now, with Skiv gone, Bob was able to take over the Pepsi Cola and dairy sales.

It wasn't easy. Here was another member of the new generation, young and college-educated, with a different way of doing things. Both L.S. and Vernon restricted and thwarted Bob at every turn, causing him to become frustrated to the point that he considered leaving. Bayard Sr. added to it by bickering with him over changing from the accepted way of doing things at the plant. Deciding it wasn't worth it and biding his time, Bob did his job and stayed around.

In the spring semester of 1952, Dick was elected president of the Alpha Tau Omega fraternity. That April, the fraternity had its biggest dance of the year. As president, he naturally had to attend. He didn't know many women at Illinois and, after the way he had treated his last girlfriend, didn't want a date from the university.

Jack Chamblin and Betty Hughes, the daughter of the divisional marketing manager of the Ohio Oil Company had broken up the summer before. She was a tall, vivacious brunette whom Dick had always gotten along well with and thought to be an extremely beautiful young woman. A senior at Robinson High School, she had been voted Miss Robinson. Then when the basketball team reached the state tournament in Champaign, she was named Miss Sweet Sixteen.

Since he already knew her and got along with her so well, Dick asked her to the dance. She accepted and came to Champaign for the weekend. At the time, he was going home to Robinson on most weekends and saw Betty often. Before long, they were dating regularly.

Betty went to Stephen's Girls School in Columbia, Missouri, in the fall of 1952 when Dick went back to Illinois. He spent much time traveling to Missouri that fall to see her. They decided that Betty should transfer to Illinois for the second semester. After she transferred, they decided to get married after Dick returned from an eight-week ROTC summer camp in August 1953. He was making up a second semester of three he had to make up to get his ROTC commission. His last semester would be in the fall. The Hugheses and Maxine Zwermann, a Robinson High School speech teacher and friend of both families, planned the wedding for August 8, four days after Dick returned from Fort Eustis, Virginia.

Nearly a thousand people attended the wedding reception held on the country club grounds. With the two biggest industries in town represented, it would have been difficult to keep it small. The wedding party itself had thirteen grooms-men and thirteen ushers. Bob was Dick's best man.

Considering the number of people and the free-flowing liquor, it was an orderly, well-behaved crowd with one exception. After Skiv's death, Dick had been given his father's company car. As a joke and a result of having too much to drink, Mary Morris poured sand in the gas tank, locking up the engine and ruining it. Bob Heath was infuriated.

"That was about as stupid a thing as I've ever seen an adult do," Bob said, his temper rising with each word he spoke. "You've totally ruined the car with your stupid joke."

"Oh, buzz off," Mary said. "I thought it would be funny."

"Do you see anybody laughing?" Bob asked, looking around at the circle of friends and family gathering.

"I wish you had never come back from Korea," Mary said. "Too bad you didn't die over there."

Bob's mother had been standing back away from the two until then. She stepped through the gathered crowd, bumping into anyone not moving quickly enough and knocking them aside.

"What did you say, you drunken bitch?" Thelma said. "I'll slap you sillier than you already are. Don't you ever say anything like that again."

Bob turned to his mother, partly in surprise and partly to restrain her from any further participation. Both of them felt very strongly about what Mary had said and never really forgot it. All Dick could think of was the conversation he had

had with Bayard Sr. in the back yard of the family home on the day his father was buried. He couldn't believe his close-knit family could behave like that and what he was witnessing and survive.

After the incident was over, Bob loaned Dick his car and the newlyweds drove to Clearwater, Florida, for a short honeymoon before going back to Illinois for the fall semester. Dick was taking the minimum of six hours for his last semester of ROTC.

L.S.'s office had an old red leather chair and matching foot stool in one corner. After Skiv died, Dick spent quite a bit of time in the chair, sitting there talking with his grandfather or listening to him talk and philosophize about whatever came to his mind.

Sometimes L.S. would be wearing a three-piece suit; other times, when he had been out surveying something or out on a farm for something else, he might be wearing bib overalls. His shoes weren't dirty, but they weren't shined, either, because of where he was trodding around.

The common loss of Skiv made Dick feel that his grandfather wanted to talk as long as he did. As a result of these long conversations, Dick learned so many things about his grandfather that his own children never knew. Earlier, it had been basketball that they talked about. But now it was about the old man's life, the way he was brought up and the way he believed.

He was in his eighties, his mind as sharp as it had ever been. He repeated how he had become a director of the Second National Bank of Robinson, the bank that wouldn't loan him the money to drill the oil well, and how Bayard Sr. had become the chairman of the board of the Crawford County State Bank, after the well had started producing and making big money.

"Money," L.S. said, "takes care of those kinds of things, Dick."

"I'm sure it does," Dick said.

The old man could cuss like a trooper when he got angry. His voice was high-pitched and shrill. "Dawddomit, Dick," he would say, "sit down here and listen to me." When he got like that, Dick knew he had better sit down, shut up and listen. Once, Dick told him about his milk costs and how the dairy was losing money. He nearly manhandled Dick getting him in the chair.

"Look," he said, standing over Dick and looking down on him, "don't you think I know what my costs are after fifty years in the dairy business?"

"You might not be picking up all the costs with the size of the dairy," Dick said, setting his grandfather off immediately.

"Now look here," he said, yelling and almost jumping up and down as he talked, "we're selling a quart of milk for twenty-one cents a quart. I know what the milk costs, and I can figure the overhead and other costs. I know we have a profit. You're beginning to sound like Bayard."

Dick agreed with him because he knew he wasn't about to win. L.S. didn't want to hear about his grandson's accounting or anyone else's that didn't agree with his.

"Anyone can make the figures come out to what they want," the old man said. "You should be smart enough to know that."

That was all of that ballgame. No need to talk about it anymore. Class dismissed.

College classes were dismissed for Dick when he graduated from the University of Illinois with a bachelor's degree in marketing in 1954. He also received his ROTC commission and orders to report for active duty at Fort Eustis in May and on to France in August.

From his graduation at Illinois until he reported for active duty, Dick joined the company in Robinson. With Bayard Jr. and Bob on board, the void left at Skiv's death was filled and the running of the day-to-day business was in good hands.

During this time, Pete, Bob and Dick decided to buy the Pepsi Cola plant in Meridian, Mississippi. They thought, as did others in the family, that it was a good opportunity to expand. After the company bought the plant, something happened and the plant never made a dime in profit. With Pepsi Cola selling wholesale for $1.10 a case, the price was too low for profit, and the price structure didn't change quickly enough. Then, too, Coca-Cola was too strong in the area, and absentee management didn't help the situation.

But before the results of the purchase were fully evident, Dick had to leave the company and report to active duty. His wife, Betty, gave birth by cesarean section to their first child, Scott, on July 30, 1954. In August, Dick was sent to Bordeaux, France, for a two-year tour of duty. Mother and child joined him ninety days later, arriving in France aboard the Queen Elizabeth. A few months after arriving in France, Betty became pregnant again. She and Scott flew back to the States from Paris in November to have the baby at home. Dick followed in December, and their daughter was born prematurely by cesarean section on December 16, 1955. The baby, Sue, was taken to St. John's Hospital in Springfield and cared for for two months until she was able to return home.

Rather than returning to France after Christmas, Dick was transferred to Great Lakes Naval Station in Chicago. Because of a troop reduction brought on by a budget crunch, he was given credit for a twenty-four-month tour and discharged from the Army as a first lieutenant in February 1956.

The company had continued its slow growth while Dick was in the Army, although not much had changed since he joined the board of directors in late 1951. Bayard Jr. and Bob provided better management. But as long as L.S. was there and essentially in charge, the thrust of the company would not change. Together with Bayard Sr., who had divested himself of some of his stock by giving several shares to his grandsons, Peter and Wickliff, L.S. dictated the company philosophy and direction.

Two days after receiving his discharge, Dick went back to work at the Heath company.

11

When Dick returned from the Army to join the family business, L.S. was eighty-six years old and failing fast. Bayard Jr. was thirty-six years old, Bob was twenty-eight and Dick was twenty-five. All three of the elder Heath's grandsons were college-educated and had their military service behind them. They were closer than at any other time in their lives and were ready to make changes in the company they believed necessary for it to grow and prosper.

Bob's office was also the conference room and the board meeting room. The real board meetings took place there daily. Every morning from about 8:15 until nine, Bayard Jr., Bob, Dick and Jack Morris would sit down and drink coffee together. After getting the past day's golf game fully discussed or the plans for the next one made, they talked extensively about the business. Pete might walk in and out a half a dozen times. When he was in town, Vernon always came by at about 8:20 a.m.

Vernon would only sit down for a few minutes. He really thought it was a waste of time, never understanding how important the time really was. The younger men thought it was pitiful how little he did understand business but never voiced their opinions except among themselves. Pete actually had a great deal of business sense to him but had no motivation after Skiv's death.

During a conversation one morning, the dairy came up as it often did. "We don't know how much the dairy is costing us, do we?" Bob asked.

"We've never known from day one," Bayard Jr. said.

"This is probably the largest company in America that doesn't have an accrued accounting system," Dick said, laughing as he remembered his conversations on the subject with L.S.

"Well, something has to be done and damn fast," Bob said. "I know we're losing a bunch."

"It would be hard to get my dad to change after all these years," Bayard Jr. said. His father was sixty-three years old and had been in the Heath family business for forty-two years, using a cash accounting method all the while.

"I think I have a solution," Dick said.

"Come on, John Henry, let's have it," Bob said, calling his cousin a nickname that a mutual friend, Dode Douglas, had given him after watching him drive an iron shot a country mile. "John Henry was a steel drivin' man," he'd said. Douglas was older than Bayard Jr. and was the character of the country club. Besides that, he'd hit Normandy Beach on D-Day plus four and went all the way to the end of the war. He had learned to play golf when he came back, and he was tough. To the Heath boys, who were all good golfers, he was one of the best putters they had ever seen. Anyway, his nickname for Dick had stuck.

Douglas had started another name that stuck, too. The company made a lot of cheese with excess Grade A and B milk. When he'd see Bayard Jr., Bob and Dick walking into the club, he'd say, "Here come the boys from the cheese plant." From then on, L.S. Heath & Sons, Inc., became known as the cheese plant.

"Okay, listen to me," Dick said very seriously, unconsciously using words he'd heard his grandfather say hundreds of times. "Bayard Sr. will never change from his cash basis. We know that. But that's all right. Let him keep the system he has. I'll run a real accrual system parallel to him."

"You're no accountant," Bayard Jr. said. "How can you do that?"

"It's simple. I'll learn how."

"You're kidding," Bob said.

"That would take a long time, Dick."

"Not really, Bayard. Not with my plan. Here's what I've got in mind: I'll call Professor Bill Thomas at Illinois. I had him for cost accounting. He's written books on the subject. We'll see if he wants to come down and set up a system and teach me how to run it. You know the family wouldn't stand for an outside accounting firm. Nobody would want to spend the money nor want outsiders to know our business."

"It might work," Bayard Jr. said after thinking about it for a while.

"Do you think you can get him?" Bob asked.

"I don't know, Bob. But first we have to get it past the board. You know that."

"Well, I'll sell Dad."

"I'll sell the one who counts," Dick said.

"When are you going to see him?" Bayard Jr. asked.

"Now."

It wasn't long before Dick was back in his favorite red chair with L.S. Slowly and painstakingly, Dick described the conversation he had held with his cousins and what they wanted to do. This time L.S. was listening, not lecturing.

Finally he said, "I see your merits. I knew you young boys

would start taking over. It's time, too. The company's future lies with you."

That's basically what he had to say regarding the subject. Of course, it took two hours to say it fully because he wanted to reminisce about the past. Dick always enjoyed that because he learned so much about the family and the business. At the time, L.S. was failing badly and seemed to have a sense of urgency about him.

"You boys go ahead with that," L.S. said after a while, a faint smile in his eyes. "But the day I die, I want you to come in here and get this stack of notes out of the safe and destroy them."

The old man stood and went to the heavy, black, double-doored safe to the left and behind his desk. He opened a door and withdrew the stack of notes.

"There," he said, turning toward Dick. "Will you get rid of these for me?"

"If you'd like me to, Father Heath. Yes, I will."

"I'd like you to, Dick."

A board meeting was unnecessary now. For all practical purposes, the meeting with L.S. to explain what the younger Heaths wanted to do had concluded the board meeting that had started with them. Dick called Professor Thomas at the university, told him who he was and what he wanted.

"I remember you, Mr. Heath," Thomas said. "It's easy to do with your name. Your idea is intriguing, but let me think about it and call you. I'm not teaching this summer, so it is a possibility."

Three days later, Thomas called. He had decided to take the job. He wanted a five thousand dollar-retainer and another five thousand dollars when he was finished. Now the plan had to go to the board. But Dick told him to plan to come to Robinson, that the board would approve it.

As far as the actual board meeting, Dick had sold Jack Morris and neutralized Vernon, and Bob had told Pete to go along with the decision. With L.S. still running the company, the arguments Bayard Sr. and Ruby had were immaterial. Dick knew the real work had been done in the red chair. It never took him long to know how to play the game. And for years now, he had done his homework.

He knew one of the most important decisions the company had to make was to change the accounting system Bayard Sr. had been using since he had taken over the books years ago. He would simply prepare a balance sheet at the end of each fiscal year, June 30, and the change in the net worth was the profit the company made that year. Somehow, he tried to separate the divisions, but it was not that accurate and always left room for an argument.

So bringing in a new accounting system was the first threat to Bayard Sr. He knew L.S. wouldn't be around much longer and considered himself the heir to the throne. The reality was, however, that it was too late. The new generation had arrived. And, because of his promise to himself and Bayard Sr. on the afternoon of Skiv's funeral, there was no way Dick was going to let his uncle take over and thought it was downhill from then on. Bayard Sr. hadn't seen how Dick could sell his way around the company.

He knew if he wanted to sell Ruby on something, he could. Or any of the rest of them. He thought he knew each of their weaknesses and each of their strengths. And he didn't think he was being devious about it. He just wanted to head the company in the right direction. Getting control of the books was a major step in his mind. He believed it would be a good, workable system and would probably prove to be the end of the dairy after L.S. was gone.

Bill Thomas arrived shortly after the board approved the plan and began to work with Dick. He had had nine semester hours of accounting in college, three separate courses that included cost accounting. With Thomas, Dick was about to learn how accounting was really done. At the time, the Heath company had the candy division, the dairy division, the bottling division and the miscellaneous division, which was everything else. Not only were Thomas and Dick going after the division breakdown, but they were going for individual product costs.

Each morning at the mini-board meeting, Bayard Jr. and Bob were anxious to know how they were getting along. Thomas and Dick used the board room office to work while Bob moved to a temporary office. They worked long and hard. The cooperation out of the south office from Bayard Sr. wasn't there, but that didn't stop them. They were installing a double-entry accrued, generally accepted accounting system. Bayard Sr. was using changes in capital assets month to month on a large spreadsheet from a cash basis.

The need for a new system had actually started at the board meetings earlier. Bayard Sr. would report a profit of $200,000 for the year. L.S. would be the first to speak.

"I know how much the dairy is making out of that figure," he would say. "Do any of you doubt that I don't know what my profit is on a quart of milk?"

No one would challenge him.

"Everybody knows what the Pepsi Cola makes a year," Pete would say, chiming in.

"Well, I happen to know the candy company made $300,000," Bayard Sr. would say proudly. "Where does that leave the rest of you?"

Where it left them was that if they had added every figure they all tossed out on the table, including what Ruby said the farms had made, they would come up with triple Bayard Sr.'s profit statement; or if they had believed his figures, they would have realized what divisions were making or losing money and that Bayard Sr. was using his change of balance sheet accounting to try and explain that the dairy was losing a bundle for the company.

That's when the biggest arguments would start. Even Vernon would pop up in his shrill voice, actually sounding more like L.S., and get angry. Usually Pete sort of came to his rescue. He knew that the best defense is a good offense, so he would pop off to Bayard Sr. to get him off the subject. That's how it started at practically every board meeting.

Then Ruby would jump in and start airing all of her deep-seated gripes, going all the way back to the days of the confectionery on the Square and the number of cherry Cokes Bayard Sr. had charged her for at the time. The five of them would all be talking at once, none of them paying any attention to each other.

Dick and Jack Morris would just sit and listen. Normally, Pete would get tired, walk out, go to his office and shut the door for a while. Finally, they would all get tired. About that time, Pete, after catching his second wind, would pop back in and reload on Bayard Sr.

"Hell, Bayard," Pete once said, knowing his crack would hook his brother, "what makes you think anybody believes you?"

"You can't change the figures, Pete. Figures don't lie."

"Yeah," Vernon said. "Those are your figures. As Pete said, who would believe you?"

"Look here," Bayard Sr. said, repeating what he always did when it got to this point. "If you will just go along with me, I'll straighten this business out."

Ruby was usually too angry at her older brother because of all the cherry Cokes he had made her pay for to side with him. Bayard Sr. would finally get enough of her and say, "Sis, you don't know what you're talking about."

Pete would eventually pop in and out four or five times a meeting. He couldn't sit that long. Finally, old L.S. would bang on the table and say, "Daddamn it, shut up." Then it would get quiet until the conversation went back to the store days, Ruby's cherry Cokes and other family matters.

And that went on time and time again. Actual company issues were rarely discussed. The board meetings seemed to be a forum for the Heaths to go at each other with their petty gripes, since it was about the only time they all got together in the same room.

When the meeting was over, and it was over when enough of them left, nothing was changed. Regardless of the arguments, L.S. dominated the meetings as long as he lived. And Bayard Sr. dominated them for a while after that. After his father died, Vernon usually wanted to talk to Dick on the way out of the meetings, giving him the gripes he hadn't had a chance to fully air in the meetings.

"Dad would never put up with Bayard like that," Vernon would say. "All Bayard wants is to be like Dad. I went along with Dad, but I'm not going to take it from Bayard."

Those early meetings Dick attended while L.S. was still

alive eventually set the stage for the idea of a new accounting system. Dick thought it would really give them something to talk about. He could just imagine the battle shaping up between Bayard Sr. and him. He would be ready and could write the script.

For nearly four months, Bill Thomas and Dick worked diligently. While the system was being set up, Dick was really learning accounting by the experience he could never learn in the classroom. One day as they were getting near the end, Dick asked, "How good do you think I am, Bill?"

"You couldn't pass a CPA exam because we haven't gotten into tax law and so forth. Accounting-wise, you know it as well as a CPA. From an operational standpoint for what you're after, you're very good."

Dick knew he was good enough to see where the problem was in the company. It was the dairy. He agreed with Bayard Sr. on that point. It was so bad, Dick shuttered. But he decided not to say anything about what he saw to anybody, including Bayard Jr. and Bob. The problem, maybe never solvable, was that the dairy didn't have enough sales. And for the amount of milk it bought from local farmers, the company was putting too much Grade A-priced milk into the cheese vat to make cheddar cheese. After aging the cheese, the company still sold it to Kraft for only thirty-four cents a pound.

That was just one of the problems. Dick had a real problem about what it would do to his grandfather. By this time, his days were literally numbered. Plenty of time would be available to solve the dairy's problems; however, everybody was now awaiting the first statement.

"Let me ask you something, Bill," Dick said one day when the work was almost done. "You know we have this big figure under administrative overhead that includes all the family's salaries, the company cars, country club dues, huge donations, depreciation on the new addition—the dairy and the offices— plus many other fixed expenses. If we sold the dairy, what would we do?"

He knew the answer before he asked the question.

"Since we are prorating them based on the sales of each other," Thomas said, "we would redistribute them to the remaining divisions based again on their sales to each other."

"You may not agree with what I'm going to do, Bill, but I'm going to do just that—for a short while. I'm not going to prorate any of these expenses. I'll list the operating profits of each division and then add them together and subtract this huge administrative expense to come up with the overall profit. I'll defend it by saying if I spread it on sales, then if a division was eliminated, I would have to respread the expenses. It will show the dairy in the best light for L.S."

"Why do that?"

"For an old man who isn't going to be around very long. It's really not deceptive since that is what it would look like if we sold the dairy."

"Well, Dick, it's unusual to do, but there are two points concerning your theory: First, the system is a tool for management to use; second, it's not to be published as a certified, generally accepted accounting statement."

"And third," Dick said, adding the main point, "it is not audited and, as yet, is not even the official company books."

"Let's do it, if you wish. I'll not say a word—I understand you."

Of course, this made a great difference. They had actually done the books for the second quarter of 1956. Thomas was going to accompany Dick to the board meeting. He had asked L.S., Bayard Jr. and Bob to be there. The latter two always attended the board meetings, even though they weren't directors and couldn't vote. They always had input.

Looking forward to the meeting was having a curious effect on everyone, particularly Dick. It's going to be funnier than hell, he thought. He wished he could sell tickets. He knew it would be worth the price of admission. Everybody expected a big loss in the dairy, even L.S., if he'd tell the truth.

At the morning meetings, Bayard Jr. and Bob continuously tried to find out the numbers. Dick played coy with them and pretended to be ignorant of the truth.

"Fellows, I really don't know what it's going to look like," he said. "The way the system is you can't tell until the end. So I have no idea."

"Bullshit," Bob said, his temper flaring one morning. "Damn it, Dick, you know what it's going to look like. We're not interested in the cents figure."

"You're playing games with us," Bayard Jr. said, laughing.

"Well, maybe yes, maybe no. But it depends on how certain overhead figures are spread."

"I don't like it," Bob said, still angry.

"Frankly, Bob, I don't give a damn what you like," Dick said, slightly bothered and hooked up by his cousin's temper and tone of voice. "You're not a director. I have my reasons, though, and you'll both find out later."

They both had an idea of what Dick was doing and why. Others, including Bayard Sr., wanted to know in advance of the meeting. He would have been the last one Dick would have told. But to tell anyone would have been to tell everyone. By arrangement with Bill Thomas, the package was typed at the university. Dick didn't even want to chance having a company secretary type it.

Knowing that Thomas would be more effective, Dick sat back and let him present the figures. Thomas was enjoying the job. He had gotten to know Dick and what was taking place within the company. Both knew what was going to happen at the meeting before L.S. nervously called it to order.

After Thomas started reading through the statement and everybody followed along on the copies provided, the room became quiet. Dick had glanced at Bayard Jr. and Bob when they got their copies. Both had quickly gone to the back of the statement to look at the meat of it.

Bob looked up and glared at Dick with a hard, cold look that Dick had seen many times in the last few months. By looking at the administrative overhead, Bob knew immediately what had been done. However, Thomas made some changes that seemed to surprise him, Bayard Jr. and even Jack Morris, the only ones who seemed to understand any of the statement.

Thomas had carried the administrative overhead undistributed to any division. He showed the operating profits, brought the totals together and then substracted the large administrative overhead total. That way it could be allocated any way anybody wanted it to be.

Before the allocation, the dairy had broken even. L.S. beamed. Vernon was relieved. Pete didn't know what to say. Ruby didn't know what she was reading, except the final profit at the end. Bob said nothing.

"This is excellent work," Bayard Jr. said. "Outstanding. Congratulations. We know where we stand."

"This is an excellent way to present it," Jack Morris said. "I've seen it done this way before."

At that point, Bob smiled and said it was good. All eyes turned to Bayard Sr. He had diligently worked up some figures.

"It may be fine," he said, unable to keep quiet any longer, "but the end figure is not right."

Thomas and Dick had been waiting for this and were prepared. Dick had planned to let Thomas handle Bayard Sr., if it was possible to sit there and hold back. It was, and Thomas slowly and carefully responded.

"Mr. Heath," he said, "you are absolutely correct. You are on a cash basis, and these statements are on an accrued basis. Your accounting recognizes the liabilities as they are paid. We recognize them as they are incurred. We allocate and charge each revenue center for expenses. At the end of the year, we would be close or exactly the same, if you changed your accounts payable increase to reflect what is outstanding."

Bayard Sr. had not done that at the time but did afterwards. "Tell them I've got the right figures," he said.

"I'm sure you do. You've done an excellent job with the system you've had to work with. Let me congratulate you."

"Why don't you come over and let me show you how I do my books?" he said, showing he was pleased and liked Thomas.

"I would enjoy that, Mr. Heath. But I've got to get back to the university. I've been gone far too long as it is."

Everybody came out a winner, but everybody now had it confirmed what the problem was in the dairy: Sales had to be increased to create more gross profits. The option was to get out of the dairy business. And something else was accomplished. Bayard Sr. was going to continue his books, but now Dick was going to keep the new set that Thomas had set up. It was a major victory because Dick's statements would become what everybody looked to.

12

Soon after the board meeting, L.S. became ill. His condition grew progressively worse, and it wasn't long until he couldn't make it to the plant only a block away from his two-story, white-framed house. Ruby and Mary alternated staying with him. Everybody else would visit on a regular basis. No way was he going to the hospital. He had never been there, and he wasn't about to go now.

Dick was twenty-six years old and was old enough, had been around L.S. enough and had been close enough to more than just say, "He is my grandfather." Because of Skiv's death, the two had formed a close bond. One had lost a son, one a father, and the two were drawn to each other by that loss.

The time spent together in those days gave Dick a perspective that few in the family had from his grandfather's more private side. To add to both his private and public persona, L.S. had written a seventy-one-page book called *My Footprints on the Sands of Time* that gave a sketch of his life up to about 1954. It was published privately in 1955.

So L.S. Heath was many things to many people. He was a saint, a tyrant, a philanthropist, a pioneer, a dictator, an entrepreneur, a teacher, a father, a son, a dedicated meddler, a brother, a friend, an enemy, a surveyor, a husband, a lover and a man as gentle as anyone would care to know; he was kind, hot-tempered, tough as nails, mean at times, extremely well educated, ruthless, ambitious, gracious, intelligent, spoiled and caring.

He had taken care of himself as well as anyone. At eighty-six years of age, he still had all of his original teeth. He had never smoked. While he didn't drink like some members of the Heath family, he wasn't a teetotaler, either, and kept a jug of Mogan David wine in the refrigerator for an occasional glass. It was widely known that he had lovers other than his wife, and it was generally known but never proved that he fathered more than six children. He was known as a storyteller who could tell stories as long as anyone would listen.

No doubt he had his favorites among his children. But he treated them equally almost to a fault. Known for his philanthrophic contributions to causes and communities around Robinson, he once gave fourteen thousand dollars for street lights in Hutsonville, a small town nine miles northeast of Robinson. By an accountant's financial statement, he wasn't wealthy. But if he needed something, he went to the company check book, wrote a check and noted, "Charge to my draw," on the check stub. This continued into the time when the Heath company was a corporation. Dick or his predecessor would make journal entries to keep the books in balance.

Whatever and whoever he was, L.S. Heath stayed true to himself in old age. His illness lingered. Everybody knew he was quite ill when he didn't go to the plant. He stayed home and his physician, Dr. Bill Schmidt, went to see him there. With those visits and the family seeing him regularly and Ruby living directly behind him in the house he had built for her and Bernard, the old man was well cared for.

Late one warm, Sunday morning, Vernon asked Dick and Bayard Jr. if they would stay with their grandfather until the middle of the afternoon to give everybody a rest. The family was worn out from staying with him constantly. Although both men had planned to join their wives for golf at the country club that morning, they agreed immediately.

L.S. was awake and alert when they arrived and pulled up chairs next to his bed. He laughed and joked with them for a while, showing his old sense of humor. At a few minutes before noon, they noticed a change. His color paled and he seemed to slip in and out of consciousness, talking one minute and fading away the next.

Dick and Bayard Jr. exchanged glances. Both were convinced he was dying. "I'll call Doc Bill," Dick said.

Before he could move, the old man opened his eyes and was keenly alert again. He looked at both of his grandsons and said, "What are you boys doing here? It's Sunday. I thought you'd be playing golf."

"Father Heath," Bayard Jr. said, startled, "we wanted to be with you."

Dick nodded in agreement. "That's right," he said.

"Okay, fine. But help me get dressed. I've got to go to the plant."

Neither man knew what to do, but they didn't want to argue with him. He sat up on the side of the bed.

"Get me my pants," he said. "They're over there with my shirt. My shoes and socks are right here under the bed."

Not quite sure it was the right thing to do, they started dressing him and soon had his clothes on and shoes tied. With a grandson on each side of him, he stood up and started shuffling toward the bedroom door. Bayard Jr. had been around a great deal of death in combat. He could recognize the signs, the looks, the smells and knew his grandfather was going quickly. Dick knew, too. L.S.'s flesh was totally white.

All at once he stopped and turned around. "This is silly," he said. "You two have probably got a golf game, and I'm interfering with it. Take me back to bed. I might as well get this over with."

Both men were stunned.

L.S. looked at Dick and seemed to be about to say something to his grandson. But the old man didn't say anything. Dick remembered a conversation in his grandfather's office.

With his grandfather's eyes locked on his, Dick nodded slightly.

A faint twinkle crossed L.S.'s eyes as he sat down on the side of the bed.

Fumbling nervously, they removed his clothes and helped him lie back on the bed. They could see and smell death. His legs were milk white. Three minutes later he was in a coma again, lying there as though he were asleep. His eyes were closed; he breathed hoarsely through his mouth. Then it appeared that his breathing stopped.

"I think he's gone, Dick," Bayard Jr. said. "You'd better call Bill."

They both knew the old man was dead, but Dick ran downstairs to the telephone to call the doctor. Dr. Bill Schmidt lived some eight blocks away and was there in less than ten minutes. While they waited for the doctor, Dick called his Uncle Pete and told him L.S. was gone.

The doctor looked at the frail body before him quietly and tried to find a heartbeat. "He's dead, boys," Dr. Schmidt said.

"What did he die of?" Dick asked.

"Old age. The heart was the last to stop. It's like a car that runs out of gas. After so long, it just stops."

Pete arrived a few minutes later. In the meantime, Dick had begun calling the rest of the family. They arrived within minutes. Dr. Schmidt stayed to make the arrangements to take the body to the funeral home. Bayard Jr. and Dick were downstairs with Vernon, waiting for the ambulance. Ruby and Mary, who had been upstairs, suddenly began yelling at each other as they stood on the stairs. They were arguing about who should have some of their mother's things.

"Let's get the hell out of here," Bayard Jr. said, looking at Dick and scowling. "I'll see you at the course in thirty minutes."

"Make it an hour," Dick said as the two headed for the door. "I have something to do."

He drove to the Heath plant, went back into his grandfather's office and opened his huge, black safe to fulfill the promise he had made to L.S. not long before in that red chair now setting empty in the corner of the office. That promise had been to get rid of the notes and IOUs in the safe the minute he was gone.

Cautiously, Dick withdrew the black leather pouch from the corner of the safe. He knew what he had to do and didn't plan to take much time to sort through the contents. So he took the thick stack of notes and IOUs, tossed the pouch back in the corner and locked the safe. Flipping through the stack of paper, Dick saw several letters that acknowledged the writer owed money to L.S.

Dick didn't count how much money was outstanding. He knew the notes would run into the thousands and thought the figure would be close to seventy-five thousand dollars. Walking to the trash barrels on the back platform, he tore the papers in small pieces and scattered them around the barrels with the knowledge that an era was over as those little pieces of paper settled to the bottom . They would be dumped by the crew at the plant the next morning when they were full of other things.

He also knew that 23 percent of the value of the paper he was tearing up belonged to him. But he didn't care and headed to the golf course. He gave Bayard Jr. three strokes for each nine holes and still beat him out of a couple of bucks.

Bayard Sr. came over to Dick's office a few days after the funeral. The two hadn't spoken to each other except on necessary company business since the day of Skiv's funeral nearly five years earlier.

"Do you know what happened to Dad's notes, Dick?" Bayard Sr. asked. "His pouch is empty. I don't understand what could have happened to them. I want to get them to record the indebtedness and set it up on the company books."

"I don't know anything about them," Dick said, lying easily. "As far as I know, he was the only one who would have had anything to do with them. Nobody else went in his safe."

"It sure is strange. I'm going to go through his things. We need to find them."

"Maybe he threw them out. You know Father Heath. He always had his reasons for what he did."

"Do you know something you're not telling me, Dick?" Bayard Sr. asked, eyeing Dick with new interest. "Do you know where those notes are?"

"No, Bayard, I don't know where they are. Maybe he gave them all back to the people somehow."

"Yeah, maybe," Bayard Sr. said, turned quickly and walked through the door.

13

With the death of L.S. Heath, the stock division was unchanged. The four sons or their families still owned twenty-five hundred shares of company stock. Mary Morris and her family owned 1,475 shares. Ruby Dowling and her husband owned 1,325 shares. Everybody had been allowed to convert half of the common stock to preferred stock a few years earlier. Other than that and a few changes in the stock ownership, nothing had been changed within the company structure except as dictated by the death of Skiv and L.S.

Then in 1956, ten years after the company was incorporated, it underwent its first reorganization following the change from a partnership to a corporation. Bayard Jr., Bob and Dick were talking and having coffee one morning when Bob said he had an idea. Dick said he had one, too.

"Okay, John Henry," Bob said, "what's yours?"

"You know with Father Heath's death we only have six directors," Dick said. "I think we should amend the bylaws and have eight. Of course, you two would be elected."

"Do you think the others would go for that?" Bayard Jr. asked. At the time, there was much conflict in the family.

"I'm sure Pete, Jack and surely your dad will, Bayard. Besides, look at the three major stockholders who would be for it. Hell, Vernon would probably agree."

"That would make it a real board," Bob said.

"Okay, that's settled," Dick said. "What's on your mind, cuz?"

"I think the company needs reorganizing on a function basis," Bob said, indicating that the change would better utilize education, training and ability. "The three functions are sales, production and administration."

"You've got my vote," Dick said.

Bayard Jr. agreed.

Bob went on to explain the nature of the functional change was to instill directors of sales, production and administration. His college degree was in management, Dick's was in marketing and Bayard Jr's. was in general business with a law degree.

"Jack Morris would be the director of purchasing and shipping," Bob said, looking for agreement on that point before he proceeded.

"Good," Dick said in agreement. "But not under any of us directly."

"Okay. That sounds good. Then you both agree?"

Both men nodded.

"Dick, since you have the accounting system and need all the administrative control, how about you being the director of administration and treasurer? Bayard will take the production and me sales."

"I've got one better and know how to get it done," Dick said, knowing that based on their backgrounds and education, Bayard should have been in charge of administration, Bob production and him sales but saying nothing because of the need for Bob's cooperation on his plan. "Let's make Vernon the chairman of the board, the three of us vice presidents. Jack could be a vice president, too. Bayard, as a lawyer, it's time you became the secretary."

Bayard Sr. was already president and treasurer. As the oldest living member of the family and only remaining co-founder, he wanted to take over control from his father. Dick didn't want that and knew Vernon badly wanted the title of chairman of the board. He had gotten involved in many committees and was going to Chicago frequently to attend various meetings. Pete and Skiv had been the company's only two vice presidents.

When L.S. died, he had left his home to Ruby and had already given the balance of his Heath stock to her and Mary. The rest of his estate was divided among his heirs. In the estate was one hundred shares of Second National Bank stock he had had to be on the board of the bank. Both Pete and Vernon had wanted it. Vernon wanted it more than Pete, so Dick went along with Vernon. The original value of one hundred dollars per share was about ten times less than it was worth, based on the bank's earnings and market value, but Dick didn't argue about that. He persuaded Pete that it might make up for the thirty-nine thousand dollars Vernon was always griping about. Pete wasn't happy, but he bought the idea. Now, Dick knew how to get a favor back and knew he could sell Vernon on the reorganization with the title meaning nothing to the younger generation but a great deal to him.

Bayard Sr. and Ruby didn't like it when they first heard about the proposal. But Ruby merely complained about it. Virtually everybody was getting something out of the plans. Before he knew what was in store for him, Vernon wanted to know how the functional reorganization affected him.

"You'll just do what you've been doing," Dick said each time he was asked. "I'm going to do you a favor shortly that you want very much."

The most important part to Dick was to get Bayard Jr. and Bob on the board. And he went along with Bob's plan because it was more important to become treasurer than director of sales, which Dick felt was his area of expertise. The plan worked smoothly.

Bayard Sr. sat and watched his power being eaten away for what he had planned on all the past years. He wanted the control, felt he deserved it, but it was too late. Nobody was going to permit another L.S. Heath. When the rest of the board voted in favor of the reorganization, Bayard Sr. could do nothing about it. And what was so frustrating to him was that his own son was a part of the team.

The functional reorganization allowed the company to expand the business. Three young, energetic, college-educated family members who grew up with the business now headed the three primary divisions of the company and wanted to move ahead.

Since he had returned from his year's service during the Korean War, Bayard Jr. had created an excellent organization out of the production department from the people who had worked there for Skiv. It hadn't taken long for Bayard Jr. to realize how he could get the production out and still handle the trucks. In his day, Skiv was also handling the sales of the dairy and Pepsi.

"Back then, who was, if it wasn't him?" Bayard Jr. said after the reorganizational board meeting and new plans were being put into operation. In his department, key people he had inherited from Skiv were still in place.

Bob Murphy was responsible for the candy production. Vaughn Kilburn took care of the cooking. Vanieta Murphy was in charge of the women in the candy wrapping room who were on the line. Art Cowden handled getting the supplies and getting the product shipped. Jesse Lutz kept the machines operating and was the head of maintenance.

In the administrative section, two separate offices still existed. With Bayard Sr. firmly entrenched in the company as president and not about to go along with any change in his methods, Dick's election as treasurer was an important victory for the reorganization. Production capacity was such that it was possible to produce three times the current volume. Consequently, sales increases to promote company growth were given a high priority.

Bob found a man named Omar Baumgarten who had a proven sales record with a dairy association selling Gurnsey Gold, a 2 percent milk produced by Gurnsey cows, to direct the dairy sales. One of the dairy truck drivers, Don White, had been just ahead of Dick in school. Skiv had hired him in 1948 just out of high school. He had started in the yard crew and worked his way into a dairy route. Dick told Baumgarten he would make a good supervisor.

It seemed that the best way to increase sales and make the dairy profitable would be to buy small dairies close to Robinson. L.S. had long ago bought out George Everingham, who had a small dairy in Robinson. So Bayard Jr. and Dick went and bought two dairies for the company, one in Paris, Illinois, forty-three miles north of Robinson, and another in Washington, Indiana, about the same distance southeast of Robinson. Baumgarten started doing a private label business with the supermarkets that had just come into prominence in the fifties.

When Dick returned to Robinson from the Army in 1956, he had bought a small home about a four-iron shot from the high school. He had wanted to buy the place his father had built next to the country club. But his mother, who couldn't stand to live in the home after Skiv died and the kids were gone to school, had sold the home to Texas oilman Bill Davidson for fifty-two thousand dollars while Dick was overseas. She got an apartment in Robinson and spent the winter months in Palm Beach. Her daughter, Joan, had gone to Simmons Girls School in the East, then transferred to Northwestern University. After a brief fling with James Jones, the Robinson author who shot to national prominence with the publication of his best-selling World War II novel, *From Here to Eternity*, she graduated from college, got married and lived in Chicago.

In the years they lived in the house, Davidson and his wife Frances, a former Las Vegas showgirl, made several improvements in it. In one of the major changes, Dick's basketball court became a small entertainment house. He attended the Davidsons' parties, marveled at the wildness of the events now taking place in his parents' old house and dreamed about living there again.

Then in May of 1957, as Betty was about to give birth to Nancy, the couple's third child, Bill Davidson called Dick and wanted to sell him the house because he was moving to Dallas. Dick took over the 4 percent mortgage, gave Davidson a note for the balance and moved the young Heath family back into the house he had spent many of his happiest early years.

The same year, Bob met a strikingly beautiful artist from Cleveland named Jean Place who was ten years his senior. Bob was twenty-nine years old and despite several attempts to fix him up, he had never gone with anyone for long. The family was about to give up on him ever finding a woman he liked well enough to marry.

During her winters in Palm Beach, Madeline had started

going with a man she had met there. Joe Lippman was a nice, kind, Jewish man who filled the void in her life left by Skiv's death. Together, they talked Bob into spending a week's vacation near them in Florida and introduced him to their friend, Jean.

After a whirlwind romance in Florida for the week, Jean came to Robinson to see Bob. She stayed in a little house Madeline had bought about a half a block from the Heath plant. In no time, the couple decided to get married at Cape Cod in August 1957.

Dick and Betty drove their 1957 Chevrolet station wagon to Cape Cod for the wedding. After the ceremony, they would fly home and leave the car for the newlyweds to use for their honeymoon and then bring their belongings back to Robinson to the apartment they had rented.

A formal wedding with white tuxedoes was scheduled for one o'clock in the afternoon at a quaint little church. The weather was unusually warm for New England. Temperatures had soared into the nineties all week. Dick had picked up Bob and was headed for the church when they saw a small driving range off to their left.

Both men's golf clubs were in the back of the station wagon. When Betty had protested to Dick about bringing them, he had said, "We'd never leave town without them. That'd be like a gunfighter leaving his guns at home. You never know who might jump up to make a bunch of speeches. Like the Boy Scout motto of 'Be prepared,' we always try to be prepared."

With fifteen minutes to kill before they were supposed to arrive at the church, the two cousins were prepared to hit a bucket of balls. Because of the spontaneity of the moment, it wasn't clear who said what to whom. But Dick pulled up to the driving range.

"You get a bucket of balls," Dick said. "I'll get our wedge."

"Okay. Shoot you for quarters, closest to that marker about seventy-five yards there," Bob said, pointing to the first flag flapping gently in the breeze.

Dick was on target from the beginning, his balls landing close to the pin most of the time. Bob got down two dollars quickly and started gritting his teeth. That look of determination Dick knew well had come on Bob's face. He wasn't about to lose. It had become a point of pride with him. Yet he couldn't close up and the gap worsened, up to three dollars.

"Get another bucket of balls," Bob said through clenched teeth.

By this time, they were sweating profusely and their white jackets were soaked inside. Jean, her mother and the rest of her wedding party drove by in three cars. They saw the two men. Dick saw the party, but Bob kept looking at the flag pole.

"They all just went by, Bob," Dick said. "I think we ought to quit."

He turned and looked at Dick and said, "I'm starting to get even and you want to quit."

Knowing that Bob wasn't going to quit, even with his bride and her wedding party going by, a church full of people and his wedding approaching, Dick knew he had only one alternative. He was hitting the wedge shots so well that he could easily hit them just a little harder. It took quite awhile and some careful shots on Dick's part, but they finally got even.

They arrived at the church twenty minutes late, red-faced

from the heat and wet with perspiration. Jean was furious. She glared at Dick for the rest of the day. It was apparent that she had made up her mind that she was going to change the relationship the two cousins had enjoyed for years. Dick wanted to tell her the wedding would never have taken place if it hadn't been for him. He knew Bob would have stayed at the driving range until hell froze over if Dick hadn't let him get even.

When Bob and Jean got back to Robinson with their wedding presents, Dick went over to their apartment at about nine a.m. the next morning to trade cars. He hadn't seen the couple or heard from Bob since he left them at the church in Cape Cod after the wedding and was thinking about the day when he knocked on the apartment door.

Jean answered the knock and said, "Oh, hi, Dick. Is there something I can do for you?"

"Why, hi, Jean," Dick said, somewhat surprised at seeing her and moving through the door without being asked. "I need to see Bob and get my station wagon. Where's the man?"

"In the bathroom. He's shaving."

"Oh, that's all right," Dick said, starting toward the bathroom. "I just wanted to tell him something and exchange the cars."

"You can't go in there," Jean said stiffly. "He's not dressed."

"Hell, Jean, I've seen him naked all his life."

"Well, he's married now."

Dick started to say something when he heard Bob yell, "John Henry, is that you?"

"Yeah, it's me," Dick said, yelling back.

"Come on back."

Jean didn't say a word. Neither did Dick. He figured she was still upset with him about the golf incident on the day of the wedding. It hadn't bothered him to take the blame. But it wasn't what was bothering her, he didn't think.

Whatever it was, Dick just wanted to get his keys and get out. He walked to the bathroom and talked to Bob a few minutes. Dick could tell his forever-relationship with his cousin was going to change. The happy-go-lucky, no-holds-barred Robert Heath he had always known was starting a new life with the marriage.

Soon after the wedding, a situation came up at the company where the new accounting system proved to be of great value. Once before, in the late forties, a union tried to organize the Heath company. Now, another union came into the picture. It was the oil and chemical workers' union. The confectionary workers' union never bothered the company because it paid its employees higher wages than called for in the union contract.

But the oil and chemical workers' union was after the several hundred employees at the Ohio Oil Company refinery in Robinson. The union's plan was to organize the Heath company as a prelude to going after Ohio Oil. Union officials knew they couldn't get enough signatures to hold an election with the entire plant, so they concentrated on the dairy drivers.

Heath executives wanted all workers to vote for the union, not just a small group. A National Labor Relations Board meeting had been set for a hearing in St. Louis. Bayard Jr. had retained a labor lawyer, Arthur Donovan, to represent the company. Bayard Jr., Bob and Dick accompanied him to the meeting.

The Heath company was seasonal within the various

divisions. In the spring and summer months, the bottling and dairy divisions were extremely busy; in the fall and winter months, the candy division was the busiest. Anybody who worked for the company was guaranteed forty hours, with the exception of the high school kids who were hired in the summer as the Heath boys had been hired when they were that age. When work slowed down in one division, people were switched to the division where they were needed. This occurred often.

In the accounting system Dick had initiated, anyone moving from one job to another had a time-transfer slip filled out. These slips were the basis of the company's cost accounting. Since so many employees, including some of the drivers, were constantly being moved from job to job, many of these slips were filled out each month.

Part of the plan was to present this information at the hearing. If the union got in the wages might have been slightly higher, but many people would not get forty hours. The Heath company had what unions were after many years later, a guaranteed annual job. Dick's time tickets would show the real story of the company.

It was never possible to present that information at the hearing, however. The union flew its international president in from Pittsburgh to impress the board and to tell the board members how beneficial it would be for Heath employees if his union could represent them.

The three Heath cousins and company executives were sitting with their attorney. After the union president had been testifying for about twenty minutes, Donovan turned to them and said, "I've got an idea I want to try when I get to question him."

"What's that, Art?" Bayard Jr. asked.

Before he could answer, it was his turn to question the union president. "What does L.S. Heath & Sons, Inc., do?" Donovan asked immediately, using the corporate name.

"What do you mean, what do they do?" the union president asked.

"Simply, what do they make?" he asked again, knowing that the man he was questioning had been picked up from the airport and rushed to the hearing and hoping there hadn't been time for much more. "I think that's a fair question since you want to represent the company employees and look out for their welfare."

"Oh, you know," the president said, hesitating and fumbling for words. "They're like Kroger's. They're in the food business."

"Gentlemen of the board," Donovan said, looking slowly at each member, "everybody knows what the Heath candy company is and what it makes. Are you going to permit a union like this to represent these people, with a president who doesn't even know what they make? I move for dismissal."

And he got it.

Later, Bayard Jr. asked Donovan how he figured out that the president didn't know what the company did.

"I didn't. But I had nothing to lose. Of course, I used the corporate name. Otherwise, how many people wouldn't know what you do? Hell, the name sounds like a farm in Flat Rock, Illinois."

Donovan and the Heath cousins laughed.

14

In the dairy division, the company had been producing a three-ounce ice cream bar consisting of the candy toffee, vanilla ice cream and an average-quality chocolate. The sale of the toffee ice cream bar in the fifteen-county distribution area consistently outsold any of the company's other ice cream novelties and had for most of the nearly twenty years it had been produced.

Late one afternoon in 1958, Bob and Dick were in a golf cart at the country club on the back nine. They weren't really going at it as they usually were when they were on the course together. Mostly, they were talking.

"John Henry," Bob said, "what do you think about expanding our Heath ice cream bar?"

"What'd you want to do?" Dick asked. "Franchise it?"

"Why not? Think it'd sell?"

"Sure. People out there are no different than they are around here."

"There'd be problems."

"What's so new about that?"

"Let me work on some costs."

"Okay. I'll help you sell the family and go out and sell the damn accounts, if necessary."

A couple of days later while drinking their morning coffee, they told Bayard Jr. about the idea. He liked it and would come up with some crushed toffee and the franchise agreement. Bob was working on getting a bag and a box for the bars. He also was talking to the Nestle company about producing a blend of the same chocolate used on the Heath candy bar, prepared in five-gallon pails or five hundred-pound drums. Nestle officials told him they could thin the milk chocolate for the bar.

Although the cousins knew it would take time to get the bar on the market, they felt they had something and kept at it. Besides the toffee ice cream bars, the dairy also sold Eskimo pies, so they knew there was a market for the product. Until they were further along with the plans, they weren't going to say much about what they were doing. They discussed where they were each morning. Bob was a methodical person and kept working at it.

In the meantime, Vernon approached Dick about John. He wasn't in college and was working at a radio station in Charleston, Illinois. Vernon and Bea's other son, Allan, was at the Heath plant in much the same capacity as Bernard Dowling. He had no responsibilities. Allan was a good person but was somewhat limited in what he could do for the company.

John had married a Charleston woman named Sheila Owens. Her father owned the radio station where John worked. But now that they were married, he wanted to join the Heath company. Vernon, knowing that Dick was the key to the others or at least could sell them on an idea, wanted to know what Dick thought.

"What would he like to do, Vernon?" Dick asked.

"I think he'd enjoy working in the print shop."

An area that had just been remodeled next door to the

garage housed the print shop. As the company grew, more in-houuse printing was done.

"That's fine with me, Vernon," Dick said. "You know that. What would you like me to do? I'll just tell the rest that he's joining us. I don't remember anyone else having a vote on them."

"That would tickle me to death."

"Give me a couple of days, and I'll be back to you," Dick said.

He told Bayard Jr. and Bob about the conversation with Vernon, thinking it would tickle L.S., too, if he knew yet another family member was joining the company.

"Hell, I don't give a damn about it," Bayard Jr. said. "If he wants to come, who would stop him?"

"Oh my God," Bob said. "Another Vernon."

Dick laughed. He could say something about Pete, he thought. But he didn't.

"Dad won't like it," Bob said, "but I don't guess there's anything that can be done about it."

"Bob, you and Bayard both know that none of us or anybody can say no. Let's accept it. Vernon has gone along with what we've asked him."

"You're right about that," Bayard Jr. said. "I don't want to talk about it anymore. What time are we playing Saturday morning?"

"Ten o'clock," Dick said. "You tell Pete, Bob."

"All right."

Jack Morris was no problem, as Dick knew he wouldn't be. On the other hand, he knew Bayard Sr. would put up a fight. That was fine with Dick. He believed Bayard Sr. would only drive Vernon farther away from him, if that were possible.

"The hell I'm going to agree with that," Bayard Sr. said when Dick told him. "I've had enough of you damn kids the way it is now."

"Okay, Bayard, I've told you about it. If it comes to a vote, you'll lose and Vernon will never forget it."

"I don't care what he thinks, either. I'm tired of carrying him. I've carried him from the time he came back from Decatur."

"Are we going to do it the hard way or the easy way?" Dick asked, not giving an inch. "Hell, all he wants to do is work in the print shop."

"How much do we have to pay him?"

"I don't know. Let Vernon decide that."

"Well, he can't be worth much."

"Since when are people with the last name Heath ever paid what they are worth around here? Either way?"

Bayard Sr. grunted and walked off. That was about all there was to it. Vernon was relieved and happy when Dick told him everybody had agreed.

"What did Bayard Sr. say?" Vernon asked.

"I don't have to tell you what he said. Just tell John to come down and go to work. Nobody will stop him. You pay him what you want to."

Vernon started laughing. "You sound like Skiv," he said.

"Nobody's like Skiv."

In fact, none of the Heaths were like one another, Dick thought. The only thing they had in common was their last name and a stake in the family business.

John moved back to Robinson in a few weeks and just showed up in the print shop one day. Nothing was said. Everybody treated it as if it were normal. And in a way it was.

L.S. Heath wanted all the family in the business and have them treated equally. It was a folly, but everybody went along with it.

They all knew that people have different abilities and talents. Meshing in in-laws and offspring of every person in the family could not work. Bayard Jr. and Allan were first cousins. But that's as close as it went. One had a law degree; the other hardly made it out of high school. Bob was the same way compared to John. It was even the same among L.S.'s children. As far as having a business sense, Pete was head and shoulders above Vernon. Ruby had about as much ability to sit on a board of directors as a post. Why was she there? Simply because of L.S. Heath's not-thought-out quirk, and she was his daughter.

L.S. himself had no more right to be the chairman of the board than Skiv or Bayard Sr. The old man had supplied the money, his sons the work and the product that brought the company its huge success. So the family ranged in business sense from one end of the spectrum to the other.

At every board meeting, Bayard Sr. gave his figures, then Dick would pass out his. The tension was always there. Everybody could feel it. The eight board members, all so different, now without L.S. and Skiv, acted as though everyone had a little kingdom and was waiting for somebody to invade his or her world. There was no one leader. Bayard Sr. was sixty-five years old. Rather than mellow with age, he became more crusty and abrasive. He felt he had developed the Heath toffee bar and deserved to head the company. And perhaps he did.

But Dick was totally prejudiced against Bayard Sr., and it took a long time to recognize his uncle's frustrations. It was too bad that he had said what he had to Dick in the back yard on the day of Skiv's funeral. Dick had never trusted him afterwards and for a long time couldn't understand him. Neither could Bayard Sr. understand his nephew. Perhaps if they had understood each other, things would have been different.

But the crisis was just around the corner with the ice cream bar. Everybody knew it, too. Bayard Sr. was just as obsessed in his opposition to the ice cream-bar franchise as Dick was with him personally. Finally, the three younger Heaths approved a blue bag and box for the Heath ice cream bar and were ready to launch it to the family in early 1959.

Before that took place, however, Pete, Bob and Dick still had the Meridian, Mississippi, Pepsi Cola plant. They wanted to open a downtown office to move all the bookkeeping on the plant away from the main Heath offices. One of the office personnel at the plant was a woman named Sharon Osborne. She was a year or so older than Dick and had a younger sister named Mary Lynn Shepard. Both women had worked in their parents' grocery store across from the high school and had virtually grown up in a business environment. Dick hired Mary Lynn, a capable, intelligent young woman, as the bookkeeper and opened the office. Shortly afterwards, Bob and Dick were talking about the ice cream-bar franchise.

"If Bayard Sr., Vernon and Ruby," Dick said, mentioning the three they felt would be against it, "give us a lot of problems and don't want to do it, let's do this: We'll buy the toffee from them and pay them a royalty on each bar sold. Mary Lynn can take care of the office. We both know she can do it all."

"What royalty would you pay them?"

"Our gross profit from the pricing schedule we prepared shows 38 percent," Dick said. "Offer them 10 percent of the sales dollar."

"That much?"

"Yes, that much. It would be a hell of a deal for everybody. It's double the net profit on the Heath candy bar. They sell us the broken toffee at cost plus 10 percent, too."

"If it comes to that, it sounds like the way to go."

"We can cut Bayard Jr. in, too. Everybody that's for it is included."

"That's fine with me."

They wanted to be prepared to offer an alternative if the board turned the franchise plan down cold. Either way, they felt it would provide a financial windfall and weren't about to let the opportunity get away.

A loud, vocal argument developed the day they presented their plan to the entire board. Bayard Sr. almost came unglued and hit the ceiling. He saw this new division as a threat to whatever control he thought he had in the company.

"Hell," he said, "it won't sell. That's the first reason it's a dumb idea."

Then he continued with reason after reason why it wouldn't sell. Vernon was passive but against it. Ruby thought it was a ridiculous idea. Even Pete was skeptical. Only Jack Morris and the three cousins were in favor of trying it, leaving the board in a four-four deadlock.

"How do we know the dairies would make it right?" Bayard Sr. asked, unaware that the younger Heaths had anticipated and prepared for most of the questions and objections.

"We have a quality-control program set up with Western

Union to fly samples from anywhere in the country to Terre Haute," Bob said. "That way we can test and grade each license."

The questions continued. It was coming to a real knock-down family fight with no real basis for rendering a decision. Bob and Dick had a plan for that. They had made some sample bars, put them in the newly designed individual bags and those in the boxes. Bob was going to head south with samples; Dick would head east for the week.

They had price lists and the franchise agreements for the units. A unit consisted of fifteen hundred dozen or eighteen thousand bars. This was a single pack. A six-pack box was called a multi-pack. A unit cost more because of the three thousand boxes. That single-bar unit, consisting of eighteen thousand bars or five hundred pounds of chocolate and 180 pounds of toffee, was priced at $412. With the company cost for chocolate at thirty-two cents a pound, toffee at forty cents and the bags at $1.26 per thousand, that figured out to be $254.68 for a gross profit or 38 percent per unit. The multi-pack profit was about 35 percent gross profit. In either case, the profit margin was substantial. Those costs were freight-paid. And the company's bag supplies would imprint the particular dairy and ship the bag to it. Using the individual dairy's ice cream and equipment and the Heath company's chocolate, toffee and bags, the bars sold for ten cents and the multi-packs for fifty-nine cents. For the company, only one secretary was needed to process the orders and bill the customers.

In the board meeting, it got down to the point that somebody had to say stop. The details had all been worked out; the pros and cons had been discussed. Yet the argument raged.

"If somebody doesn't say, 'No, you stop,' we're going ahead," Dick said, laying it on the line in the midst of all the bickering. He wished somebody would say stop, so he could present the other proposal. The company could save a couple of vice president's salaries that way, and the franchising of the Heath toffee ice cream bar could still be accomplished at a considerable profit for those involved.

While everybody was still fretting, Dick called a man named Patterson at the Borden company in Indianapolis. He was the division president. His secretary put the call through after Dick told her he was a vice president and treasurer of the Heath candy company. With an appointment at Borden's in hand, Dick dry-iced several dozen samples and headed to Indianapolis on Monday morning. He planned to be gone until late Friday night and wasn't going to call in through Indiana, Ohio and Michigan, hoping for a surprise and knowing that everybody would still be in Bob's office, still arguing.

For the trip, he had taken the ice cream bars, franchise agreements and price lists. It was one time in his life that he left his golf clubs at home. As far as he was concerned, it was show time and no time for golf. Borden's had an ice cream bar called the Elsie bar, but the quality of the Heath bar sold Patterson. Dick persuaded him that it would not hurt sales for the Elsie bar. The company had the space in the cabinet, and it could take advantage of the Heath name to adult candy eaters. Before heading on east, he nailed Patterson with a twenty-five-unit order or ten thousand dollars worth of ice cream — the equivalent of 536 cases of Heath candy bars, a case consisting of twenty-four boxes of twenty-four bars. The profit on a dollar sale of ice cream was six times the profit on the equivalent sales as candy.

With that sale and his confidence soaring, Dick headed on east to Frecker's Novelties in Columbus, Ohio, where he marked up another twenty-five-unit order. He got a twenty-unit order at Kolten Buckeye in Lima, a ten-unit order at Stroh's Ice Cream in Detroit and a twenty-two-unit order at Short's in Ft. Wayne on the way back to Robinson or 102 units in all for more than forty-three thousand dollars in sales.

While Dick had traveled east, Bob had taken samples south to Memphis where he would introduce the product to High's, a large independant novelty maker that supplied many dairies not making their own. Pulling his car into his parking space at the Heath plant on Saturday morning, Dick wondered how Bob had done at High's. The two hadn't talked during the week, although Dick hadn't been able to resist sending word that he had good news.

If Bob never forgets a day the rest of his life, it will be this one, Dick thought, as he walked into the room. Nothing had changed. He nodded at Bayard Sr., Vernon, Bayard Jr. and Bob.

"Well, look who's here," Bob said. "I thought you just kept on going east, John Henry."

The two older men nodded but said nothing.

"I thought about it," Dick said, a slight smirk on his face, wondering where Bayard Jr. and Jack Morris were this morning. "Any luck in Memphis?"

"Some. I sold High's a test order for them to try on their dairies. It'll be a big order, if they go for it. What about you?"

Bob knew Dick and his little smirk. And he knew if he hadn't been successful or had had a problem, he wouldn't be playing it the way he was, either.

"Okay, John Henry, where are the orders?" Bob asked.

"You look like you just marked your second shot on a par four eighteenth hole two inches from the cup."

Dick laughed. "What orders?" he asked.

"The ones you've been collecting all week," Bob said, playing it to the hilt.

"Oh, you mean these orders," Dick said, taking them out of his back pocket all wadded up and tossing them nonchalantly on the table.

At that point, all eyes were on the table. Bob jumped out of his chair and came running around his desk to look at them. Dick didn't pay any attention to what Bayard Sr. and Vernon were doing or how they looked but watched Bob carefully as he counted the orders.

"Only 102?" Bob said. "What the hell's wrong with you?"

"Bad week."

"Damn, I thought you had sold something with all that time out there."

"What's good?" Vernon asked, not knowing anything else to say.

Bob turned to him with a straight face and said, "I don't know, but forty-three thousand dollars isn't much."

"It looks pretty good to me."

Bayard Sr. still hadn't said a word. He knew it was a fantastic beginning; he also knew Bob and Dick's actions were all an act. He finally said, "I've got to go."

Bob started laughing after Bayard Sr. left and said to Vernon, "I'm only kidding. Bayard Sr. knows that, too. Vernon, this is phenomenal. It proves it all. Borden is one of the biggest in the country. Don't you really know what this all means?"

"Probably not, but I do know that forty-three thousand

dollars is a lot of sales," Vernon said, rising to walk to his office. "That's pretty good."

That was an understatement to Bob and Dick. It was one of the sweet times to them. "Another oil well, I do believe," Dick said.

After Dick's return, everybody was convinced the company had a big winner. The major problem was going to be how to get around the whole United States. They couldn't drive everywhere, and commercial air lines wouldn't take them where they wanted to go.

Getting everything together at the plant was simple. A single secretary, already working, took the orders and separated them under single units and multi units. She sent a purchase order to Jack Morris for X number of bags of toffee crushed from the scraps or broken pieces. Jack shipped the scraps as he received the orders; Dick transferred the cost of the crushed toffee to the ice cream bar division.

The secretary sent an order to Nestle for the necessary chocolate to be shipped to the ordering company in either five hundred-pound drums or five-gallon pails, according to what the company required. She used the same procedure with Bag Craft and John Strange Carton Company. These companies all billed the ice cream division. Dick charged these bills to the ice cream cost of goods sold and credited accounts payable. The secretary then billed the dairy for the order. That entry was to credit sales of the ice cream bar franchise and debit accounts receivable.

The sales would appear on a separate division. Less the cost of goods sold gave the gross profit. Dick also had an account, a lump-sum account for any expenses like travel and entertainment. This was substracted and known as operating profit before administrative overhead. During those times, the profit margin was phenomenal. Dick was so busy that he had little booze, no women and no golf losses. The huge profits impressed just about everyone in the company.

Bayard Sr. remained cool toward Dick and the idea in spite of the obvious success. Eventually, Dick sold some forty accounts all over the United States. With the Heath name behind him and the ability to reach the top man of each company, it wasn't too difficult. Many of the later sales were made on the golf course. Dick was totally baffled by Bayard Sr.'s attitude toward the ice cream-bar franchise and discussed it with Bayard Jr. He had no answer. All Dick could think of was that it had become a thing with his uncle, that he had made so many speeches against it that he couldn't back up and say he was wrong. And he never did. Apparently, this was the issue he had made to make his stand against the "kids." He couldn't have picked a worse issue.

Sometimes Dick thought the resistance was because of his relationship with Bayard Jr. But that didn't really make sense. The ice cream-bar franchise was Bob's idea from the beginning. He had done much work in getting it put together. Bayard Jr. and Dick had helped a great deal. But he knew, if it meant anything, that Bob got the credit for the idea. Centuries later, then, there wouldn't be any of this stuff by anybody who wants to rewrite history like the old days with the Heath candy bar when everybody started wanting to take credit for it. Dick wasn't there in 1914 to know who did what or what happened in the early thirties, either. It wasn't until the forties that he really got to know anything. He was there in the cart that afternoon when Bob first told him his idea.

But it took a team effort to get the franchise going. The

team was there, on and off the golf course. Besides Bayard Jr. and Dick, Jack Morris, or "Uncle Weak Eyes" as his golfing partner Dode Douglas called him literally because of his poor eyesight but figuratively because he missed so many short putts, was also a key to getting the franchise off the ground. Thinking about how they had worked together, Dick remembered little incidents from the past.

Golf great Ben Hogan had written an article on golf that was published in *Life* magazine in 1951. The article told about the Hogan secret in his swing (being able to fade a shot, not draw it as everybody else had). Bayard Jr. read it and kept going to Dick's office every morning to discuss it. Because Bayard Jr. was so hung up on the theory, Bob and Dick started calling him "Hogan." And Dick started calling Pat "Valerie," Ben Hogan's wife.

These were silly things, Dick thought and laughed. But they showed the relationship. As part of the history of the family, the inter-relationships were important. At least the first three men in the third generation of the Heath family had fun. The first generations had very little, if any, fun. This generation put out the work, though. More quality work than quantity work, too.

And Dick would guarantee that the three of them could work for a couple of centuries for what they were being paid in comparison to what the ice cream-bar franchise contributed, and would continue to contribute, to the kitty.

15

By 1959, Bayard Jr., Bob and Dick knew the dairy was not going to last much longer. The reason was the same one that was a part of the other 650 that went under or were about to go under in the state of Illinois: With cost cutting and price wars continually going on, small companies couldn't get enough volume to show a profit. No matter how hard they tried or what they did, nothing was going to save the dairy. Both Bob and Dick thought their efforts were needed for the ice cream bar, anyway.

To sell or visit the many ice cream-bar accounts around the country, the company had started chartering a single-engine Mooney airplane from a St. Louis firm. Word was going around at the time that Mooney planes were having problems with tails falling off in flight. That was probably untrue, but flying in a single-engine plane was always a nerve-wracking experience for the three Heath cousins who were making trips selling the ice cream bars.

Bayard Jr. and Dick had been caught in a driving snow storm going to Pittsburgh to sell the Borden Dairy. The Mooney wasn't equipped for IFR or instrument flight. And because the plane had no instruments, they got lost for a while. The snow had blinded the pilot, who had been flying from visual sightings from the ground. They sold Dick Waggoner at the dairy, but they were scared in the single-engine plane.

The pilot, Jim Reese, was good at his job. But the regular risky flights were getting old and were costing the company large sums of money. Other dairies that had only heard about the ice cream bar began calling the Heath company. Finally, after Dick had flown to Mayfield, Kentucky, to sell the Mayfield Dairies the bar, an incident scared Dick so badly that he decided to do something about making other flight arrangements.

On the return flight from Kentucky, they again ran into a storm and were flying in the clouds. The plane picked up ice. Without instruments, it was a serious situation.

"Goddamn it, Jim," Dick said to the pilot. "Where did this mess come from?"

"I don't know. We don't have radar in this little plane, so we're flying by the seat of our pants."

"Well, this is the last time for this. If we go down, I'll have to throw this order out the window and hope somebody finds it and sends it to the plant. Wait until I get home—if we ever make it home."

Only Reese's experience and calm professionalism got them back on the ground safely in Robinson. And, true to his word, the next day at the mini-board meeting with his two cousins and Jack Morris, Dick slammed the order down on Bob's desk and said, "This is it. We hit an ice storm at Evansville last night, and I thought it was all over. I was scared shitless. Jim probably was, too, but he somehow brought us through it. This thrill-a-minute flying is getting old. And I'm through with it."

"What can we do about it?" Bob asked.

"Buy a larger plane, like we've talked about," Dick said. "I'm going to get Vernon and Pete in here."

With the others solidly behind the plan, both of the men agreed. The larger plane they were talking about was a Cessna 310 twin-engine plane that came with everything, including radar, necessary for instrument flying. The plane seated five besides the pilot and cost about $240,000.

Dick told Bayard Jr. to tell his dad that the company just bought the twin Cessna and stole the charter pilot to fly it. At this point, Dick could care less about what Bayard Sr. or Ruby might say. Without another plane, it was agreed that none of them was going out again. Neither of the older family members liked the plan, but they never complained much about it. Ruby did say later that she took the train to Chicago and carried a sack lunch.

"I don't give a damn how you get to Chicago or what you eat," Dick said, thinking that he and Ruby had a personality conflict with each other similar to that of Winston Churchill and Adolph Hitler. "You're not selling a million dollars worth of ice cream, either."

Ruby had constantly talked about driving to Sullivan, Indiana, to catch a train to Chicago. She always took a brown-bag lunch for her husband and her. And she had been criticizing the younger Heaths about how they wasted their money entertaining the ice cream-bar accounts.

Shortly afterward, the company purchased the Twin Cessna from the company it had been charting planes from and hired Jim Reese, the charter pilot.

The family decided to paint the plane brown and white (Heath candy wrapper colors) with a Heath bar on the tail. Everybody felt much safer as they continued the company assult on the nation's dairies. Dick made trips to Chicago; Boston; St. Louis; Des Moines, Iowa; Sheboygan, Wisconsin;

Johnstown, Pennsylvania; Wichita Falls, Texas—all successes except the one in Wichita Falls.

There, Dick had made an advance appointment for nine a.m. with the president of a large dairy. This was Dick's usual approach. He went right to the top, not wasting time talking with some purchasing agent. Who Dick was got him to who he wanted to see. Being an officer of the Heath company didn't get him any advantage on the golf course, but it did give him one in getting appointments that he needed to sell the ice cream bars. At the time he hit the Texas city, he was virtually undefeated and almost had to give points to his cousins on a kill.

When he walked up to the receptionist, a light-skinned brunette with a Texas drawl, she said, "Mr. Wadell had to leave town yesterday, Mr. Heath. He asked me to tell you to see Mr. Lyons, our purchasing manager."

"Okay," Dick said and thought, he was sure glad Bob and he didn't have a bet on this one. It was his first go at anybody less than a president or general manager.

A few minutes later, Lyons took Dick's hand without rising, waved a hand at the chair in front of the desk, took off his watch and lay it on the desk in full view. "I'm very busy this morning," he said. "You've got five minutes. What do you have to show me?"

Dick looked at him, thought a second and said, "I'm sorry. I have nothing to show you. But thanks for your valuable time. Tell Mr. Waddell I'll see him at another time."

Lyons simply looked at Dick and said nothing. There was no way Dick would begin to try to sell Lyons. He probably wouldn't know what he was being offered, Dick thought, and more importantly, he couldn't or wouldn't make a decision.

After asking the receptionist to call him a cab, thanking her and riding back to the airport, he left town. Dick knew their supermarkets would eventually put pressure on the company, and someone would be calling Heath.

When Ross Fife, Nestle's national bulk chocolate sales manager, called on the Heath company, he met with a Heath or Jack Morris. Fife had told Dick early on that the secret of selling something like chocolate was to make sure to get to the right man, the one who could make a decision. And when Fife called on the Heath company, he usually, if possible, ended up in a golf cart playing golf with one of the Heaths. He sold the company so much chocolate that it became Nestle's number-one bulk chocolate account. Out of the forty or so accounts Dick eventually sold in the next few years, seven of them were sold on the golf course.

On the call in Texas where Dick struck out, he knew it was the first inning of the game. He knew there would be other days. "I got tapped out," he told Bob when he called in that morning. "The son-of-a-bitch was a no show, and I wouldn't talk to the purchasing asshole who wanted to give me five minutes of his fucking time. Go tell Bayard Sr. he was right: I found a guy like him and didn't sell him."

"That's tough, John Henry. But that counts. You're not undefeated anymore."

"You can't win 'em all. Guess I lost for the first time, huh? I'm on my way back in. Any late crises?"

"No, not really. Bayard Sr. made a raid over to see Vernon about letting us kids run around the country. That was just after you left."

"How's old Vernon's pulse?"

"Dad said he's all right. Vernon wants the plane to go to

Chicago to some meeting Friday."

"Who is he selling?"

"The higher education board of the state of Illinois."

"I'll bet he doesn't bring back any orders," Dick said and wondered what Bayard Sr. thought about that trip.

Vernon always cringed when Bayard Sr. would come to see him and would later spend an hour relaying the conversation to Dick to get it out of his system. Dick would listen sympathetically. He knew Vernon would cause them no problems about the sales trips.

One morning a few weeks later, Bob said, "You know we need a sales manager to run these sales. We're getting all these accounts, Dick, but somebody had to manage them while we hit the rest of the country."

"You're right about that. Selling them is one thing, taking care of them is another. You know how valuable these accounts are—each one is worth a thousand candy accounts to us."

"Let's find a sales manager then."

"Why don't we steal Ross Fife from Nestle?"

"Do you think he'd come with us?"

"I don't know. Let me try to nail him."

"Go get him, John Henry. I'll tell the family what we're going to try to do. Let's see what Hogan says."

Later, after Bob had spoken to Bayard Jr. about the plan, the two younger cousins got together again. "Hogan's for the idea," Bob said. "But he says the old man will hit the ceiling."

"Hell, he's been there all along. So what's new about that?"

"Hogan wants a meeting with Dad and Vernon over this."

"So what's the problem?"

"Bayard Sr. thinks it would ruin us with Nestle."

"What are they going to do? Walk away from a six million-pound account between the candy and ice cream-bar divisions?"

At the meeting, Bayard Sr. ranted and raved, but in the meantime Dick had called Fife and told him he wanted to see him. Fife was going to be in Detroit in a few days. So Dick set up a meeting with him at the Hilton Hotel while all the discussion about the situation was continuing at the plant.

The meeting took place at the hotel bar. For the first two martinis, the two men visited and talked about their golf games. By the third drink, Dick said, "Ross, we want you to come and join us as the ice cream bar national sales manager."

"You do," Fife said, taking a small sip of his martini but showing no emotion. "Well, I'm flattered. I like you guys, and you've got a helluva product."

After the fourth drink, the two men had cut a deal. Fife said it wouldn't be a problem with Nestle. The main problem was that he was making more money than Bayard Jr., Bob, Dick and Jack Morris and almost as much as the senior members. Dick knew that wouldn't bother the younger members, but it might bother some of the older ones—particularly Bayard Sr. and Ruby. Finally, Dick said the hell with it. Fife was top quality. He wasn't getting any stock. All he would do for the company was make everybody more money. It wasn't that Ross was overpaid, anyway, Dick thought. It's just that the rest of them were underpaid. So at ten p.m. that evening, they shook hands and had a deal. Dick would take the flack later.

Ruby started with the flack at the next board meeting about the deal Dick had made with Fife. Bayard Jr., Bob, Pete and Jack Morris backed Dick's action. And by that time, Bob had

Pete in line for good. Dick had shown an eighty thousand-dollar profit for the quarter, matching the candy division before the flack had started.

Fife's salary had been set at only one thousand dollars a year under the salaries of the three older family members. Dick solved that with a motion to raise the salaries of his three uncles. Bayard Sr. even raised hell about that, but Pete and Vernon were satisfied.

No sooner than the crisis over hiring Ross Fife settled down than Dick did something to make everyone forget about Fife's salary. If they think hiring Ross was bad, Dick thought as he and Bob sat at the bar in the Warick Hotel in Philadelphia, they ain't seen nothing yet. He was waiting for a man whom he wanted to hire to head sales in the eastern part of the United States. The man's name was Eddie Bertaine, one of the best natural salesmen Dick had ever seen.

The East Coast market was a game of its own, a market so huge that it was virtually impossible for Dick and Fife to go out there and try to handle the many prospective accounts. Dick had sold H.P. Hood, one of the largest dairies in the East. But the company had to have someone who lived in the area and could take care of the market.

Bertaine wanted a commission or a salary with bonus to take the job. The company opted for the salary with bonus, and he soon became the highest-salaried employee in the company, including the elder Heaths.

"That's outrageous," Bayard Sr. said about the amount of money Bertaine made.

"I wish he made double you all," Dick said. "If he did, he'd be making us a ton of money. He's earned what he makes, and he's worth every penny of it. What would you say if one of your brokers made a commission of more than your salary. Would you cancel him?"

"Obviously I wouldn't," Bayard Sr. said.

"Obviously not," Dick said. "The secret of this company—or any company for that matter—is to attract top-quality people who will make this company money. But it's a fight every step of the way."

About this time, Bob and Dick had an appointment with Bowman Dairies in Chicago. They wanted the account badly. Their wives, Jean and Betty, had accompanied them to Chicago to do some shopping. The meeting lasted longer than expected, and it was dark flying back to Robinson. They left Meigs Field in Chicago about 8:30 p.m. It was a clear night. The flight was about an hour. Dick was sitting in front with Jim Reese. Bob was in back with the two women. Just south of Danville with Terre Haute in radio contact, Reese said, "I can't land this plane, Dick. I'm sorry, but I can't do it."

"What the hell's going on, Jim?"

"I'm sorry," he said, his hands trembling, lips quivering. "I can't do it. I've got lumbago."

Dick couldn't understand what lumbago had to do with landing a plane. He didn't know what was going on or how it happened so quickly, but he knew that somehow Reese had lost his composure. Bob began to suspect something was wrong. He leaned forward.

"What's going on?"

Not wanting to panic anyone, but shaken himself, Dick said, "This son-of-a-bitch says he can't land the plane."

There was silence in the back of the plane. Dick could see the lights of Terre Haute in the distance to his left. He grabbed Reese by the shirt just under his throat, half hit him with the back of his hand and drew his face over to his.

"If you don't land this plane," Dick said through clenched teeth, "I'm going to beat the hell out of you and land it myself. Tell me now because I'm going to take it in at Terre Haute."

Apparently what Dick said and did had an effect because Reese snapped out of whatever had happened to him long enough to land the plane in Robinson. Bob fired him on the spot before Dick could do it. Everybody was shook up and on edge.

Later, when the company hired Woody Blaha, an older and more experienced pilot, Dick told him about the situation that night and asked, "Could I have landed this plane at night at Terre Haute, Woody?"

"You would hardly have hit the county, let alone the airport," Woody said, laughing. "Remember, Dick, you said you had three drinks before you took off, too."

Dick smiled weakly, knowing Woody was undoubtedly correct. Bob said he had known that all along when Dick relayed the conversation to him.

"Don't worry about it, John Henry," Bob said. "You can't do everything. In fact, I'm going to give you a real challenge in your ball park. And I'll bet you ten bucks you can't sell the guy on the first shot."

"You're on," Dick said, without knowing who he was supposed to sell. "Who is this one?"

"Harvey Barrett, the president of the Borden Division in Florida and Alabama."

"What's so special about him?"

"Ross said he would be the toughest sale in the country."

"Is that right? Well, then give me two to one odds if he's so tough," Dick said and went to find Fife to learn a little more about the man, to find out what made him so tough.

"He's a no-nonsense man," Fife said. "He's the complete and total boss of his operation. What he says goes. If he wants something, he gets it. I sold him some coatings when I was with Nestle's. But he's hard to see by people just calling on Borden's to sell them something. He is very wealthy, has a rather aloof personality and doesn't seem to want to get into the details of the running of the company."

"Does he play golf?" Dick asked.

"Everybody plays golf in Florida."

The next Wednesday, Dick called Harvey Barrett in Tampa. His secretary put him on the phone after Dick told her who he was.

"Mr. Barrett, this is Dick Heath, vice president of the Heath candy company. I'm in New Orleans with my pilot. We're heading for Tampa tomorrow afternoon to play some golf at Doral Friday. I've heard a lot of nice things about you and would like to meet you to discuss something I think will be to our mutual benefit."

"Fine, Mr. Heath," Barrett said without hesitation. "What time are you arriving?"

"About five o'clock at the Jake Flying Service there at the airport."

Barrett hesitated a moment, then asked, "Do you have reservations?"

"No, I don't. Not yet."

"I'll make them for you. I assume you want two rooms."

"Yes, that's fine."

"I'll tell you what, I'll pick you up if that's all right—oh, by the way, what's your handicap?"

"The same as it is when you look at the sky."

Barrett laughed, knowing Dick's handicap was zero.

Dick didn't tell Bob about the conversation because he would have made Dick give him the two-to-one odds. As it was, Dick knew Bob's twenty bucks was a goner.

Not only did Barrett pick Dick up, but he asked him to have cocktails at his home and meet his wife. Then the three of them had dinner that night at a restaurant, tastefully decorated in simple Spanish style, that specialized in seafood. No matter how insistent Dick was about paying, he was Barrett's guest. During dinner, Dick told him all about the ice cream bar, the dairy and the family. Barrett enjoyed the story. His family had sold its dairy to Borden's a few years earlier, and he had continued in the business as president of the two-state region.

The conversation and party continued well into the night. What the older Heaths never realized was how the ice cream bar was going to be sold. These were huge accounts. And one-on-one was the only way the selling could be done successfully. The younger Heaths' personalities, their golf abilities and their lifestyles fit what they were doing. The average candy sale was about a six-case order. That was about $140. The company had some ten thousand accounts in the candy division. At the peak of the ice cream-bar business, the company had about 115 dairies. So with the ice cream-bar franchise, it was definitely a one-on-one show.

Both Barrett and his wife liked the bar and thought it was a winner. He arranged for Dick to meet with Borden officials the next morning. Although Barrett would have to leave early, it was downhill on the sale. The boss was sold.

The next morning all the key Borden people were present. It became even more apparent that Barrett was the boss. He introduced Dick, explained the plan, told his people to take care of the details and they did. Just to fill the pipeline with back-up product for both states took 240 units. That was 4.32 million ice cream bars. The order was $98,880, all single pack or twenty-four loose bars in a plain box to start. This was the second largest sale in the company at the time, second only to the $175,000 candy order from the Army back in 1942.

As much as the sale pleased Dick, the twenty-dollar bonus he would get when he got home pleased him no less. Even the prospect of playing golf at Doral didn't interest him. He called Bob and told him to get his twenty dollars together for when he got back Friday night, knowing that Bob carried hardly any cash. Dick didn't tell him the size of the order.

Pete, Bayard Jr., Bob, Jack Morris and Ross Fife were waiting for Dick Saturday morning. While Dick hadn't told him the size of the order, Bob knew it was a huge order because of the call. But he hadn't told anybody. This was the fun of it for Bob. Nearly everyone had asked him if he had heard from Dick late Friday afternoon. Bob just nodded and said Dick would be in Saturday morning.

Saturday morning was like many other Saturday mornings that Dick had come into the office after being on the road all week. That morning, Bayard Jr., Bob, Jack and Fife were in Bob's office before Dick arrived. Fife had sort of prepared everybody not to be disappointed in case Dick came back empty-handed.

At a little after half past eight, Dick walked in, impassive and poker-faced. Bob had said nothing for the twenty minutes it had taken for everybody else to drift in. And when Dick got there, Bob went to get Pete from his office down the hall.

"Well, King Richard, I see your briefcase," Fife said. "Did you get an order? Let me see it."

Dick scooted the briefcase across the table to Fife. He opened the briefcase, rummaged through it but couldn't find an order.

"Did you get tapped out?" Bob asked.

"He wouldn't be that smug if he had gotten wiped," Bayard Jr. said.

"Better shake him down, Ross," Bob said.

"What's in his back pocket?" Bayard Jr. asked.

"That's my schedule for the opera the next time I go to Chicago," Dick said, pulling out some papers.

"Let me see them," Fife said.

Dick threw them across the table to Fife.

"I'll be damned," Fife said. "He hit the jackpot."

Vernon, dressed in a suit as always, walked in to see what was going on. "Hit what jackpot?" he said.

"How many units is it?" Bayard Jr. said to Fife.

"Two hundred twenty-five units."

"That's pretty good, isn't it?" Vernon asked.

"You'd never realize how big, Vernon," Bob said, handing Dick a twenty-dollar bill. "You done good, John Henry."

These years were Dick's most productive time with the company. He spent little time in Robinson. In addition to selling the ice cream bar, he was also responsible for doing the accounting. So he had no time to sit around and argue with anybody when he was in the office. Bayard Jr. and Bob handled the inter-family squabbles.

But with Fife taking over sales, Dick wouldn't be taking more sales trips. He fully enjoyed both the trips and the selling. Before Fife took over completely, though, Dick knew of two other big accounts that were highly important to the company that he wanted to sell. He mentioned them to Bayard Jr. one morning.

"Why don't you come with me on this one, Hogan?" Dick asked. "I've got Foremost in Jacksonville, the other large dairy in Florida, and Meadow Gold in Dothan, Alabama, that I want to see before I hang it up. These are big and important accounts, probably a million and a half initial bars."

"Okay, I'll go. But let's take the girls. We have the plane, and it wouldn't cost that much."

"Fine. How do you want to do it?"

"Let's fly to Sea Island first, play golf and stay all night. We can go to Jacksonville the next day. You tell me Ed Volkwine, the big daddy, plays golf. Let's get a game with him. We can hit Meadow Gold at Dothan the next day, stop at Point Clear that evening, play golf there and come on in the next day."

"Sounds good. Let's work it out. I'll call Volkwine for golf and Dothan for appointments. You make the reservations on the rest."

So it was all set. They would be gone three nights. Bob thought it was a great idea and had the itinerary. Bayard Sr. was beside himself, still fighting the ice cream bar despite its success.

Nevertheless, Bayard Jr., Pat, Dick and Betty left for Sea Island, Georgia, early in the morning. Four sets of golf clubs and two boxes of ice cream bars on dry ice were stowed in the rear of the plane. Because of a weight problem, each couple took only one suitcase. Dick sat in the co-pilot's seat with Blaha and watched the sun rise as the plane headed southeast out of Illinois. By the time the trip was over, things at the Heath company would never be the same again.

The Heaths arrived at Sea Island, played golf in the middle of the afternoon and had dinner that night. Bayard Jr. and Dick, sitting with their wives over cocktails later in the evening, talked about the situation at the plant and the increasing power struggle brought on by Bayard Sr.'s disagreement with the company's direction with the ice cream bar.

"I don't know how much longer this can go on," Bayard Jr. said. "Dad just won't look at the facts."

"I know what you mean," Dick said. "Everybody's miserable there. Pete just comes in and closes his door and says nothing."

"I told Mother how bad it is. All she would say is, 'You know Bayard.'"

After that, the two cousins and sons of the co-founders of the Heath company, didn't talk about it anymore. The day had been a good one, warm and sunny with a cold breeze blowing in off of the Atlantic Ocean. Both Bayard Jr. and Dick had shot well at golf. Life was something to be savored like a fine, rare wine. The two couples drank, danced and enjoyed their good fortune well into the night.

The next day, they flew to Jacksonville, Florida, where Bayard Jr. and Dick met with Ed Volkwine. They referred to him as "Daddy White Bucks" because of his white shoes. He is a daddy all right, Dick thought, a Big Daddy, the head of all Foremost Dairy operations in Florida. But the Heaths got along well with him and signed him to a sixty-unit order, more than a million bars.

While Dick was getting the purchase order and taking care of all the details, Bayard Jr. was up in Volkwine's office negotiating strokes with him and his sales manager. Dick thought he and his cousin had the right jobs because Hogan was tough on the strokes. Because he had a twenty-five thousand-dollar order in his pocket, Dick would have given them an extra stroke on the side. Not Bayard Jr. Business was one thing to him; golf was another.

It took Dick an hour to work out production details and selling information with Volkwine's people. Before it was completed, Bayard Jr. and Volkwine came to the office. "All right, you guys," Volkwine said. "We have a tee time in a half an hour. You've got five minutes to wrap it up."

Bayard Jr. stood behind him laughing. He had done a good job of negotiating the strokes. The important work had been done. Dick was about finished with his part and soon had a signed purchase order. Within minutes, the foursome was on the way to the picturesque golf course at Ponte Vedra Beach.

"Do we count this twenty bucks as a sale?" Dick asked later after he and Bayard Jr. had taken Volkwine and his sales manager for ten bucks apiece. "You know Ruby. She would think we were really something if we added it in. I could have a separate line item on the statements."

"Hell," Bayard Jr. said, "none of them could read it anyway."

The next day, they landed at Dothan, Alabama. Meadow Gold had to have the ice cream bar because Borden had it. Actually this was true in many situations. Companies had to keep up with their competition.

"This is a cripple, Hogan," Dick said to Bayard Jr. "You handle this one and earn your dinner tonight."

Bayard Jr. promptly went and signed Meadow Gold to a fifty-unit order worth twenty thousand dollars. He was smiling widely when he returned to the plane with the order. Dick had never seen him so tickled about anything. They celebrated with their wives by playing nine holes at Point Clear later that afternoon. Located at the southern tip of Alabama, the Point Clear course consisted of three nines winding through the pine trees. The Grand Hotel was rustic and had some of the best food Dick had ever eaten. It was his favorite resort area in all of the United States.

"This guy was so tough you can't imagine," Dick told Pat and Betty that night in the hotel dining room at their table overlooking the picturesque setting in the pines and the last rays of the setting sun. "He screamed, 'No, no, no. ...' It took Hogan's best sales effort. We have to drink to Bayard for doing a fantastic job."

Actually, the president of the company almost had the order ready when Bayard Jr. and Dick walked into his office. His largest supermarket chain had been demanding the bar. At the moment Dick was raising his glass for the toast, a waitress stopped at the table.

"I have a call for a Mr. Heath," she said.

"Take it, Dick," Bayard Jr. said. "It has to be Bob."

Dick hurried to the lobby and the phone. He couldn't imagine what was so important that Bob couldn't wait until they returned to Robinson to discuss it. His mind was racing as he walked.

"John," Bob said almost before Dick said hello, "Bayard Sr. has thrown in the jock."

"What the hell does that mean?"

"He told Dad and Vernon that he wanted them to stop us from running around the country or pay him a million dollars for his and Pat's stock. He wants out and wants a million bucks cash is what it amounts to."

Bayard Sr. had given Bayard Jr. and his two boys 325

shares, and L.S. had given him fifty shares. The million dollars Bayard Sr. wanted was for the 2,225 shares he and his daughter owned. He never thought Pete and Vernon would permit the company to pay him that much money.

Dick was quiet for a few seconds, thinking quickly, before he said, "That'll be no problem."

"Dad and Vernon are upset," Bob said. "That's what we have in the Second National."

"Tell them not to worry about that. I'll get it by Wednesday. Set a meeting for Friday."

"Where are you going to borrow it?"

"Probably Indianapolis."

"Okay, Dick. Tell Hogan what's going on. By the way, how did you do with Foremost and Meadow Gold?"

"More than a hundred units between them."

"Great. Tell everybody hello. See you tomorrow."

Dick went back to the table and relayed the conversation.

"I wonder what finally brought it to him?" Bayard Jr. asked quietly, thinking about his father's move and what it would mean to their relationship.

"Us here with the girls."

"He's not kidding."

"I know he's not."

What was happening or had happened was that Bayard Sr. was sticking it right at Pete and Vernon. His ultimatum was either "we" run the company, which meant he ran it, or the company buy him out and pay him off. He stuck the million dollars at them, thinking they wouldn't deplete the company bank account. And that's why Dick was planning to borrow all the money for the buyout. The company could pay it off easily out of the ice cream bar profits, which would be ironical considering Bayard Sr.'s opposition to the bar. But the price was fair to him and to the company.

Pete and Vernon didn't think the price was fair to the company, but Bob and Dick were able to persuade them it was fair. In the meantime, Bayard Jr. gave Dick the address of Lester Irons, an Indianapolis lawyer with the large and prestigious firm of Barnes, Hickman, Pantzer and Boyd. Bayard Jr. had met Irons when he worked with Lester Ponder, another lawyer with the firm, on company business and had told Irons about the present situation shortly after returning to Robinson.

When Dick called Irons about helping him secure the money from the Indiana National Bank in Indianapolis, he agreed to make the necessary appointments. A short time later, he called back and said he had an appointment with Hugh Funk and James Lentz, two senior vice presidents, at eleven a.m. Wednesday and would meet him at the bank.

At the last annual meeting, Dick had been made treasurer of the company. So when the men met at the bank, he brought with him the last financial statement he had completed. Actually, there was $1,200,000 cash in the Second National Bank in Robinson and $200,000 in the payroll account at the Crawford County State Bank there.

After telling Funk and Lentz his story, Dick said, "If you loan us the money for a three-year loan, I'll move a million dollars to your bank. We may get it down to $500,000 once in a while, but it'll average out at a million. It depends on when Jack buys chocolate, almonds or butter. I want the money today in two cashier's checks, one made out to Bayard E. Heath Sr. for $820,000 and the other to Patricia Heath Keisling for $180,000."

They agreed with little discussion. Dick signed a corporate note for a million dollars and agreed to transfer the company account the following Monday if the deal with Bayard Sr. was completed. Bayard Jr. would send the bank the corporate resolution. If there was no deal, Dick would send the checks back, and they could tear up the note.

"This is the fastest transaction to loan a million and pick up a million in deposits I have ever done," Lentz said. He was in charge of national accounts. Funks was in charge of the Indianapolis accounts.

"It's the fastest transaction I have seen, too," Irons said to Dick on the way out of the bank. They were on their way to see an Indianapolis CPA firm. Dick had agreed to have a certified statement prepared that the Heath company had gone to a bank to borrow money for the first time in its history. Irons had made a call from the bank to make arrangements to meet right away with members of the Bailey, Cord and Williams CPA firm. The firm's offices were close by.

Dick explained to Skipper Bailey and Noel Cord what had happened, including his books, Bayard Sr.'s books, all about Dr. Thomas and his role in setting up new books and the bank's requirements. It was apparent that Bailey and Cord were elated over the prospect of being the Heath company's CPA firm, if Bayard Sr. went through with the deal.

In less than three hours, Dick had Lester Irons to act as the company's general counsel with Bayard Jr., a new CPA firm and a million bucks in his pockets. As he left town for the two-hour drive back to Robinson, his thoughts were of his dad and his grandfather. Dick was wondering if they would have approved. Knowing all the circumstances, he had no doubt both would have approved. He also knew it would have great ramifications with Bayard Jr. only having 375 shares of company stock. Dick, however, also knew several other things. With his 2500 shares, which included his mother and sister, he could insure Bayard Jr. would have a seat on the board with him. If the company retired Bayard Sr.'s 1,850 shares and Pat's 375, it would take some 1,337 shares to legally hold a seat. Together, Dick and Bayard Jr. had enough to insure two seats out of the eight.

Although Dick was fairly confident, he still didn't totally believe Bayard Sr. would sell out once his bluff was called. Bob didn't believe he would; Bayard Jr. wasn't sure, but he said if he had to bet, he would bet he would. Pete thought he would; Vernon didn't think so.

"I don't want to say either way," Jack Morris said. "But I can't believe they would let you walk out of that bank with a million dollars without any collateral."

"They weren't totally surprised," Dick said. "Hogan had called Irons, so they knew we weren't kidding. Lester is the bank's lawyer, you know."

Friday wasn't a board meeting day, but everybody was there except Ruby. Bayard Sr. was making one more move on Pete and Vernon in Pete's office. The rest of the group was sitting in Bob's office board room next door. The older men had been together for nearly a half an hour. Dick was sure Vernon had told Bayard Sr. they had the checks waiting for him and felt sorry for Bayard Jr. Dick didn't care what anybody said, that was the man's father. Bayard Jr. had shown just what kind of a man he really was all along. He would not compromise right and wrong. And if the deal went through, he knew he would be at a complete disadvantage to everybody in stock ownership. But he also knew he had Dick's respect, and Dick would see that he would get what he rightfully had earned. The same feeling that had once existed with their fathers against their father back in 1914 was the way they felt now.

"What's he doing now?" Bob asked, everybody knowing the he to whom he was referring.

"Making his final move," Dick said. "But he also knows all that money sets here. What he doesn't know is that leaving will lengthen his life. He has the bank up there to have something to do."

At this point, Dick knew it would be futile whatever he was saying to Pete and Vernon. What he still wanted was to run the place. And that was the last thing Pete and Vernon wanted, so it was not going to work.

Finally, all three came in, nobody saying a word. None of the group in Bob's office really knew what Bayard Sr. would do to the last minute. He didn't say a thing but reached in his coat pocket and pulled out various shares, both the green-printed preferred and the brown-printed common ones. Obviously, this was not a spur-of-the-moment decision as he had Pat's signatures and her stock. He laid them on the table and pushed them to the middle. It reminded Dick of a poker game. Bayard Sr. had called the bet.

Dick opened a folder and withdrew the two checks, giving them to Vernon rather than Bayard Sr. The room was totally silent. Nobody said a word, most untypical of the members of the Heath family and the board members when they gathered in the room. Vernon handed the two cashier checks to his older brother.

Bayard Sr. glanced at both checks. He apparently hadn't realized that the money had been borrowed until he saw the Indiana National Bank's name on the checks. His face tightened and a look of surprise crossed his face.

"I see you've been out of town, Dick," he finally said. "For that kind of money, you couldn't get it here."

"How do you know? The Crawford County Bank has a correspondent bank," Dick said and almost started laughing. Instead he thought, here it is 1962. He's picking up a million dollars, and he's worried about why you didn't go to the Crawford County Bank. Wonder what it would have been like to have gone to the bank where he is the chairman of the board and chief executive officer. It would have taken two months to get the money, a first mortgage on not only the company, but everybody's homes plus personal signatures.

"I didn't want to bother your loan committee," Dick said, "with something that might not happen."

"Will you leave the payroll account there?"

"Absolutely. We all have friends there. In fact, I think we should keep a higher balance."

That seemed to please him. At that moment, Dick really felt sorry for him. All the feelings of bitterness were gone. It happened just like that. The private war between the two men was over, and they could be friends again. There was no winner. Looking at Bayard Sr. across the table that morning, Dick had more respect for him than he had for any of his brothers and sisters. Maybe for the first time, Dick could see how his anger and frustration had built up. The very least Dick saw across the table was a real man. He was as tough as they came, but he was what he was.

Since Skiv's death eleven years earlier, Dick had fought his uncle tooth and toenail. Sure, Dick thought, Bayard Sr. was absolutely wrong on the ice cream bar, but that's business. At least he never held back and believed what he believed until the very end. You can say one thing for him: He fought like hell for what he believed, right or wrong. And now that it's over, the game finally played, the score in, he's acting like a real champion. There's no bitterness in him. He's tired and he's leaving. He saw the only brother or sister he really cared about die here just as his father died here.

When Bayard Sr. got up to leave, Pete and Vernon had already left the room. Bob and Jack left immediately, everyone wanting to leave him with Bayard Jr. Dick started to leave.

"Wait a minute, Dick," Bayard Sr. said.

Dick sat down again. Bayard Jr. was across the table to his father's left.

"Well, you boys have got it, and I don't know what you're going to do with it. Look out for the rest of them. You don't know them like I do. They are more treacherous than you know, especially Bob."

Feeling a bit uncomfortable, the younger Heaths didn't respond to his comments. Dick shook hands with his uncle and told him not to worry about his bank.

"I'll do more business with them than you did," Dick said laughingly. Then he walked out, knowing another era had ended.

16

When Bayard Sr.'s stock was retired as treasury stock, the number of company shares issued and outstanding fell from 12,800 to 10,575 shares. Pete's family had its original 2,500 shares (.234 percent); Vernon's family still had 2,500 shares (.234 percent); Dick's family had 2,500 shares (.234 percent); and the daughters had the 2,800 shares they had been given when the company incorporated in 1946 and by their father a few years later. Mary Morris' family had 1,475 shares (.138 percent), and Ruby Dowling's family had 1,325 shares (.125 percent). Bayard Jr. had the 375 shares (.035 percent) his father and grandfather had given him years earlier. Together, Mary and Ruby had a greater percentage (.263 percent) than any one of the three major interests.

A few days after the buyout, Bayard Jr. got a letter from his sister, Pat, chastising him for betraying their father and letting him sell out. The letter hurt Bayard Jr. deeply. He brought the letter to Dick and let him read it.

Although Pat really didn't know the issue of the ice cream bar and her father's stance on it, she said any son who would turn on his father for any reason would have to be a horrible person with no respect for his father. She berated her brother in every way she could and said Bayard Jr. had humiliated their father and could kill him over it. At the end of the letter, she said she would never forgive her brother for what he'd done.

"She cuts to the bone, doesn't she, Hogan?" Dick said, glancing up from the letter at his cousin's flushed face. "Of course, she's only heard one side of the story. I'd like her to hear the other side some day when I get a chance to tell her."

"It wouldn't do any good, Dick. He's her father, and what he says is all she'd listen to. You know this family as well as I do."

"Maybe. But I'd like to tell her anyway. Life goes on, though. We've got a board meeting to go to now."

It was the first board meeting after Bayard Sr. had left, and nobody knew quite what to expect. Vernon had come to Dick earlier and said with Bob on the board Pete had two seats, considered Bayard Jr. as Dick's other seat and wanted his son John as a director. After thinking about it a minute, Dick saw he had a point and agreed but added another twist.

"I'd go along with John," Dick said. "But you know we're going to have to elect new officers. I think you should be president and let Pete be chairman of the board."

Vernon beamed.

Knowing that he would like the president's title as well as the agreement about John becoming a director, Dick continued. "Bayard Jr. should be executive vice president," he said. "He certainly is qualified and deserves it."

Vernon agreed and backed Dick in the board meeting. The changes didn't make Bob too happy, but he went along with them because he couldn't do anything about them, and Dick's reasons were sound. Ruby didn't like the changes at all. Dick listened patiently to her, then went ahead with his agenda as he could care less what she didn't like. He didn't think she knew what she wanted. So the old players were getting moved around a little.

"It's time to get back to running the business," Dick said after it had been settled. He was thinking he should have said, Let's get back to doing what we had been doing before this Bayard Sr. episode came about.

Nobody disputed that assessment, and the new era started off smoothly. For some time, everyone active in the day-to-day operation knew the company was going to need some more office space. That was one of the reasons Bob's office was the desk in the board room. The Heath company owned twenty-five acres on the west edge of Robinson. This property on West Main Street and State Route 33, that ran west nearly fifty miles to connect with Interstate 70 in Effingham, had a rail siding to the rear running parallel to the highway. Across the track was a large tract of land that could be purchased if necessary.

The company had purchased the twenty-five acres in the late forties for one thousand dollars an acre. The thinking at the time had been that maybe someday the land would be needed as a site for a new candy plant, bottling plant and office building. Too, the family members making the decision knew they couldn't go wrong with that much land at the city limits of Robinson for twenty-five thousand dollars.

Plans for a new office building had actually been drawn. But before the building could become reality, something else came up. Even though the company had increased its dairy sales, the dairy was losing more money. This was true before the overhead factor was considered. A consensus had been reached to sell the dairy, but no buyers were in sight. So the dairy kept on running and kept draining company profits.

One day a man named Carl Hottenstein who owned American Dairy, a fairly good-sized dairy in Evansville,

Indiana, came to the office looking for Vernon. When the receptionist couldn't find him, she called Dick to see if he would meet with him.

Hottenstein walked into Dick's office, the same office L.S. had used, minus the red chair and black safe. The Evansville dairyman wanted to sell the Heath dairy cottage cheese because he felt he could provide it for less than it cost the company to make it. He didn't know what the Heath's cost were but felt he could do the job for less. He also didn't know he had that right. It wasn't long before Dick was happy that Hottenstein hadn't found Vernon.

As Hottenstein went through his sales pitch about the cottage cheese prices, Dick only pretended to pay attention. He was thinking and figuring out how to turn the sale around.

"What do you think about my price, Dick?"

"It's so good you can sell us all of our products, Carl."

"All your products?"

"Yes, all our products. You wanted to sell cottage cheese to us, so sell everything."

"That's like buying your business, isn't it?"

"You have the right idea."

Hottenstein shook slightly, visibly shocked by the implication. "What are you saying to me?" he asked.

"You can buy the whole thing pretty cheap."

"I don't have the kind of money to do that."

"I know that. But hear me out." Dick knew the man didn't have the required capital to buy the Heath dairy outright, but he also knew that the Heaths wanted out of the dairy business.

"Let me hear your proposal then," Hottenstein said.

"We keep the building," Dick said, measuring his words as he articulated the offer that had been formed while

Hottenstein had quoted the price of the cottage cheese. "We'll sell the production equipment. You buy the inventory, the trucks at our book value and the ice cream and dairy cabinets the same way. You get the five million dollars worth of business free. You pay us fifty thousand dollars and give us a note for the balance for 5 percent to be paid over three years. I don't know what the exact figure will be, but I'd say it will be around $200,000 after everything is figured. You couldn't pick up sales like that, Carl, and you know it."

"You're not serious?"

"Yes, I am."

"Can you make the deal?"

"Yes, and the board will approve it."

"How soon do you want to do this?"

"Do you have the fifty thousand dollars?"

"Well, yes."

"A week from today from our side."

"Can we do this in Evansville?"

"Certainly. I'll get my cousin Bayard to draw up the agreement and note. We'll be down with the titles, and you have your lawyer and fifty thousand dollars."

"My God, Alice will kill me. That's my wife."

"I'll call you to check out the time in a couple of days."

"You don't know my phone number."

"I'll find it."

"You are serious, aren't you? How can you sell a dairy just like that after forty-five years?"

"Just by shaking your hand like this," Dick said and stuck out his hand to Hottenstein. He took it instinctively.

Leaving the office a few minutes later, Hottenstein shook his head. "I heard you Heath boys are movers."

"Might be, Carl. But in this case we are sellers."

Both men laughed. It was that simple.

Dick's next move was to persuade the board that he had made a good deal for the company. That was fairly simple, too. The dairy was about to shut down anyway. With the sale, the company got its inventory dollars out, and everything, including the ice cream and dairy cases, sold at book value. The trucks with the refrigeration bodies cost a lot of money. The large Pure Pak machines were leased.

"We have saved a half a million dollars on an office building, too," Dick said as he explained the deal to the board. "When you look at the financial statement, we won't lose any net worth. We just shut down a big loss."

The more everybody thought about it, the better they liked the idea. L.S. was undoubtedly in the back of everybody's mind. His love for the dairy had kept it around for years.

Finally Bayard Jr. said, "I think you did a hell of a job the more you look at it."

Everybody else except Vernon nodded. He had been fidgeting in his seat and jotting something on the pad in front of him.

"What about you, Vernon?" Dick asked. "What do you think?"

"What am I going to be president of with the dairy gone?"

"L.S. Heath & Sons, Inc. Just the same thing you've been doing."

That satisfied him. A week later Bayard and Dick drove to Evansville with the paper work. Carl Hottenstein had the fifty thousand dollars, and the deal was closed. The Heath company was out of the dairy business for good. Everybody breathed a sigh of relief.

What Dick had told everybody about the sale not affecting net worth proved correct. It just took some journal entries to make the adjustments to turn inventory ice cream cabinets and trucks from those assets to cash on a note receivable. The rearrangement of assets on the balance sheet would be completed for cash or notes receivable. So the sale had no effect on the net worth as Bayard Sr.'s stock sale had done. His sale had lowered the net worth, but now fewer outstanding shares had to be divided into the value of the company.

Before Bayard Sr. and his daughter sold their stock, the book value was about three hundred dollars a share on the 12,800 outstanding. When the company paid them one million dollars for their 2,225 shares that amounted to a little more than $468 per share. The company lowered its net worth by one million dollars, and the stock (12,800 minus 2,225 shares or 10,575) made the book value of the stock drop to $266 per share.

The dairy was a business that was subject to all kinds of price fluctuations and was extremely capital intensive. The ice cream-bar franchise, on the other hand, was the least capital intensive business Dick had ever known. He did buy the secretary a new typewriter once in a while. But with the dairy gone, so were some of the company's best people. All the sales people and sales supervisors, except Don White, went with American Dairy. He became Ross Fife's assistant in the ice cream-bar division. What few production people that had been required were absorbed throughout the company.

After all the equipment was moved out, the officers decided to remodel the interior of the dairy to add more office space and moved the candy offices over to combine them with the new administrative area. Only Bayard Jr. maintained his office at the old plant so he could meet more easily with production workers.

The upstairs area above the dairy cooler was made into an expansive board room with paneled walls and thick, plush carpeting on the floor. L.S.'s and Skiv's pictures were hung on the wall with small lights hanging over them. A long conference table and heavy, comfortable chairs sat in the middle of the room. Board members could scream at each other without everybody else in the company knowing what was going on. Bob moved out of the old board room, which would now be used as a conference room. The retail room, complete with soda fountain, bar stool and several tables and chairs, was kept intact for use by employees and sales purposes.

Not long after the new offices were completed and during the first board of directors meeting in the new board room, another crisis erupted. Vernon had given Pete a copy of Ross Fife's expense account for his trip to the West Coast, mainly to San Francisco. Fife had flown out there specifically to see the Foremost Dairies, Inc., at its regional West Coast office. Foremost was the largest dairy in California.

Like Dick, Fife dealt with only the highest executives. He knew how to entertain and do it right. He had stayed at the Fairmont Hotel and had taken the company president and the executive vice president and their wives out to dinner at the hotel. The bill for the night was $586. This had set Vernon off, and he had taken it to Pete to complain. Instead of Pete going to Bob for an explanation, he had popped it out at the next board meeting.

"Five hundred eighty-six dollars for dinner?" Ruby said, screeching and jumping on the bandwagon.

Bob's face flushed as he turned to his dad. "Why in the hell didn't you bring this to me instead of bringing it up now?" he said, blowing up at his father.

Vernon and especially Pete and Ruby had no idea what it cost to go first class at a restaurant in the Fairmont Hotel. The bill seemed totally excessive to them. It was a huge account, so Fife spared no expense and didn't hold back on the wine. The older Heaths simply didn't understand doing business that way.

"Hold on, stop, be quiet and let me talk," Dick said, hitting the table with his fist. "I know about this. Pete, first off, do you know what Ross sold in units that night?"

"No, and I don't care."

"One hundred and sixty units. Which caused Carnation in Los Angeles to go before their competitors. Carnation's initial order was one hundred units. That sale to Foremost broke the West Coast market for us. Now look at the expense account in detail. What do you see for wine?"

"Four hundred dollars," Pete said.

"Was a $585 dinner worth an initial order for eighty thousand dollars, carrying a gross profit of twenty-six thousand dollars? Some of you still don't understand the nature of this business."

"Dad, I can't believe you not asking me about it," Bob said, still red in the face.

"Let me say something, too," Bayard Jr. said. "For three years, we've been through all this, especially with Dad. Bob and Dick are right. And if you don't like it, sell out to them; if you don't want to sell out, I suggest you shut up."

All three of the younger men jumped on their two uncles and father. Time had passed them up in some respects. The Fife incident made that clear to everyone and effectively

silenced their voices and management. Ruby and Dick, however, weren't quite through with each other. No sooner had
everything quieted down than she started on her tirade about
all the cherry Cokes she had been charged for at the Heath
Brothers Store more than thirty years earlier. This time Dick
was ready for her.

After she brought it up and complained how many times
she had had to pay for them, even though she was a part of the
family and worked for the business, too, Dick said, "You're
absolutely right, Ruby. You shouldn't have had to pay for
them. How many do you figure you paid for?"

"A hell of a lot."

"A hundred? Three hundred? Maybe a thousand?"

"Probably a thousand."

With that Dick pulled out a company check, made it out to
her for fifty dollars expenses reimbursed and handed it to her.
"Now you're even," he said.

Ruby took the check and never said a word. The saga of the
cherry Cokes ended once and for all, too.

The main problem with the board of directors running the
Heath company was that of the eight board members, four
were highly educated in business, accounting, management
and law. Ruby, Pete, Vernon and John had no formal education in any of those areas. None of the four could actually
understand or read the financial statements which were designed for management. They didn't understand that things
that were done got accomplished by making deals.

Certainly, Dick knew, this was the way it had been in the
eleven years he had been on the board. And as business grew
and more people were needed, the company was going to
change even more. Vernon was only concerned with the items

on his little white pad. Pete's drinking had become worse, but it was overlooked. Besides, he didn't have any responsibilities at all.

Even with the family still controlling the board of directors, the day-to-day operation and administration of the company was in capable hands of both family and non-family members. Bob Ward was the office manager; Verdi Mitchell had been the cashier and a Heath employee since the twenties; and Ross Fife led the growing ice cream-bar franchise.

By 1962, a competent and talented organization was in place and growing. Dick was somewhat restless with time to spare and looked around for new challenges. His mother lived in Palm Beach most of the year, returning to Robinson only for long visits. Dick's sister, Joan, had married Paul Copello, a Chicago insurance broker, had four children in forty-four months and lived in Lake Forest, Illinois.

More and more Dick returned to golf, his favorite pastime, for his challenges and let the Heath company move smoothly along. When Jack Brown, a local jeweler, was elected president of the Crawford County Country Club, Dick was elected vice president and spent more and more time at the club and the golf course.

17

The younger Heaths all spent a lot of time on the nine-hole, non-irrigated golf course. Dick and Betty played with Bayard Jr. and Pat each weekend. Bayard and Bob started playing Dr. Keith Correll, an optometrist, and Dick. Bob and Dick were scratch-handicap golfers. Bayard and Keith were about twenty-three handicappers. With a little coaching and the competition, the other men got down to five handicaps, even with Bob's temper flaring up frequently. He was notorious for throwing his clubs when he wasn't shooting well. Bad play on the golf course brought out the worst in him.

Jack Morris Sr. and Ross Fife were four to five handicappers and could play the game almost as well as Bob and Dick. Morris had played on his college team at the University of Minnesota. His son, Jack Jr., a pretty good golfer, too, had played on the Robinson High School team Dick had started again upon his return to town.

After high school, Jack Jr. enrolled at the University of Kentucky but flunked out. He tried a second time but flunked out again. Morris Sr. approached Dick about giving his son a job with the company. Dick talked to Vernon and Bayard Jr., pointing out that it would be difficult to say no with Bernard Dowling, John and Allan all there. It was decided that something could be found for him. Dick liked Jack Jr. and did what he could for him, even loaning him money for dates.

During a conversation with Bob one day, Dick brought up the condition of the golf course. The Crawford County Country Club was started in 1924 with Bayard Sr. and Skiv as charter members. The club was in poor condition overall. Besides the non-watered greens and fairways where the grass withered and died under the hot summer sun, the clubhouse was a concrete building with a linoleum floor and florescent lights. Everything was in need of repair, updating or replacement. Even though the club was the only recreational facility in the area and Robinson had a lot of industry for a small town, the club membership had shrunk to 151 members.

"It's a disgrace, Bob," Dick said. "With the expansion of sales and the increase of employees, the club is becoming more important to the company."

"Do something about it, John Henry," Bob said.

Doing something about it was what Dick had had in mind all along. He went to see club president Jack Brown at his jewelry store and told him he would like to make something out of the club during their tenure in office. Without many specifics and little idea about what Dick had in mind, Brown told him to do anything he wanted. So Dick had a green light, a reason and a plan.

Living in Robinson, Illinois, the country club was the center of the Heath family and company's recreational and social life. It was that for Bayard Jr., Bob, Jack Morris, Ross Fife and all the other employees Dick knew the company needed to attract. Robinson was a relatively wealthy community, and seeing a number of country clubs around the country as he was selling the ice cream-bar accounts had made Dick realize that the same quality was possible at home.

In 1962, he was a little burned out after the many battles.

He was only thirty-one years old but felt much older. A letdown had followed the Bayard Sr. buyout, and Dick felt hollow and drained emotionally. He had hit the ice cream-bar sales trail like someone possessed. Now it was only a matter of methodically going out and picking up the rest of the accounts. And the company had the organization with Ross Fife to do that. The fight of do or die, which stimulated Dick, was no longer there on a regular basis.

As his plans for the country club began to take shape, his longtime friend Jack Chamblin returned to Robinson from New Orleans where he had worked for the California Company as a geologist. His father, Don, had used his retirement fund as a down payment to buy Bradford Supply Company, an oil field supply company with five outlets in southern Illinois, and was struggling to get it started. Dick and his mother had bought twenty-five thousand dollars worth of stock, and he had sold a few shares to some of the older Heaths. But the company was still having financial difficulties.

Bradford's main office set just across the Illinois Central Railroad tracks from the Heath company offices. Chamblin walked over to Dick's office a week before a real deadline. Unless Don could come up with $150,000 within a week, he would lose the five stores back to the company in Bradford, Pennsylvania. The area bank politics had prevented Don from getting a loan. Dick understood that and forgot the country club for a moment.

"We'll get the money, Jack," Dick said, knowing Bradford's financial statement justified the loan. "Let me make a call."

The phone call was to Jim Lentz at the Indiana National Bank in Indianapolis where Dick had borrowed the money to buy out Bayard Sr. The bank had become the Heath company's prime bank and carried a million-dollar checking account there. He made an appointment for Monday morning and told Jack he had an idea to get the money with a poker game.

Monday morning at nine a.m., Dick and Chamblin were in Jim Lentz's office. Hugh Funk, another senior vice president of the bank, was there, too. The Heath company had paid pretty well on its loan and had the million dollars in the bank to easily pay off the loan. Dick introduced Chamblin and explained his problem.

"If Bradford Supply Company doesn't have the money by Friday," Dick said, "the company is history. And I can't let that happen to a friend of mine. So if your bank doesn't loan the money, I'll loan it to them from the Heath company.

"And if I loaned it to them, I won't be treasurer any longer. I won't be fired because of my last name and the amount of stock my family owns. Once I'm not treasurer, however, the loan and the account goes to the Second National in Robinson with Vernon sitting on the board of the bank."

Lentz and Funk asked a few questions, looked at the Bradford financial statement and decided the bank could make the loan, adding some working capital to the required $150,000. Dick smiled. The power of money had always fascinated him. Later, Lentz asked him if they had refused to make the loan, if he would have had the guts to write out the check for Bradford.

"Yes," Dick answered. "When it's nut-cracking time, you do what you have to do."

"Would they have fired you?"

"No."

"Would they have taken the treasurer's job away?"

"Maybe, but the vote would have been close. A lot of them wanted me in the job, but you never know."

"Hugh asked me, when you left, if I thought you were bluffing."

"What did you tell him?"

"I knew you were dead serious."

Dick told Bayard Jr. the story the first time they were alone. "Who do you think would have voted not to fire me as treasurer?"

"Jack and me. I don't know about Bob."

Dick thought over the answer. He found it strange. With Bob voting with the younger Heaths and Jack Morris, the vote would have been deadlocked at four to four; with him voting with the elder Heaths and John, Dick would have been fired. He hadn't considered that Bob would vote against him.

Back at the Heath company, Dick had the accounting system in place that had been desperately needed. He was going to hire a comptroller who would automate the whole system with a computer. He was left with the administration, which was no real challenge to him. The dairy's yoke around the company's neck had been removed. Few other problems existed. But Dick knew with his family in charge of the company that there would always be crises over nothing.

As for his own situation, he felt he was a world-class sprinter all primed with no real races to run. He knew Bob and he were each in the wrong areas of the company. Bob, with a management degree, wanted the sales division where all the development lay and was possessive about his territory as Dick, with a marketing and sales degree, found out when he started making deals within the family to accomplish what was necessary for the company. L.S. had made those deals from the very beginning to the end of his life. Dick had merely picked up the reins and made the deals necessary to get the company where it needed to go. Not everybody agreed where that was. That sometimes caused problems.

For some reason, there was a deep hatred of Bob by some family members. Dick had seen it with Bayard Sr., Ruby, Vernon and Mary. Ruby and Dick would get into it outwardly, right on top of the table. When it was done, the two of them went their separate ways with no deep-seated resentments. All problems Dick had with any of them were outward. Bob, on the other hand, was not so open with everybody.

At any rate, Dick felt the country club and golf course would be an outlet from the family strife as well as the challenge he needed. He could easily do his job at the company the way the functional organization was set up. In his mind, there were fifteen things which needed to be done to get the club moving forward. What he liked about the job was that the club was in a shambles in 1962 and had no way to go but up. With Jack Brown giving him the green light and his experience in working with the Heath board, he knew he could work with the board of trustees.

The first step of his plan was to prepare a simple set of books and put in an accounting system. He took his secretary, Sharon Osborne, to the club with him. When the two of them walked into the club, Dick terminated the manager but retained the waitress and the kitchen staff.

"Reconcile the bank statement and add up the IOUs, Sharon," Dick said. "Ester Moore, you inventory the place. I'll count the cash."

George Hayes was keeping the books on a cash basis. He was a longtime club member and an old friend of Skiv Heath.

"Keep the membership and don't worry about the books, George," Dick said to him over the phone. Hayes agreed and told Dick the club had a loan of ten thousand dollars from the Second National Bank and a ten thousand-dollar certificate of deposit at the bank, too.

A few minutes later, Dick called Chuck Correll at the bank and told him to cash the CD and pay off the loan. That took two minutes. By then, Osborne had completed her task. Dick told her to add up the unpaid bills he had dug up.

Within two hours, Dick had valued the assets, conservatively, he thought, and had a columnar pad. Shortly, the club had its first balance sheet. Osborne had typed a general ledger, and Dick had made out the chart of accounts and the subsidiary ledger. At the end of the day, Dick had a handle on the finances, and the club had a set of books. He was really alive again. The fun of winning and losing was back.

It wasn't long before membership started increasing. Members had been advised to remove their liquor from the club since they owned it, the only way it had been possible to have alcohol in a dry county. Dick implemented a refreshment fund, sidestepping being in a dry county, and worked out a way for the club to sell liquor by the drink. Instead of charging fifteen cents for ice, glass and set-ups, the club could now charge what a drink should cost and deposit the proceeds in the refreshment fund for the membership. Next, he implemented a charge system and added a 15 percent service charge. If members didn't spend twenty-five dollars a month at the clubhouse, the service charge was levied against them, unless they happened to be out of town for the winter. Finally, he installed the existing slot machines which had been stored for quite some time in the maintenance building. He reasoned that they would do no good in storage and would help with revenues for as long as they stayed in operation.

With everything in place and moving forward, some remodeling was needed. Dick felt he could invest eight thousand dollars in the clubhouse, get the membership excited and possibly draw new members, both resident and non-resident. To raise money, he sold eighty-one hundred-dollar debenture bonds to the members and raised the necessary funds. Dick bought thirty of the bonds and later gave them back to the club as did nearly everyone else. The bar was remodeled, creating a new atmosphere, and a more formal cocktail lounge was opened in the large dining room. Dick was elected president in 1963 and continued to help elect trustees, people who shared his vision for the club. It was making money, and Dick had many plans on the horizon.

One of those plans looked insignificant at the time, and some people thought it was a gamble. Golf seemed to be dead after Labor Day, so Dick decided to host a thirty-six-hole weekend pro-am tournament late in September 1962 and put up two thousand dollars for prize money to be paid from entry fees, outside concessions, slot machines and inside sales. Because some members thought it was too much of a gamble, he collected one hundred dollars from twenty people to bankroll the purse. Pete Heath was the first to kick in a loan of a hundred dollars to guarantee it.

To help with the volunteers, Dick enlisted the help of Maxine Zwermann, his old high school speech teacher and wife of Robinson Mayor Carl Zwermann. She had come to the Heath plant some time before with Eula Schmidt to see if Dick would make a crate to send a huge scrapbook of articles and pictures on the city's "fix-up, clean-up" campaign to enter a national contest sponsored by the National Municipal League for cities with less than twenty-five thousand population. Dick agreed. Robinson won. The Zwermanns went to Washington, D.C., to receive the award. So Dick traded that favor for the favor of helping in the tournament. It was a good tradeoff as Maxine was good at staging events. The club realized a profit on the tournament, everybody had a good time and Dick announced that the prize money would be raised to twenty-five hundred dollars the following year.

At the Heath plant, the candy division was selling mostly five-cent bars and was in a profit squeeze. The market for the Heath English Toffee Bar that had made the company famous was quite narrow. Dick used to say, "If everyone was eating a Heath Bar who told me it was their favorite candy bar, we couldn't produce enough." So the company had begun to venture into fund-raising sales with its miniature candy, toffee chips. And Bayard Jr. was working on plans to build a new automated candy plant on company property on the west edge of Robinson.

"What do you guys think about hiring an advertising agency?" Bob asked Bayard Jr. and Dick during their morning meeting one day. "Some of these markets need to have some small media marketing."

"Who do you have in mind?" Bayard Jr. asked.

"No one in particular," Bob said.

"Why don't we get the word out and see what various agencies have to say?" Dick said.

"I'll make some calls," Bob said.

In a couple of months, three men from J. Walter Thompson Agency in New York showed up with a major presentation. All three wore pin-striped suits and were as formal and professional looking as anyone the Heath clan had ever met. As had been the tradition since Skiv Heath's days, most of the company officers wore sweaters to work. That was true of Pete, Bob, Dick and Jack Morris. Bayard always wore a sports coat and tie and like L.S., Vernon always wore a suit and tie.

For most of the family, the sweater was a symbol of informality. Business might take any of them anywhere throughout the working day. The business could be in the kitchens or the break room of the candy plant; it could be in the old armory building where all the supplies were kept; it could be where the trucks loaded and unloaded or the garage. Everyone operated that way, mingling with the employees.

And everyone's doors were always open unless they were in conference or in a private conversation on the phone. Any employee could walk in and talk to any of them. Dick particularly felt that informal dress made the whole atmosphere conducive to making employees feel at ease. Robinson wasn't a major city where dressing more formally was necessary. He thought this atmosphere was one reason why the company had so few labor problems. Also, any one of the younger officers might be hitting the tees early at times.

It was apparent by their looks how much disdain the men from J. Walter Thompson had for the informal dress of the Heath officers. Dick was amazed at how they attacked the company as a client. Even in his advertising class at the University of Illinois, he had studied how to sell a client, depending on who the client was.

"I think you should allow us to create a national image to tell the people who you are," one of the Thompson men said.

"That would involve a lot of money we aren't ready to spend," Bayard Jr. said.

"What we need to do is take a market," Dick said, "and do some media so we can measure the results for dollars spent."

The Thompson men looked at each other. One of them said, "That's a good observation. But that comes later."

Still, Dick knew the men from New York made an excellent presentation, but they hadn't done their homework on the Heath company or the Heath family. The Thompson men were talking in abstract terms. The Heath men were interested in specific terms. The officers were polite, courteous and attentive. From the beginning, however, they all knew that in no way did they want the J. Walter Thompson Agency to represent the Heath company.

Several more agencies came in to make their pitches. Finally, the officers decided to try the Bittle Company from Bloomington, Illinois. It was a relatively small agency that had the Beich Candy Company. The Heaths felt the Bittles would understand a candy company better that was also a family-owned business. Everett Bittle, the company founder, had turned most of the handling of the business over to his son, Dale. The younger Heaths immediately tagged him "Big Daddy" because of his thick, heavy-set stature, tremendous girth and need to let everyone know he was running the Bittle Company.

The Bittles were golfers and talked about their exploits on the golf course during the first meeting. No one said much as Dale talked about the company staff's golf abilities. The Heaths were interested in how they scored in the advertising game rather than the golf game.

As it turned out, the company had scored rather well. It had put together the "Goren on Bridge" show on television at the time. The Heath company agreed to give the Bittles a try. And they made several market breaks immediately with the theme, "Love at first bite," for the ice cream bar.

Before that materialized, however, the Bittles wanted the Heaths to all bring their wives and spend two days in Bloomington. Everett and Dale planned to entertain everyone at the Bloomington Country Club the first evening after a tour and a meeting at their office. The next morning everyone would play golf before driving back to Robinson.

"We'll really show you a time," Dale said to Dick in a phone conversation. "Be sure to bring some extra money for the golf game."

"We'll try to accommodate you," Dick said.

The next morning he was drinking coffee with Bayard Jr. and Bob and said, "Bob, have you told Dale or any of them about our golf game or our handicaps?"

"No, not much. They all know we play. That's about it. He's always talking about how good they are."

"Why, Dick?" Bayard Jr. asked. "What's going on?"

"Well, these guys think they can beat us. Can you believe that one?"

"Surely not," Bob said. "They don't know us. Hell, this Carter told me they are four to ten players."

Dick laughed. "I've got an idea they think they're going to have some fun," he said. "What a shock they are going to get if they jump up, Bob. We're zero handicappers. Jack is a solid three. Ross is a four. And, Hogan, you're a six. This is one tough team, believe me."

In Bloomington, the Bittles hosted the Heaths to an elaborate affair at the country club. Pete, Vernon, Jack Morris, Bayard Jr., Bob, Ross Fife and Dick and their wives all attended the affair that was kicked off by a cocktail party and concluded with a formal sit-down dinner. Everett and his wife, Thelma, a striking blonde, Big Daddy and the Bittle people were all there, planning to make the two-day event memorable. The booze flowed freely, and everybody seemed to feel pretty loose after a while. Dale was making speeches in front of his friends. With everybody's attention, he said, "Tomorrow, we're going to beat the Heath boys on the golf course. But tonight we want you all to have a great time."

While the Bittle contingent hooted and clapped, Dick sidled up to Bob and said, "This Big Daddy is something. This irritates the hell out of me."

"Yeah," Bob said, "he's really laying it on in front of everybody. What's the Cincinnati break going to cost?"

"We budgeted ten grand with newspapers and radio advertising."

"Shall we go double or nothing?"

"Sounds good to me. Tell Pete and Vernon what we're going to do. If it's okay, let me know."

"All right," Bob said. "But slow down Weak Eye and Hogan on the drinking the rest of the night. Bayard looks like he's getting ready to bench press Thelma Bittle."

Bob was talking about how Bayard Jr. felt about working out with weights. He was so proud of how he was doing that he was always wanting to grab someone and lift them.

Fifteen minutes later, Bob was back with Dick and said, "Dad didn't give a damn because he knows how we play. Vernon was nervous, but I told him he could take the ten grand out of our checks if we lost."

"Hell, if we let these clowns beat us, he ought to," Dick said. "Okay, I'll bring this to a conclusion."

Dick threaded his way through the crowd, finding Dale

still talking about the golf game. By now, he was at his best. It seemed to be a thing with him.

"Dale," Dick said, "you know this is your home course. We've never played it. However, since you think your guys are so good—which you probably are—I've got a proposition to make to you that you'll lose."

"What's on your mind, Dick?" Dale asked, laughing loudly and slapping Dick on the back as he looked around at his friends, winking grandly. "You boys did bring your money, didn't you?"

"Yes, we did. And we'll take our five guys and play any of your five guys. If you win, we'll play you twenty thousand dollars for the Cincinnati market break, which is ten thousand dollars; if you lose, you pay for it. You have the best deal since you have 15 percent commission. So if you lose, it only costs you eighty-five hundred dollars. That's what the Heath boys think and will do. You've made all the speeches, so let's get it on."

Dale was stunned, as were the people around him. There was silence. He knew Dale had to call it, though. He was the one who had dug the hole, not the Heaths. After a moment, he said, "Okay, we accept your challenge to play double or nothing on the Cincinnati advertising break. The lowest team total wins."

Later that night, Dick had a change of heart and told Pete and Vernon, "Don't worry. I'm going to call it off tomorrow on the first tee. The game's not fair. We'd murder them. But this will shut him up for the rest of the night."

Dick told the rest of the family he was going to call it off, too.

"The hell with it," Bayard Jr. said. "They made the speeches. Let them pay."

"You know we wouldn't really do that to anybody, Hogan."

"Yeah, I know, but they deserve it."

In the past, Bob and Dick had played many games for money. They once took on some Terre Haute gamblers who thought they could play. Every New Year's Day, Bob and Dick played anybody who wanted to show up. It was the Heaths' best ball versus the best ball of the ten or fifteen guys who showed up. It was for a quarter a hole, to each player on the winning side from each player on the losing side, best ball under any conditions, unless there was more than a two-inch snow on the ground. Dick thought it looked like the old days with the Heaths against whomever wanted to play.

Everyone was at the tee the next morning. Just before Dick could call the game, Everett Bittle walked over to Dick and said, "I want to call the bet off."

"That's fine, Everett," Dick said. "You beat me to it. I was going to do it before we teed off."

"It got out of hand last night," Everett said.

"Yeah, it certainly did. It was the booze and the crowd that made Dale rib us. The game wouldn't really be fair with our handicaps. Somebody didn't do their homework on how well we can play."

"I'm sure. I'm sorry it happened."

"That's okay. We'll just go and play a nice, friendly game of golf."

It was a quiet and subdued game, played for a few dollars. The Heath group beat the Bittle group badly.

"How bad did we beat them?" Bayard Jr. asked Dick after they were through playing.

"Eighteen strokes. I thought we beat them twenty-five, but it was pretty one-sided anyway."

"I didn't like the whole thing," Bob said. "In fact, I'm not sure we have the right agency with these guys."

Dick agreed. He knew the company would keep the agency for the time being; he also knew that Bob would eventually change agencies.

18

The Heath company continued to build the organization. Ross Fife had been the first non-family member executive hired from the outside in company history. Up until then, it had been hard enough to have enough jobs to take care of the family coming into the business.

Dick was looking for a comptroller and had his eyes on one in Robinson. His name was Jim Reedy. The problem was that he was cashier of the Crawford County State Bank, which was Bayard Sr.'s bank. He had become chairman of the board after leaving the Heath company. And Dick knew hiring Reedy would cause an explosion.

After giving it some thought, Dick went to Reedy one day and asked him if he would help find a comptroller for the company. Dick told him the qualifications and the kind of man he was looking for to fill the job.

"How much does the job pay, Dick?" Reedy asked.

"Oh, I thought I'd start him at fifteen thousand dollars."

Reedy's eyes widened. He was surprised. Dick knew he was making eleven thousand dollars. At the time, banks didn't pay their employees well.

"How about me taking the job?" Reedy asked.

"Jim, we would love to hire you. But you know it would have to come from you with Bayard Sr. sitting as chairman."

"I'll go tell them I heard about the job but not from you."

Bayard Sr. called Dick shortly afterwards and said, "What the hell are you trying to do in taking someone like Jim Reedy from the bank? He's one of our best employees. Don't you realize this is the bank you're talking about?"

"What's the difference between the bank and us, Bayard? You're in the business of making money like us. What do you think the bank is, some kind of church or something?"

"You can't go around and steal the bank's valued employees like Jim."

"Well, the comptroller's job pays fifteen thousand dollars, and I'm looking for one. I'm sorry that you're paying him probably thirteen grand, and he's decided to better himself. Besides, if you think so much of him and he's such a good friend of yours, you ought to be happy to see Alice and him get the opportunity. You know the bank could never compete with us as we continue to grow."

What could he say? Dick wondered. Jim Reedy became the Heath comptroller, and he wasn't going to be the last good man the company hired. Bob had been looking for a sales manager to run the candy division similar to Ross Fife running the ice cream-bar franchise.

Bob interviewed several prospects before deciding on Jesse Texiera. He had a solid background in the candy business and was an Easterner with a slight New England accent. Age-wise, he was just past forty, older than Bob but not quite Bayard Jr.'s age. With the board's approval, Texiera was offered the position of candy division sales manager. He accepted.

Tex, as everyone called him, was the kind of sales manager who believed in deals and promotions. By deals he meant if the retailer would buy five cases of candy, he would get one free. So Tex came to the company with a different type of background and philosophy in a man than the company had ever employed before. He had a dry sense of humor and called his wife Candy, not because he was in the candy business but because she was "so sweet." He became closer to Bayard Jr. than any of the rest of the family.

Shortly before Tex was hired, Pete had decided to build a new home across the street from his present home on Locust Street, the same street on which Vernon lived. Tex bought Pete's old house as soon as Pete's new one was finished. At the end of the concrete driveway in Pete's old house was Bob's old basketball goal. Bob and Dick had shot many a basket there in their youth. The lights had allowed them to shoot at night. As Dick watched the new sales manager move in his uncle's old home, those days seemed like a long time ago when he and his cousin were really like brothers growing up.

By this time, Bob had been married for six years. He and Jean had three boys: Craig, Brad and Ted. When Craig was born, Bob and Dick were still close enough that Dick was with him in Vincennes at the hospital at the time. But since Bob had gotten married, Dick could see slight changes in him. Dick remembered how Bob used to be "a real cut-up and had fun." What Dick meant by a cut-up was having a fun personality. Bob always laughed and played jokes. Slowly but surely, Dick saw his cousin's entire personality changing. It wasn't just Dick noticing the change, either. Bayard Jr. saw it. So did their friends Keith Correll, Bob Jones, Dode Douglas, Jack Chamblin and others who mentioned it to Dick.

No doubt Bob and Dick were working hard, growing older and going through many incidents and battles which brought on change, but Dick thought it was something else. Bob became serious and lacked his old sense of humor. However he looked at it, Dick could see nothing causing the change like his marriage. That seemed apparent one Sunday morning when Dick dropped by Bob and Jean's house unannounced to talk business. Jean answered the door.

"Oh, Dick," she said rather coldly. "It's rather early. What do you want?"

"Well, uh, want?" Dick said, at a loss for words for a moment. "I need to see Bob, I guess."

Jean opened the door wider, motioned for him to come in and said, "Bob's just getting out of the shower. Please sit down, and I'll get you a cup of coffee."

"Don't bother," Dick said. He started toward the bathroom, but stopped abruptly and turned on his heels when he remembered Jean's reaction the last time he had come by when Bob was in the bathroom. "Well, I guess I could take a cup. Thanks."

"Please have a seat and wait here," Jean said stiffly. "I'll get you some coffee."

He sat down on the couch and put his feet up on the coffee table. While he was waiting, he wondered what possessed him to stop by Bob's house on a Sunday morning. Dick knew it would be better to talk about business some other time and decided to drink a cup of coffee and go.

"Dick Heath," Jean said harshly as she carried a cup of coffee into the living room, "get your feet off of my coffee table. Have you no manners? Whatever would make one think that one could go into another's home and prop one's feet up on the coffee table?"

After he recovered from the initial shock, Dick took his feet off the coffee table and stood up quickly. "I'm quite sorry,

Jean," he said. "I never even gave it a thought."

"That is much of your problem, I'd say," Jean said. "You never give a lot of things any thought. I'd appreciate it if you'd stay away from Bob and stay away from here."

Dick nodded sharply, spun and walked to the door. "You got it, lady," he said, not looking back.

After that, he didn't stop by the house or see Bob as much. While Dick and Betty spent many evenings at the country club dining with friends, Bob and Jean rarely ate there. But the golf games between the two cousins continued as always. Neither Dick nor Bob ever mentioned the incident at the house that morning.

The ice cream-bar franchise continued to grow. Ross Fife often told Dick that many of his old accounts asked about him. That wasn't surprising since he had personally sold some forty accounts. Don White told him the same thing.

"Perry Short sends his regards," White said one day, chuckling slightly.

"To me?" Dick said, laughing and remembering Short's Ice Cream Company that he loaded with chocolate. "Perry is a good man. I was so fired up. Guess I kind of oversold him. I told him he could send some of the supplies back."

"I know. He told me. He said neither of you realized at the time how much he bought."

"Well, he didn't."

"He said he had to rent space to store all those supplies."

"Really? That's funny. But those were fun days, Don. I really miss them."

"He told me he had finally sold that first order and gave me a four-unit order instead of the twenty-two units you sold him."

"I was kind of wondering where he was going to put twenty-two five hundred-pound drums of chocolate. I didn't really want to sell him that much, but, Don, he really insisted on it."

"I'm sure he did, Dick. Practically forced you to sell it to him, didn't he?"

Dick laughed. He was proud of Don White. He was working hard, as he always had, had grown up with the company and was now traveling all over the country. It gave Dick a good feeling to see someone who had come up through the ranks and was making good. He and Ross Fife worked well together, too.

"You've got to go and straighten out all my work, Don," Dick said, kiddingly. "Back then, I was selling them as fast as I could get to them. We had a battle with Bayard Sr. in those days telling everybody I couldn't sell the product. I had to prove I could."

"You must've done a good job," White said. "They all remember you. About anywhere I go, they all say to say hello."

Not everything went as well or gave Dick the same feelings of success as did the ice cream-bar franchise. After the company had sold the dairy, American Dairy had built a warehouse on the west edge of Robinson. The finished product was shipped to this distribution center, and the trucks would deliver the product. Dick regularly saw many of Heath's old employees. They were good men, and he had hated to see them go.

Then Jim Reedy became extremely ill. Local doctors had diagnosed the illness as Hodgkin's disease. The prognosis was not good. Dick made the arrangements to have him see a physician at Barnes Hospital in St. Louis, Missouri.

"Woody will fly you down," Dick said, referring to the Heath company pilot. "If anybody can cure you, Dr. Charles and Barnes Hospital can."

Dr. Charles, or the "thin man" as Dick called him, was known as one of the best diagnosticians in the country. Dick had become convinced because of the several Heath employees who had been sent to him and recovered after local doctors had given up on them. But Reedy's case was a tough one. It took the help of Bethesda Naval Hospital in Bethesda, Maryland, to find a way to arrest the illness, allowing Reedy to return to work in a few weeks.

"The only thing I think Dr. Charles can't cure is Keith Correll's golf slice," Dick said when Reedy came back to work. "I'm coming closest to that because it's costing me a lot of money when we play Bob and Bayard."

19

With the country club moving ahead and making many improvements and Dick Heath the main force behind it, he was elected president in 1963. Each year, three new trustees were elected to serve with six holdovers. Dick had encouraged Bayard Jr., John Gwin and Friday Chapman to run for trustee. They were elected and worked with him to make the club a special place.

The Robinson Open Golf Tournament was a success again. Twenty-two pros, mostly club professionals from the area, played in the field the previous year. The 1963 field had a better group of amateurs and a few pros out of Chicago and St. Louis competing for the twenty-five hundred-dollar purse. This was a good purse because it hadn't been long ago that PGA tournaments were paying fifteen thousand dollars in prize money.

Originally, the idea had been to keep golf going after Labor Day and give the members a little excitement and something to look forward to. But with the entry fees and concessions, the club was making some money. At the end of the tournament, it was announced that the prize money would be raised to three thousand dollars the following year. The St. Petersburg PGA Tournament had paid only twenty thousand dollars in 1963.

Dick was reelected president at the club again in 1964. By

this time, he also had Jack Chamblin and Mort Imlay on the board of trustees. This organization was vital to what Dick wanted to do in the expansion of the club. He wanted to take some idle land on the east side of the lake on the old nine holes and build some overnight lodges to help the club with additional revenues. People staying there as guests of club members or companies like Heath and Marathon Oil would have a rather luxurious place to relax and enjoy the country club atmosphere.

The land on the east side of the lake was a mess. It was all grown up in weeds, from the shallow bank on away from the lake, and needed to be cleaned up anyway. Dick had Frank Reese Jr. contact his cousin, Frank Doughty, a professor of architecture at the University of Arkansas in Fayetteville. Doughty designed twelve rustic lodges of redwood with cedar shaker-shingled roofs, each unit having a balcony overlooking the lake and off to the ninth hole.

To raise the funds to build what would be called Old Lake Village, the club board authorized a corporation called Old Lake Village, Inc., and twenty-five hundred shares of stock to be issued and sold at fifty dollars a share. After selling shares to twenty club members, an attorney registered the issue. Some 143 people bought stock, ranging from one share to one block of one hundred shares to raise fifty thousand dollars. The Crawford County State Bank loaned the balance needed of seventy-five thousand dollars to build the first twelve units.

The smallest sale of one share had been to Margie Butler, the receptionist at the Heath plant. She asked Dick one day if she could buy a share just to be a part of it. The largest sale of one hundred shares had been to Elizabeth Flynn, the widow of an oil man. Most sales were ten shares. Dick wanted a large number of investors to get more people involved. That plan proved to be highly successful and was a real key to the success of the club.

The corporation made money the first year, paid some dividends, reinvested in more units, bought back some stock and paid on the loan. During the first five years, the book value of the stock doubled, and Old Lake Village contributed heavily to the success of the club. People could now come to the club and stay at the village. While they stayed overnight, they spent money in the clubhouse, pro shop and paid cart and green fees. This was all plus business against a fixed expense. And the club was rapidly becoming a first-class facility.

In the fall of 1964, the Robinson Open was still a thirty-six-hole event. It went to three thousand dollars in prize money and increased the quality of both the amateur and professional field. Maxine Zwermann continued to help with the tournament, and more club members were either playing or getting involved. Neither Bob nor Dick played in the event. Dick was busy. But Bob wasn't. The two continued to play together frequently, and Dick wondered why his cousin didn't play in the tournament but never mentioned it. Others noticed it and mentioned it to Dick.

"When I play you in the club championship, John Henry," Dode Douglas said, using the nickname he'd given Dick, in the conversation the two were having about Bob not playing in the tournament, "I have so much fun competing with you. Your cracks keep me loose, and I play my best."

In the club championship the year before, Douglas had shot a seventy-one to Dick's seventy-two.

"When I play Bob, though," Douglas said, continuing, "nobody says anything. I want to beat him worse than anything, but I shoot horrible. I shot an eighty-four the last time I played him."

Several other people, including Bayard Jr. and Frank Reese Jr., had told Dick the same thing. During a match in the club championship, Bayard Jr. had given Dick his worst beating ever. Bayard had it two under par at the end of fourteen holes, and Dick was gone. Against Bob in the next round, Bayard shot a horrible eighty-five, thirteen over par.

"What gives, Dode?" Dick asked, knowing the answer before he heard it.

"When you play Bob, you're waiting for an explosion and for clubs to start flying. Don't you remember the day on old number four tee, playing with Earl Greenwell when he was the pro, you, me and Bob? He hit a bad three-iron shot with the wind behind him to knock it down the hill. He wound up to throw the iron but didn't let go and released it behind him. It whistled next to Earl's head and hit the cart below me.

"I said at the time that I'd never play with him again. That was the fifth time something like that happened. I have to play with him in a tournament, but that's it."

Dick knew what Douglas was talking about. He had seen it since they were kids. He thought some day the temper would go away, but it never had. Bob's sister and father knew about it. Joyce had said something to Bob once when he lost control on the golf course.

Bob and Dick were playing; Pete and Joyce were riding in a cart. Bob missed a five-iron shot to an elevated green. The ball spun back to a deep valley in front. He repeatedly beat the club into the ground. When Joyce said, "Come on, Bob, stop that," he threw the club.

Pete yelled for his son to stop, too. Dick just never let it bother him, but he always knew the temper was there, never far from the surface.

Another temper surfaced for Dick and the Heaths to get involved in that was totally unexpected, unlike many of the past crises. Dick got a call at seven p.m. one evening in 1965 from Jack Stevens, a retired Heath company bottling manager and second cousin to L.S. Heath. Stevens could hardly talk.

"Dick," he said haltingly and gasping for breath, "Bus has killed Peggy. He's in jail in Atlanta. You're the only one I can turn to."

Dick was stunned. He and Bus Stevens had grown up together, had played together as far back as he could remember, had played basketball and football together in high school, even though Stevens was one grade ahead. They were close friends in those years. Stevens was an all-state end in football and captain of Robinson's last undefeated football team. He had gone to the University of Illinois on a football scholarship and was the place kicker on the 1953 Rose Bowl team. After graduation, he had become a pilot and went with Delta Air Lines where he was now a captain.

"What happened?" Dick asked, still unable to believe what he had heard. Peggy Sackrider, Stevens' wife, was a Robinson woman Dick knew well. She was two years ahead of him in school and married Stevens when they were in college. They had two small girls. Dick hadn't seen any of them for several years.

"They had an argument, I guess," Jack Stevens said. "You know Bus' temper. He had a .22 caliber rifle and accidentally shot her in the neck. He said it was accidental, and I believe him."

Dick knew his friend had a temper, but he didn't believe

he had deliberately killed his wife, either.

"They've got him charged with first-degree murder, Dick," Jack Stevens said. "Will you help us? Margaret is about to go crazy."

His wife worked for the Heath company in the ice cream department. Dick thought highly of both of the Stevenses. They were family.

"I'll go to Atlanta in the morning and see what I can do," Dick said, plans racing through his head. "I'll be in touch. Tell Margaret to hang in there."

After hanging up the phone, Dick called the Heath company pilot. "Saddle up for a 6:30 takeoff to Atlanta in the morning, Woody," he said. "I'll fill you in on the details on the way." Then he called Jack Chamblin, also a good friend of Bus Stevens', and told him the story.

"I'll go with you," Chamblin said without hesitation.

The two old friends were in Atlanta talking to Stevens the next morning. He was a wreck, unkempt, unshaven and had bloodshot eyes. A look of hope flashed through his eyes as he saw his two old hometown friends.

"Hi, guys," Stevens said as Dick and Chamblin came up to the cell door. "I guess I really did it this time. What am I going to do?"

"Are you all right, Bus?" Chamblin asked.

"As good as I can be," he said. "Can you believe this?"

"No, I can't," Dick said. "I know what happened, but I know you wouldn't intentionally kill her."

"No, it was an accident. I did it. But, God, I wish I hadn't."

"Do you have any money?" Chamblin asked.

"Not much. And I don't know what the girls need."

"We're here to help you," Dick said. "We'll find a way."

With little money and a first-degree murder charge hanging over his head, Stevens was going to need help. And he was going to need the best lawyer money could buy.

Dick called one of the Heath company customers and got the name of Bob Edwards, who was said to be the best around. His great-grandfather had been a famous judge in the Reconstruction days after the Civil War. Dick and Chamblin met with him to see if he would represent their friend. He agreed but wanted thirty-five thousand dollars cash up front and a plane load of Stevens' friends in Atlanta for the trial. The second part of the request was easy; the first part presented a problem.

When they got back to Robinson, Dick called Mae Espey, Stevens' aunt in nearby Palestine, to see if she would help. She gave him fifteen thousand dollars, all she had. Dick kicked in ten thousand dollars of his own money. That left the fund still ten thousand dollars short, so Dick went to Pete and Vernon and explained the situation to them. Because Stevens was related to the Heaths and the family had worked for the company for a long time, they agreed that the company should help. But Vernon didn't want to hurt the company image and wanted Dick to borrow the ten thousand dollars from the Second National Bank, leaving a company check with Chuck Correll at the bank as collateral for the loan. They said that could pay for the loan at a later date. That made no sense to Dick, but he wanted to help Stevens and went along with the plan.

Many of Stevens' friends, including Dick, Chamblin, Merle Crosby, his old high school football coach, and Bill Tate, the Illinois fullback on the 1953 Illinois Rose Bowl team and then head coach at Wake Forest University, made the trip to Atlanta for the trial. Dick testified on behalf of Stevens. During the course of the testimony, defense attorney Edwards asked Dick about his relationship to the Heath candy company. He answered that his grandfather, father and uncles had started the company as a family business years ago. At a recess, the judge asked to meet with him in his chambers.

"Mr. Heath," the judge said, "I find your company and your grandfather intriguing. My dad started a similar business with almost the same background."

"That's interesting, your honor. I guess many companies started that way."

"I'd like to know more about the history of how the Heath company got started."

So Dick told him the story of the store on the Robinson square and how L.S. wanted a family business to keep the family provided for and together.

"Bus Stevens' mother and father have worked for us for many years," Dick said. "His dad, Jack, was our foreman of the Pepsi Cola plant. They were both solid citizens and hard-working people. Bus is related to us."

"Was this boy different?" the judge asked.

"Not really. He had a temper that got out of hand once in a while. But he wouldn't have deliberately killed his wife. I knew Peggy Stevens in high school, too, as I said on the stand. Bus loved her, but his damn temper would go out of control."

"I see," said the judge. "I'm glad we had this talk, Mr. Heath."

"None of us would be down here if we thought Bus killed her intentionally."

"I know. Thank you for your time."

"It was nice to have had a chance to meet and talk with you,

Judge," Dick said, offering his hand to the man.

Back in the courtroom, Stevens subsequently was convicted of manslaughter and sentenced to five years probation. Within two years, he died of a heart attack at the age of forty-two and was buried in Robinson next to his wife.

With everything going well at the country club, Dick began one of his major moves. Just barely touching the club's property, across a blacktop road, lay four hundred acres owned by Dr. Samuel S. Allen, the son of the doctor who sold Skiv Heath the acre for his house. The property had a sixteen-acre lake on it. For months, Dick had been trying to get Allen to give the club a hundred acres that adjoined the club to the west.

The Allens were multi-millionaires, but it was almost impossible to get him to donate the land. Allen was somewhat eccentric, a practicing physican, the largest shareholder of the Second National Bank and, by most accounts, a tough son-of-a-bitch to deal with. He was rough and opinionated to go with everything else. His huge home, complete with a bomb shelter that some said was second only to Strategic Air Command Headquarters, set on top of a small hill in the middle of the property a few yards off of the lake that was well stocked with bass, crappie and blue gill. In the basement in his shelter, he had a bar thirty feet long. The whole place was his domain.

"You want what?" Bob Jones said to Dick in his living room one night. Jones was the local Chevrolet, Oldsmobile and Cadillac dealer and a supporter of the club.

"I want a hundred acres and that lake for the club," Dick said, taking a measured drink of his vodka and tonic.

"I know him, Dick. You're crazy as hell to think you could even buy it from Sam Allen, let alone get it for nothing.

You've finally joined the rest of the crazy Heaths."

"Maybe. But I'm going to get it."

"You don't have a chance."

"You'll see in a week. I'll be ready to attack him then."

"Hell, Dick, he'll throw you out himself or get the sheriff to throw you in the jailhouse."

"We'll see," Dick said, thinking that Jones would bet his car dealership on this one. "I'm going to give it my best shot, anyway."

What Jones didn't know was that Dick had hired Jim Spear, a Chicago-based golf course architect to do a colored layout of a nine-hole course around the lake on 96.6 acres of Allen's land. But that wasn't the one Dick was going to show Allen and his wife, Bernice. Spear had completed a second layout with all the real estate plotted around the course. The four hundred dollars-an-acre land was worth a fortune with the golf course there.

Spear completed the layouts and delivered them to Dick within the week. After he had the second drawing all wrapped and sealed in brown paper, he called Allen.

"You want to see me?" Allen said, growling. "It's colder 'n hell outside. But come on over. We'll have a drink."

Ten minutes later, Dick was sitting with Allen and his wife, drinking a vodka martini. He put the large covered package against the chair and said nothing about it.

"Okay, Buster, what's up?" Allen asked bluntly. "What brings you out on a cold night like this?"

"I want to discuss something with you," Dick said, sipping his martini and lighting a Viceroy. He had no intention to rush things, planning to have two or three drinks before he got to the point.

"Bernice, get me another drink," Allen said gruffly. "Get Dick one, too."

Dick made small talk.

"Boy," Allen finally said after the second drinks were almost gone, "what in the hell did you come over to see me about? What's in your package?"

"Sam, I want one hundred acres of your land for a second nine."

"You're crazy."

"You're the second one who has called me crazy this week."

"Bernice, damn it, get me another drink and get Dick one, too."

Bernice got the drinks again. While she was making them, Dick slowly unwrapped the package, then began telling and showing them both his plan after she returned with the drinks.

"You give up one hundred acres and make twenty times what the whole thing is worth. And you can sit up here and look down on this beautiful golf course. Besides, the club will give you a lifetime membership like it did Jim Donnell."

J.C. Donnell, the president of Marathon Oil Company, had been given a lifetime membership for his contributions over the years. No one else had ever received one.

Dick had the Allens' attention.

"Who is going to build the course?" Allen asked, scooting up to the edge of his chair, his eyes narrowing.

"I am."

"Where're you getting the money?"

"Your bank."

"Who's going to help you?"

"Charlie Dees, Bill Wyke, Ray Luton and you as members of an executive committee with me."

Luton was a retired vice president of Marathon and was on the board of directors of the Second National Bank. He and Allen controlled the bank.

"Have you asked them?" Allen asked.

"No, but they'll do it. You know that. Bill and Ray are on your bank board, too. It'll change your damn image."

Allen didn't answer. He kept looking at the layout. One more drink and it'll be a deal, Dick thought. He had known Allen would be ready to make a deal after he saw the layouts.

"Okay," Allen finally said, "here's what I'll do: You raise thirty-five thousand dollars cash from the members. You say you can build the course for eighty-five thousand dollars with help on the construction from Charlie, Jack Chamblin and Mort Imlay. If you raise the thirty-five thousand dollars, I'll see that you get your loan of fifty thousand dollars. One more thing: If it is ever not a golf course, the deed comes back to me. Bob Whitmer will draw up the deal."

Dick shook hands with him and said, "Sam, I might make people think you aren't as bad a son-of-a-bitch as they think you are."

They both laughed. By this time, they were both half drunk. Before he left, Dick promised to put the Allens' picture in the tournament program, thanking them for the donation, in addition to the other arrangements.

"Wonder what old Bob Jones will have to say to that?" Dick said aloud as he shivered against the bitter cold and headed his car back towards Robinson.

All terms were met and construction started. Besides needing the new nine holes irrigated, the front nine needed to be irrigated and some major changes were needed in traps and trees. Charlie Dees, Skiv's old hunting buddy, was county commissioner of highways and supplied equipment and labor. Mort Imlay, a close friend of Dick's, was president of the gas utility company and provided a backhoe and a driver. Jack Chamblin contributed the required plastic pipe from his Bradford Supply Company.

With Dick raising the money and the help of these key people, both nine holes were irrigated, traps were redone and the second nine holes were completed within the estimated budget and money available and required for a modern, first-class golf course. The completion of the eighteen-hole course made the next step in Dick's plans for the country club possible.

20

Bob Heath had been developing his idea about getting the Heath company into the fund-raising business because Heath candy adapted so well to it. Bayard Jr. was working on the production of various sizes of packages. Jack Morris Sr. went to his package suppliers to get costs and samples. Dick worked on costs so they could set the selling price and get started.

Everyone knew that fund raising was a big business. With groups and organizations having a constant need to raise money, the market was virtually unlimited. Many groups vary what they buy each year; some, like the Girl Scouts who always sell cookies, stick with the same products. The Heath company wanted a piece of both markets. By generating enough volume, the fund-raising division could be a profitable one.

To make it profitable, the company needed a sales manager who understood business and had experience in soliciting and selling an item to an organization for fifty cents and providing the organization with help in having its members sell it to the ultimate buyer for a dollar for a 100 percent profit.

In this setup, the company has to wait on its money until the product is sold. It's also customary for the organization to return any unsold merchandise. The company has to produce the item and pay for the shipping, sales commission and all administrative costs.

The name recognition and quality of the Heath candy bar made it possible for the division to start out doing well. It wasn't long before the company hired a good sales manager who knew the fund-raising business. Ed Core had worked in the business for nearly twenty years and immediately put his expertise to work.

Soon afterwards, Bob and Dick went to Franklin, Indiana, to hire a quality control man for the ice cream-bar division. Don Stuart was the general manager of a local dairy. Both Bob and Dick liked him. He moved to Robinson with his wife, Inez, a month later.

These last two acquisitions demonstrated that the younger generation was continually going outside the company to fill jobs that were needed. Both new employees were college graduates and top performers. And the Heath cousins weren't through, either. Bob wanted a marketing manager who would be in charge of all the marketing programs of all divisions. Jim Hanlon, a Notre Dame graduate who had several years experience in national marketing, came aboard in that position.

Despite the hiring outside the family, nepotism was still the rule at L.S. Heath & Sons, Inc. Four of the family members continued to draw salaries but didn't do much of anything. Besides Ruby's husband, Bernard Dowling, there were Vernon's two sons, John and Allan, and Mary's son, Jack Jr. All three of the third generation and the founder's grandsons in this group, except Allan, had attended college and had no other skills. Still, Ruby, Pete and Vernon thought it was a shame with all the available family members that Bob and Dick had gone out and hired from the outside.

John remained in the print shop; Allan was taking the deposits to the bank and running errands; Jack Jr. spent most of his time going from office to office talking to various people. Dick asked Jesse Texiera if there was something he could find for Jack Jr. to do. Tex said he would try.

This was the result of L.S.'s theory of wanting everyone jammed into the place. Bayard Jr. and Bob had told Dick they feared getting stuck in the company when they got out of college. That was why Bob had gone to work for Owens Fiberglass and Bayard Jr. had gone to law school. But both were trapped or coerced into coming back to Robinson by circumstances and family loyalty.

Jack Morris Sr., although only a son-in-law, had much the same feeling. He was sitting in Dick's office one morning, talking about leaving his brother Chuck and moving to Robinson and going to work for the Heath company as an outsider.

"I loved Mary so much I would have done anything for her," he said. "But, Dick, can you imagine what it's been like to be an outsider in all this bunch? From the day I got here, I've tried to do my best for this company. I've been caught in the crossfire of every fight. You know Mary and I get into it at night. You've been over dozens of times and witnessed my frustrations."

"Hell, yes, I have, Jack. I must have been at your house fifty times, having a drink and talking about it. That's a lot of booze you've consumed, that we've consumed."

"Yeah, well, my sons don't like me. The only time I can sleep is to drink enough so that I do. And I know Jack has no idea what it's been like."

"Jack Jr. is young. How would you expect him to be any different? He's a good kid. Someday he'll grow up."

Jack Sr. looked away. He was always a loner. And although he did drink more martinis than was healthy, he was always at his desk by eight a.m. and was an asset to the Heath company.

"I wonder what my life would have been like if I'd stayed in Chicago with Chuck," Jack said softly.

"You, Vernon and a lot of the family wonder that about yourselves, Jack. I never wanted to be anyplace else."

Vernon walked into Dick's office and sat down one afternoon. That was something unusual. So Dick sat back and listened as his uncle made small talk for a while before getting to the purpose of the visit.

"John has this acquaintance from Charleston named Marshall Poole," Vernon finally said. "He contacted John the other day and asked if he could set up a meeting with a few of us. I don't know what it's about, but John asked me to ask you if you can get Bayard Jr., Bob and Jack together here at 1:30 in two days."

"Sure," Dick said. "Let me find out if they'll be here."

Before Vernon left, Dick walked next door and asked Jack. Dick knew he would be there. Then he talked to Bayard Jr. by phone to the enrobbing room. He said okay. Bob was in his office when Dick called him.

"What's it about?" Bob asked.

"I don't know, Bob. Vernon just wants to accommodate John. Vernon's in my office now."

Bob agreed. Dick put the phone down and said, "It's all arranged for Thursday in the conference room at 1:30. You can tell John that."

"Thanks, Dick, I'll tell him," he said and left.

On Thursday, Marshall Poole arrived promptly at 1:30 p.m., dressed in a well-tailored suit and made a polished presentation. Everybody was there as directors except Pete and Ruby. Pete was in his office next door with his door closed. Dick almost knocked and asked him if he wanted to sit in but thought better of it and didn't. It wasn't a director's meeting, only an informal get-together with Poole.

What Poole wanted was for the Heaths to buy stock as one of the initial incorporators for a new motel and restaurant in Olney, Illinois. Olney was a town slightly larger than Robinson about forty-five miles southwest near the intersection of U.S. Route 50 and Illinois State Route 130. Even though there was a Holiday Inn there, Poole said another property there was more than feasible.

Since the rest of the family present only cared about doing something for Vernon, and Poole knew it, he didn't take much time. Everyone was busy, and it was a short meeting.

"What it amounts to," Poole said, concluding his presentation, "is that we want to build a first-class restaurant and motel. It'll be good for the area and good for the investors. We'd like you to invest with five thousand dollars worth of stock."

The Heaths main Coca-Cola competition had a plant in Olney. Poole planned to build a nice restaurant first, then register a public issue with the state of Illinois as Dick had done with Old Lake Village at the country club and build the motel from the proceeds of the public issue.

John was for it because Poole was his friend. That made Vernon for it. The rest of the family could care less. It wasn't that big of a deal either way. No one wanted to make an issue out of it with Vernon over an investment of five thousand dollars and lending the Heath name to a worthwhile project. The company was doing too many things where his support was needed. It was worth five thousand dollars for that reason to say yes to Vernon and John. This was the first time they had asked the family to do something for them.

After they had agreed to buy the stock, Poole asked the group to name two directors to be on the board and represent the investment. Although he didn't say as much, everybody knew that getting the Heaths involved by investing and serving on the board would open some doors to see other people.

"Why doesn't Bob and Dick represent us?" Vernon asked, looking around the room at the rest of the family.

Everybody agreed, including Bob and Dick, without giving it a second thought. They agreed to it as they would to a tee time in golf. They were so eager to be doing Vernon a favor that they were actually happy about the situation.

Dick went to his office and wrote Poole a check. Bayard Jr., Bob and Dick stayed in the conference room a few minutes after everyone else left."

"Finally," Dick said, "we could do something that Vernon wanted. But I thought you looked like you were going to object, Bob."

"Not really. I want his vote on something else."

"What's that?"

"I want to do some magazine ads. Only this time on the Heath candy bar. Tex is working out the details."

Bayard Jr. and Dick didn't say anything. Neither of them knew if he would buy the idea without hearing it. And they didn't want to hear about it. Dick changed the subject but wondered what Bob had on his mind.

Advertising was something new to the Heath company. At that time in the mid-sixties, the profit margin was so slim with

90 percent of company sales in five-cent Heath bars and gross profits were small that there was no money for advertising beyond what was already being spent through the Bittle Company for other media buys. In fact, Dick thought the costs at the time hardly justified hiring Texiera and was going to show them some interesting figures the next day. The company had no money for promotional deals or sales managers.

And what Dick showed them the next day was that the candy division was on the verge of losing money for the first time in company history. In the past, that had been true only of the dairy.

"The candy doesn't look very good," Bayard Jr. said as he looked at the figures Dick had given them. "I can cut the bar from seven-eighths of an ounce to three-fourths. But that's all we should do."

"It's a damn good thing we have the ice cream-bar franchise," Bob said. "These are really spectacular figures for it. The bottling looks good, too. We have to build that new bottling plant pretty soon."

"At least the price structure is good," Bayard Jr. said. "It's ridiculous that the candy industry is still basically at a nickel."

"Looking at this gross-profit figure," Bob said, "I'd better sit on Texiera."

Through the years, the company had offset rising costs to make the Heath bar and the stationary nickel price of the bar with the increased volume. The bar also had been reduced in size from an ounce to seven-eighths of an ounce. No one had ever touched the quality. Now something had to be done. Added to the situation was the fact that the company needed a new candy plant. Everyone had talked about that for the past ten years. To stay competitive, the candy division had continued to automate the old plant. But almost twenty-five years had passed since the oil well had paid for the present plant in 1941.

Dick thought it was amazing what Bayard Jr. and his people had done to keep up production. Without them and their ideas of improvements, the company would have been hurt drastically. As it was, the company had a host of goods sold to put the finished product out for 65 percent of the sales dollar. The company could barely pay production, shipping, commission and administrative costs and make much profit. The ice cream-bar franchise had made up for the shrinking candy profits and more.

"What if somehow they would have stopped the ice cream bar in those early years?" Dick asked Bob.

"We would be richer than hell, and the rest of the family would be broke," Bob said, laughing.

"Hell, the dairy would still be draining the place if Vernon had really had his way."

The three of them talked a long time that morning. Bob and Dick told Bayard Jr. to go ahead with his plans to build his new automated plant. He told them he was experimenting with a margarine that had butter flavor. Dick got up and shut the door on that one. It wasn't that he thought that it hurt to think about things like that. But he didn't want anyone else to hear about it just yet. It was obvious to him that if the industry didn't get to a dime for a candy bar soon that the Heath company would have to consider the margarine as a substitute for the more expensive butter.

The ice cream-bar success had been because of the pricing. If it had still been a nickel item, the company would have had no chance to launch it. It seemed to Dick that once you get off the nickel barrier, you could more easily change to the right price. The theaters were higher and so were vending machines. But those markets were a small percentage of Heath's business.

The company had gone through the pricing situation in the bottling division. And it hadn't been long before that Joe Vecky had actually changed the price structure. He was about to go broke as a Pepsi Cola bottler in Taylorville, Illinois. In fact, he had gone broke selling Pepsis for eighty cents a case. Before he had to actually shut down, he decided to try raising the price.

Vecky told his route salesmen one morning to raise the price from eighty cents to $1.40. He didn't expect to sell anything. His drivers started calling in at nine a.m. They were actually selling the cases for the new price. The merchants just marked it up accordingly. Coke followed suit and hardly lost a sale. Vecky gambled because he had no choice. His competitors were in the same condition but had held back until he led the way and saved his business.

The Heath company's bottling division had the second highest per capita Pepsi Cola franchise in the Midwest and outsold Coke two to one. The price structure was good, and the company was making a good profit. Many times, family members talked about buying other franchises that were available. Four factors undoubtedly kept this from materializing.

First and foremost in the company not purchasing other Pepsi Cola franchises was the ice cream-bar franchise. If anyone in the family would have pursued the soft drink business further, it would have been Bob or Dick. During much of the time franchises were available, in their time, they were completely tied up with the ice cream-bar franchising.

Secondly, and equally prohibitive, was the dairy and L.S. It would have been smart business to purchase more Pepsi franchises and the company to have owned three states had it been done in the early days rather than pouring all the capital and energy into the dairy. The elder Heath simply would not have permitted it if it meant dumping the dairy.

Thirdly, and an important factor, was the early accounting system that hid the profit and loss of the respective divisions. Had the system Dick got the company to adopt been in place earlier and given credence, it would have shown the losses of the dairy and the profits of the bottling division. With L.S., that may not have been enough, but perhaps he could have been persuaded to go in the profitable direction of franchising with the figures before him.

Finally, if Bayard Jr., Bob and Dick would have had the control of the company even six years earlier, they would have tried to purchase the soft-drink franchises. Even then, to have bucked L.S. and Vernon would have been virtually impossible. Again, the dairy would have been protected at all costs.

Vernon looked at the dairy as some place he could hide. He knew little about it from marketing to costs. He thought the secret was in production and was always for any good production manager whom he could theoretically manage.

But the problem was that the best production equipment was leased on a full-time basis and was only needed part time. The quart machine was in operation only two and a half hours a day, the half-gallon machine only two hours.

Vernon was always interested in how something looked, not what profit was made. This is why his whole world was on a scratch pad where he would write things down that he wanted to fix. Nothing on his pad was for the candy plant.

In fact, Dick never saw Vernon upstairs in the candy plant. Dick asked Bayard Jr. if he had ever seen Vernon up there one time unless he was showing the plant to somebody. That was the only time Bayard remembered. With the dairy gone, Vernon really had time on his hands.

At any rate, as 1964 ended and more than fifty years after the opening of the Heath Brothers store, Bob and Dick were feeling mixed emotions about everything. Dick knew their relationship had changed, but it was something he couldn't quite figure out. On the other hand, Bayard Jr. and Dick had grown closer as time passed.

Thinking over the situation, Dick knew he was making fabulous progress at the country club. Bob had seen his success at the Old Lake Village at the club, had seen the membership respond to everything Dick had asked them to do, had seen what he had done with the accounting system at the company and had realized that he had sold some forty key ice cream accounts.

Dick wondered if it was going to be a repeat of his basketball abilities in high school or his success in winning two Kentucky Amateur Golf titles, while Bob didn't even qualify and headed back home almost in a rage. Everybody Dick knew was talking about what he had accomplished at the club where all of the company's social and recreational life was spent. But possibly the biggest thing sticking in Bob's craw, Dick thought, was the fact that Dick made sure Bayard Jr. was elected executive vice president of the Heath company, thereby forfeiting any claim Dick had to a presidency that Bob wanted.

What Bob didn't appear to understand was that Dick was

on the same level as Pete and Vernon. That was even true when Bayard Sr. was still there. Dick had the stock and power of Skiv. Even though Dick was three years younger than Bob, business-wise he was in a different generation. If the circumstances had been reversed and it had been Pete who had died instead of Skiv, Dick wondered if the relationship would have been different. But it wasn't. Now when Dick talked, he was talking about the power of twenty-five hundred shares of stock. When Bob talked, he was talking about the power of 375 shares of stock, or one-seventh of Dick. Because of this, Dick could say and do things Bob couldn't. Nevertheless, he sometimes acted as if he had the founder's share of stock behind him. That was why Dick thought the resentment toward Bob by some was so deep.

Bob also knew that Dick had no designs to be president and never did. But it was no secret and hadn't been for a long time that Dick wanted Bayard Jr. to be president some day. Nor was it any secret that Dick could sell the rest of the family on it, too. He didn't think Bob was the person who should lead the company. Bayard Jr. had demonstrated that he earned the leadership by making correct decisions for the company with the very strong possibility that he would be disinherited by his father. Further, Bayard Jr. was eleven years older than Dick and eight years older than Bob. It was time for him to be president. Bob's deep feelings of resentment were something that Dick had never realized, but they were becoming more and more apparent to him.

21

In 1965, the purse for the September Robinson Open was raised another five hundred dollars to thirty-five hundred dollars and an even better field was attracted. For the first time, the tournament started advertising the club by bringing people to the tournament who otherwise would never have been there and getting them to join as non-resident members. Dr. Keith Correll, Dick's golfing partner and friend was elected president, and Dick moved up to chairman of the board. The trustees stayed intact to give everything continuity.

Almost everybody gave Dick and the board compliments after the second nine holes were being built. But outside of Bayard Jr., not a single member of the Heath family said anything. Nor did any Heath except Bayard Jr. drive the mile or so outside of town to see the project under construction.

Dick didn't understand the family's seemingly cool reception to the country club project. While he knew that much would change in the community, the improvements at the club were more permanent and would benefit the club, the company and the community for years to come. He was attacking the club and the projects there much as he had attacked the ice cream-bar sales in 1959-60. One good thing about no Heaths coming around on the project, Dick figured, was that there were none of them to fight him about anything. The people he was working with at the club were helpful and fun to be around.

With that atmosphere and attitude, Dick felt that people hadn't seen anything. The membership had already tripled since he'd started working to improve the club, and he had many more plans. The momentum was there, he believed, and he knew that when that happens, anything is possible.

After the second nine holes were finished, Dick thought the next step would be to build a new pro shop and locker rooms, expand the 19th Hole Lounge and dining room and put a facing on the club that matched Old Lake Village in decor. It was estimated that nearly $200,000 would be needed to accomplish these additions. Dick and Correll began laying plans for them. The time table called for things to get underway in early 1967 and have the project completed by the summer of 1968.

It was a time of happiness for Dick because of all that was going on at the club and the company.

While the construction of the second nine had been going on, Jim Reedy came to Dick and told him he wanted to get back into banking. Dick didn't blame him at all since it was his career choice. Reedy had an offer from the Mercantile Bank in St. Louis. With Dick's understanding and approval, he accepted the offer and went on to become president of one of Mercantile's large branches in West St. Louis.

To replace Reedy, Dick found and hired Don Roads as the new Heath company comptroller. With his wife, Pat, and children settled in Robinson, Roads set about his first objective of purchasing a computer and putting the accounting system and attendant company business on it—no small task. Dick also had hired Pat as his secretary. After listening to many proposals from many companies, they decided to buy an NCR computer system and get busy.

On another front, the Fountain Lodge restaurant and motel project in Olney had moved smoothly forward after the Heath company bought into it. Marshall Poole, using the fact that the Heath company was a stockholder and the company's vice president of sales and vice president and treasurer, Bob and Dick Heath, were on the board of directors, sold several other companies and individuals stock in the venture. One of those buying stock was Reese Lumber Yard, in which Dick and Jack Chamblin had an interest. The lumber yard also extended credit. Other companies and individuals gave the Fountain Lodge a large amount of credit. The Heath company name carried a great deal of weight in that part of the country.

Dick went to several directors' meetings with Frank Reese and to others with Bob. Things looked good. The restaurant was completed and opened. Business was brisk. But there was a large debt. Much more money was in the place than stock. Poole assured everyone that the prospectus would be finished and ready to file soon. A final board meeting was scheduled before the public stock was to be offered.

The Heaths and other board members were properly notified of the board meeting and that the prospectus was finished and the stock would be available on the following Tuesday. Bob and Dick planned to go to the meeting together and decided to take Dick Eagleton, their attorney in Robinson, with them. They had dinner at the meeting, listened to the presentation and read the prospectus, which was now ready to file. L.S. Heath & Sons, Inc., was prominently displayed as the chief promoter in the prospectus.

Later, Dick was enjoying the drive home in the bright, moonlit southern Illinois night. After he turned east on a less-traveled road that was a shortcut back to Robinson, he could see the moon directly in front of him. Bob was sitting up front with him, and Eagleton was sitting quietly in the back seat listening to the two cousins talk about the possibilities of the new venture.

"Fellows," Eagleton said when there was a break in the conversation and they were twelve or fifteen miles out of Olney, "Uncle Vernon isn't going to be very happy about going to jail."

"What?" both men said at once, their heads snapping around in unison to look in the back seat.

"I'm afraid Vernon will go to jail on this because the prospectus is illegal. So is the manner in which the stock is being offered. They haven't complied with the Blue Sky regulation, and it's too late to change directions now. But they can't raise money legally as it stands."

"The wha—?" Bob asked.

"If they can't raise the funds, how can they pay the bills and get the units built?" Dick asked, interrupting.

"They can't." Eagleton said. "It's a real mess."

"That makes it real simple for us then," Bob said. "We'll just throw our stock on the table and walk away."

"Hold on, cuz, it's not that simple," Dick said.

Eagleton agreed.

"That's not the answer," Dick said, continuing. "The stock is nothing, I agree. But all kinds of people are in this because of us. And how about all the creditors who have been duped because of us being in it? The thing will blow up in our faces, legally and morally.

"Since we're on the board and the company is included as a stockholder in the prospectus, the SEC will look to Vernon as liable because he's president of the company and to us as liable because we're board members."

For the rest of the way back to Robinson, Bob and Dick argued as they had never before done. Bob was angry, his temper flaring when Dick tried to explain that if they let the stock be sold to the public with the Heath company as a stockholder, it would be in legal trouble.

"And if we 'throw our stock on the table and walk away,'" Dick said sarcastically, "we could be sued by not only our stockholders who bought stock because of us, but by creditors who extended large amounts of credit with the two Heaths on the board. Everyone who bought stock or extended credit would lose money because of our involvement."

"What else can we do?" Bob asked.

"We can straighten it out. Clean up the financial and legal mess Dick says things are in," Dick said.

"And just how would we do that?"

"Dick's the lawyer," Dick said, turning to Eagleton in the back seat. "What would it take?"

"Well," Eagleton said slowly, measuring each word as he spoke, "it looks to me like you'd have to take over the restaurant, pay off the creditors and buy out the stockholders who bought the stock because of you—if you feel morally obligated to do the latter—and then sell the restaurant."

"How much would it take?" Dick asked.

"I don't know for sure, but I'd say somewhere in the neighborhood of $200,000-$250,000."

"That's crazy," Bob said, exploding again. "I—"

"We've made good deals and bad deals," Dick said. "We've made a lot of good deals. So this is a bad one. You've got to accept both. We were used in this one, it looks like, and have the responsibility to clean it up. Besides, we can deduct the losses."

Bob totally disagreed. "I thought you would have watched this closer, Dick," he said to Eagleton.

"Nobody could have foreseen this," Eagleton said quietly.

"By God, I'm not for doing anything," Bob said loudly.

"The way you are now, that doesn't surprise me," Dick said. "One time, things like this would have mattered."

"It's about time we let the board of directors start settling things," Bob said.

"Looks like the board will have to decide then," Dick said, finding it almost impossible to believe what he was hearing. The whole conversation was so foreign to him that he wouldn't have believed it, if he weren't in the car. He really knew that the Bob he was hearing was not even close to the person he had known throughout his life.

"The way things are going," Dick said, continuing, "maybe a lot of things should be done by the board. You can't just throw clubs on this one."

"We'll see what I can do."

They left it that way and called a meeting of the board. After going through the whole situation, discussing it and arguing for about an hour, it came down to a vote. The vote was to walk away; only three wanted to clear it up as Dick suggested. He, Bayard Jr. and Jack Morris Sr. voted for the latter; Vernon, John, Pete, Bob and Ruby voted for the former. Dick was disgusted.

He had no doubt now that the present Heath family was a bunch of phonies. L.S., Skiv and even Bayard Sr. wouldn't have stood for this. Vernon didn't realize the implications of the vote. And he and John were the two that got everyone involved in the first place. The biggest factor to Dick, though, was Bob. They grew up together and were as close as brothers.

That had changed. And it was things like Bob's stance on the Fountain Lodge deal that made Dick aware of the change, after all the little things he had overlooked before. But he never thought Bob's principles would change. After his temper tantrum last night, Dick knew one thing for sure: his cousin and their relationship had changed forever.

No matter how much Dick explained that the Heaths were the ones who were duped and that they were responsible for the people who bought the stock and the credit that was extended, the vote remained five to three.

During the meeting, Vernon was quite sheepish, and he and John sat there hardly saying a word. Dick thought they surely knew it was their fault all along. It's easy for them to make mistakes, he thought. Everybody makes mistakes. But he believed it was unforgivable not to correct them once they were known.

Dick knew there weren't many like Bayard Heath Jr. He had the guts to vote his convictions against his own father. The rest of them were lacking in conviction. Dick believed Pete knew what was right but wouldn't go against his son no matter what. Pete never looked at Dick once the whole meeting. Of course, that didn't surprise him. Nor did Ruby's vote surprise him. She could care less about morals, principles, rights or wrongs, as far as he could see. All she could see is that it would cost her.

Thinking of the costs, Dick made a last effort. "We're all in the 52 percent tax bracket," he said. "If it cost us $200,000 to make it right, it would actually cost us about $100,000 — or in Ruby's case about $12,000. I didn't know you valued your moral responsibility so cheaply.

"Do you think this would happen if Father Heath or Skiv

would have been here? Bayard Sr. would not have stood for something like this, either. My God, their principles were the most important things they felt they had."

But they were not there, and Dick had to deal with who was there. He found it interesting, though, that on the stock side, if Bayard Jr. had had his father's and sister's stock, slightly more than 51 percent of the stock would have been for clearing it right up. Of course, that wasn't the reality, either.

Although he didn't have a dime of his own money in the project, Dick decided to try and straighten out the mess himself to correct what the family had walked away from. He was a Heath and had the pride of what he believed the real Heath family represented. With that frame of mind and reference, he simply couldn't walk around and do nothing.

"My principles are more important, too," Dick said. "I'll clean the mess up personally if I have to."

What he did was get the outstanding bills together and pay them off. Then he tried to work a couple of ill-advised deals to salvage the situation but stopped after about thirty thousand dollars in losses.

When the deals finally fell through, Dick put up his Heath stock as collateral to borrow $300,000 from the Indiana National Bank in Indianapolis to pay the bills. Each of the directors, except Bob, agreed to help Dick make the monthly payments. Now nobody could blame the Heaths or the company.

While the company's reputation was intact, the decision had more serious ramifications than anyone could conceive. The worst of them was that it finally broke the relationship between Bob and Dick. Both men lost their respect for each other. To Dick's way of thinking, it was Bob who had changed and was no longer the Bob Heath he had known and was close to for so many years.

Regardless of the situation, however, there was a business to run, and Dick was going to do everything he could to operate the same with his cousin as he had in the past. For the sake of the family, he couldn't change his business relationship with Bob or any of the rest of the family.

But as time passed, Dick began to realize that the family not only had different principles, but they also had different goals. Bayard Jr. had finally gotten the new candy plant approved. And the company began building a new Pepsi Cola plant next to the proposed site of the candy plant on the twenty-five acres on the west edge of Robinson but didn't expand the Pepsi business beyond the six counties. No one had the motivation to expand and utilize the new modern plant capable of much more production. Being the slow place it was, especially in rural America with only six counties with a total population of fewer than 100,000, the small franchise was rare and not exactly good business.

And few bottling plants in the country would match the one the Heaths were building. It was being built with panelized bricks and without many offices; it would primarily be a manufacturing plant to produce Pepsi Cola and the various Heath-labeled flavors. Few soft-drink bottlers would build this kind of plant with this kind of building. Nor were there many bottlers who planned to build a candy plant next to a bottling plant. The Heath company did what the family could decide upon.

In the early thirties and forties, despite the jingle and the twelve-ounce bottles, the Pepsi Cola company wasn't a major force in the soft-drink business. An early advertising jingle said, "Pepsi Cola hits the spot; twelve full ounces is a lot." Later, a part of the advertising kept repeating the price: "nickel, nickel, nickel." Still, before 1950, Coca-Cola outsold Pepsi Cola nearly twenty to one. Pete Heath and Harry Crisp Sr., a Marion, Illinois, bottler, used to take their wives to the bottling conventions back in the early years to listen to the Pepsi company's plans. Pete always laughed about having to buy the Crisps, who were in the chicken business, too, dinner, because they barely had enough money to attend the conventions in those early days.

So the six-ounce Coca-Cola virtually dominated the soft-drink business. The executive vice president of Coca-Cola in 1950 was a dynamic man named Al Steele who kept the company ahead of the competition. But because he owned little of the company, Pepsi Cola went after him and was able to persuade him to become the president of Pepsi. What was even worse for Coca-Cola was that he took some fifty of the company's youngest and brightest marketing people with him. Pepsi Cola offered Steele and his people fabulous stock options to get them to change companies.

And that was when things began to change with Pepsi. It wasn't long before people began seeing new advertising jingles like "be sociable" and "the new Pepsi generation." Al Steele knew that advertising wouldn't change the old-line Coke drinkers. So he went after the young to create a new generation of Pepsi drinkers. He knew that the coming of television to a widespread audience in the fifties was changing people's habits, and Pepsi could gain on Coke.

With the company advertising, Steele went for the take-home six-pack carton. Coca-Cola had its little red cartons and six-ounce drink in the bottle and wouldn't change from that size. While the company sat in its cozy pre-ordained position with its little, highly prized bottle and coolers, Pepsi began gaining ground and did even better in Heath's six-county franchise area. Before Coca-Cola woke up, Pepsi Cola had made the soft drink business a two-product enterprise. It was the perfect time for the Heath franchise to expand, if the family had been so motivated.

As a tribute to the Heath company and its new plant, Pepsi sent Joan Crawford, Al Steele's wife and popular movie star, to Robinson for the grand opening of the new plant. She stayed overnight at Pete and Thelma Heath's house for a big party at the country club and another at the plant site. Pete provided the house, and Dick provided the Smirnoff vodka he was told she drank. He took two quarts by the house in spite of Thelma's longtime ban on liquor at home. Pete didn't drink vodka, anyway, so Dick thought it would be okay. After Crawford's two-day stay in Robinson, Dick went by to pick up what was left of the vodka and found none.

At the party at the country club, the Heath company gave out black and gold ash trays with the imprint of the new plant on the face of it. Joan Crawford gave a boost to a product the Heaths were already selling twelve million bottles annually in its small franchise.

"I wish Skiv could have been here to see this," Pete told Dick that night, happiness and pride shinning in both of their eyes and on their faces. "I can remember when we both put five cases on a flatbed truck to go around trying to sell some bottles and sneak in those coolers."

Pete was referring to pop cases cooled by ice and filled with rows of products, mostly Coca-Cola. Dick remembered them well back into the forties when he had his city route.

"I wasn't as nice as you and Skiv," Dick said. "I just waited until the Coke man left and took some of his rows out, put them back in his cases sitting next to the cooler and put Pepsi in the cooler."

That night, Dick was especially proud of the country club, too. The 19th Hole had been paneled with rough siding, a new formal cocktail lounge had been installed and new carpeting, soft lights and nice furniture had been installed and added to the dining room. Paneling and nice paintings had transformed the old concrete walls. This was one night that it was apparent just how important the club was to the Heath company.

22

The Robinson Open prize was raised to five thousand dollars in 1966. This was the fifth straight year the tournament had been held. Instead of increasing the purse five hundred dollars as in past years, it had been upped fifteen hundred dollars. Everybody knew the full eighteen holes would probably be ready by the following year.

Pursie Piper from Mount Vernon, Illinois, continued to dominate the amateur division. But more good players were coming in from a wider area. One of the better ones was Lee Elder, a young black pro just beginning to establish himself.

Each fall the volunteers looked forward to meeting and seeing the new players, both professional and amateur, coming in. It was part of the volunteers' jobs to make them feel comfortable and welcome. Dick's mother, Madeline, met Elder's wife, Rose, in 1966 and asked her to dinner at the club. Other volunteers did the same with other wives.

Meanwhile, and even before the tournament was over, Dick and Keith Correll were starting work on a new pro shop and men's locker room addition planned for the southwest side of the clubhouse. The exterior would match the facade of Old Lake Village. In addition, the dining room would extend toward the putting green and have windows looking out over the course. The plans also included tripling the size of the 19th Hole Lounge with all glass on the west and north sides and a formal cocktail lounge added to the east end of the large dining room. The old men's room would be turned into a new women's locker room. With additional air conditioning, it would be about a $175,000 addition.

Chuck Correll, Keith's brother and cashier at the Second National Bank, made arrangements with the American National Bank in Chicago to secure a loan for the club to complete the project. Heath company pilot Woody Blaha flew Dick and Keith Correll to Chicago for the meeting.

Dick was armed with the club's accounting statements when he and Correll sat down with bank officials, expecting the statements and his presentation to be all that was required to secure the loan. But bank officials viewed the club changing presidents each year as a weakness. They wanted continuity of management and finally agreed to make the loan as long as Dick agreed to remain as chairman of the club's board as long as the loan was outstanding. That simply required Dick to run for trustee every three years.

With the loan in the bank, construction on the addition began. While it was under way, Dick wanted to change the exterior of the clubhouse with redwood to match everything. The concrete-block, painted exterior looked out of place with Old Lake and the new pro shop addition.

Each morning at 6:30 a.m., Dick arrived at the club to eat breakfast with Keith Correll and some of the other members. "Doc," Dick said one morning, "I've got an idea about how to get the extra funds for the facing of the clubhouse."

"I hope so," Correll said. "We're really tight on funds. What have you got in mind?"

"I'm going to sell members so many board feet of redwood with the installed cost as a donation."

"Can you sell it that way?"

"Why not? I'm going to hit Beth with it when she and Bayard come in this morning. I've got the cost down to each running foot. I think two and a quarter a foot would take care of material, labor and staining with enough left over to do the stone work in the front. I figure if I can sell Beth, I can sell anybody."

Bayard Sr. and Beth Heath came in every morning between 7:48 and 7:52 a.m. and sat at the same table. Bayard Sr. would read the *Chicago Tribune* while Beth just sat. By this time, Dick's relationship with them had improved considerably. The elder Heath actually looked healthier and happier than he had in a long time. Dick was always kidding him but never about the Heath ice cream bar.

At 8:01 a.m. that morning, Dick attacked Beth with the proposition and soon sold her twenty feet. His uncle, the old-warrior look in his eyes, looked over at Dick and shook his head. "You're at it again," he said, "trying to sell your way to what you want."

"Do you have any better ideas about how to get it done?"

Bayard Sr. laughed and said, "No."

Selling Beth on the project was like Marshall Poole selling the Heaths on the Fountain Lodge. How could anyone say no if Beth set the pace? And it was all sold out quickly, the proceeds and work really changing the looks of the club. Helping that along was having the same rock spread around the entrance to the clubhouse that was used at Old Lake. That cost had been built-in with the running board feet cost of the redwood facade.

Things were going well at the country club.

Sometime later, Dick walked into Bob's office and was surprised to see him in a suit. They had a golf game scheduled at one p.m. And they rarely wore a coat and tie.

"Who's coming in this morning?" Dick said. "What's going on?"

Bob fidgeted around, then said, "Nobody's coming in and nothing's going on."

"Why the suit?"

"Jean thinks that since we're officers of the corporation, we should look the part."

"That's fine," Dick said, laughing and forgetting all about the tee time. "I think I'll stick to wearing sweaters. I don't think it'll hurt my image."

As he walked out of Bob's office, Dick was thinking again about how times had changed. The two used to say to each other, "If they want to sell us, they'll have to take us like we are. That's the way we've always been."

Perhaps it was not a big point, but it showed Bob's change in the philosophy as the Fountain Lodge situation had shown the change. Up to this point, the only time the two had really talked about being officers was when it helped them get into somebody's office to sell something. Dick laughed again, thinking how Bob had to change clothes before teeing it up just like the guys downtown.

Trying to clean up the Fountain Lodge was the nightmare Dick had expected it to be. In killing the sale of the stock, Dick saved the company but killed the project. And the $300,000 he had borrowed to clean it up had to be paid back. Each director was still sending Dick his share to make the payments. But he didn't know how long everybody would continue with the way many of the family felt about the situation.

The Reese Lumber Yard was really hurt over the deal, too. That upset Dick as much as the rest of it had. He finally told Jack Chamblin, "I'll take your 20 percent of the lumber stock I got you in and give you the shares of Bradford in exchange. Mother and I bought them for you anyway."

That didn't completely take care of Reese's involvement, but it helped ease Dick's sense of obligation to his friend. Chamblin had been like a brother to him and a second son to his mother. He had eaten many meals at the Heath house in the early days. Exchanging what Chamblin had once said was the third largest block of Bradford stock behind his dad and Roy Parker and had been originally purchased to help Chamblin anyway seemed to Dick to be the least he could do on a bad deal.

Bayard Jr. continued to work on the new candy plant plans and talk with equipment suppliers. Now that Bob had moved from the conference room to another office, the three cousins no longer met each morning for coffee. To Dick's way of thinking, this was something that really hurt them. In many of these meetings, they had done much planning and, equally important, had kept excellent communication among the three of them.

Dick mentioned this to Bob, but it didn't seem to bother him that that aspect had changed. And Bayard Jr. simply came over to Dick's office each morning. Since Jack Morris was next door, he would usually come in to sit down and talk, too.

About this time, the Heath company had the Metropolitan Life Insurance Company as its group insurance carrier. The agency had come in and sold the younger directors a $100,000 term policy, payable to their wives. Pete, Vernon and Ruby didn't qualify, but Vernon had handled the policies with the agent. For some reason, Bayard Jr. was especially concerned whether the coverage was in place.

"Are we covered yet?" he asked Dick one morning.

"I don't know. I keep asking Vernon, and he can't find out. I don't know what the problem is."

Time passed, and it became a thing with Bayard Jr. Finally, after hearing him ask the same question again, Dick said, "I'll find out if you're covered."

He picked up the phone and called the agent.

"This is Dick Heath," he said. "Bayard just kicked the bucket, and I want to know if he's covered."

The agent started nervously asking questions but finally said, "I'll call New York immediately and find out."

Bayard Jr. shook his head and laughed when Dick replaced the phone receiver.

"I was tired of screwing around," Dick said. "We should know shortly."

About half an hour later, Vernon walked in Dick's office as angry as Dick had ever seen him. The agent had called him about Bayard Jr.'s supposed death.

"You can't do that, Dick," Vernon said. "It's not done like that."

"For two months," Dick said, standing up behind his desk, "Bayard has asked me about this coverage. I've asked you. You couldn't find out nor could anybody else. Hell, we're the customers, and I want to know whether he is or isn't covered. Suppose it did happen. It if takes what I did to find out, that's tough."

Vernon started to leave.

"Well, is he or isn't he?"

"He is," Vernon said as he walked out.

For some reason, the agent also had told Dr. Bill Schmidt about Bayard Jr.'s "death." Before long, it got around town. Bayard Jr.'s wife, Pat, heard it at the club after she and Betty had played a round of golf. Pat called the office and got Bayard Jr. on the phone. He immediately told Dick.

"What did you tell her, Hogan?" Dick asked.

"I told her I was alive."

"What did she say?"

"She was relieved, I think. The way it spread around town, I'm not so sure that was the best way to find out if the coverage was in force."

"Well, it's the only way I could find out. Besides, the way you've been playing golf, you look dead to me."

Bayard Jr. laughed, and Dick felt it had kind of paid him back for a gag he had played on Betty some time earlier. She had been so proud of their son Scott's grades in the fifth grade and had told anyone who would listen. Finally, Bayard Jr. had called Betty, disguised his voice and told her that he was the principal of the grade school. After congratulating her on Scott's grades, he told her he had given Scott a double promotion. Betty believed Bayard Jr. for a while, then felt like a fool. Pat had disapproved of his gag and reprimanded him severely.

With the question of the insurance coverage out of the way and answered, Bayard Jr. concentrated on the new candy plant. His big concern was the new, automated, continuous-cooling process that would be in use. Up to that time, the Heath company had always cooked the toffee in batches in copper kettles over an open gas fire. In the new plant, it was designed to feed in the crushed almonds, sugar and butter to automatically come out as the finished toffee and to be cut automatically to feed to the giant chocolate coater. The bars would be fed automatically to be wrapped, boxed and the box put into a case for shipment.

Bayard Jr.'s concern was maintaining the homemade flavor of the toffee. Nobody would really know what it would taste like until it was on line and the final product was available. A great deal of money had to be spent without knowing the effect on the taste of the Heath toffee bar.

Bayard Jr. and Bob were playing golf against Keith Correll and Dick about twice a week. Both Bayard and Correll had greatly improved their games. They weren't playing for much money, but the competition was fierce. They played the two-points-a-hole, low-ball, low-total-team game for a quarter a point.

The golf game started taking on a serious side, more so than usual, about this time. That they were playing for a quarter a point wasn't the issue. The money didn't matter; the only thing anyone cared about was winning. When one team got down a point or two, it could press, or double the bet, making it four points a hole. Another press on the next hole would raise the points to eight per hole, with four points for low ball and four points for low total. By the last few holes, they could be playing for sixteen or thirty-two points a hole or more if each team pressed when it had the opportunity — anything to increase the pressure.

To make things even more interesting, Bob and Dick always had an individual Nassau game on the side. This game was for the lowest score on each nine holes and the lowest total on the eighteen holes. The side bet was for a dollar for each low total. Presses were also possible at appropriate times.

The foursome decided among themselves that they were

going to play strictly by USGA rules. Everybody agreed. That way there could be no disputes of any kind. On the fifteenth hole of a particularly close round, Bob missed a ten-foot putt. He got so angry he broke his putter. None of the other three said a word.

"I just want to see what he does on the sixteenth hole, Keith," Dick said. "He'd better not ask Bayard to use his putter this time."

It wasn't the first time Bob had broken his putter. And he had used other putters in the past. On the sixteenth green he said, "Hogan, let me use your putter."

"If you do, it'll cost you," Dick said. "You know the USGA rules."

Dick thought maybe that would finally stop all the club throwing. Bob knew the rules. He said nothing, walked over to his bag on the cart and grabbed his two iron. He had an eight-foot birdy and calmly made it. Everybody laughed but Bob.

At the eighteenth hole, he didn't get by so easily. He had missed the green on the seventeenth hole but chipped to within six inches. On eighteen, he was thirty feet away from the pin and was lucky to three putt the hole. It cost him the match.

"I'll pay you tomorrow," he said and went to his locker and on home. It was the first time he hadn't gone to the 19th Hole for a drink after the round since they'd been playing as a foursome.

After he had gone home, Bayard Jr., Correll and Dick had a drink and discussed Bob's temper and the putter-breaking incident.

"He can't help it," Correll said.

"You would think that after all this time it would stop," Bayard Jr. said.

"I don't think it will ever stop," Dick said. He had seen it all his life and didn't think Bob would ever be any different. He was forty years old and was always going to be the way he had always been.

The next morning he was fine. He even apologized to Bayard Jr. and Dick for not going into the bar. Dick told him not to worry about it, and everybody went on with business.

Computers had changed much in the way business was conducted. Don Roads had come up with programs for the whole system for every division and function in the company. The general ledger which gave the company the financial accounting and the cost accounting was programmed. This provided accounts payable, billings and receivables in less than half the previous time.

The company had space in twenty public warehouses around the country for the candy division. Jack Morris shipped the candy to these warehouses from the plant, packed in various ways and with different counts.

Candy orders came in from brokers, chains and individual accounts. The Midwest orders and those close by would be shipped by common freight out of the Heath plant. Orders that were near the various warehouses would be shipped from them. The computer allowed Bob Ward, Jack's assistant, to know what he had and when the warehouses needed to be restocked and streamlined inventory control.

When an order came in after the computer system was in operation, a notification would be sent to the appropriate warehouse, and the order would be sent to the customer. The computer would then bill the customer, notify the warehouse, subtract from the company stock and charge accounts receivable in the manner called for by the accounting system. Roads had earned his money and brought the company up-to-date.

The entire administration section was in good shape, too. Improvements could always be made, but the section was competent and efficient. Noel Cord and Bob Richart of the Indianapolis CPA firm Bailey, Cord and Williams audited the Heath company books annually. The company was making some $400,000 net profit each year. By 1967, the company had paid off the loan for buying Bayard Sr.'s and Pat Keisling's stock and was ready to start building the new fifty-four thousand-square-foot candy plant.

While Bayard Jr. was building the candy plant, Dick was building the back nine holes for the country club. As the top soil was removed for the new plant, it was hauled to the golf course and used there. It cost ninety-two thousand dollars to build the second nine holes at the Crawford County Country Club. But had all the free labor, use of equipment and material like the yards of top soil been considered, the cost of the addition would have been considerably higher. Members of the club and the community had a first-class facility for an extraordinarily low cost.

That was apparent when the course opened for play in July 1967. While the course was still a bit rough, it wasn't anything that time and patience wouldn't smooth out. The bent grass on the greens and tees were exceptional. It would take awhile for the fairways to mature and become real turf.

Illinois Democratic Governor Otto Kerner and Dutch Harrison, a PGA tour professional from St. Louis known as "The Arkansas Traveller," were on hand for the official opening of the course. Kerner had been mentioned as a possible nominee for the president of the United States in 1968. Although Robinson had always been a strong Republican town, Kerner's appearance was considered quite a coup for the opening of the course.

Victor L. Smith, the editor of the weekly *Robinson Argus* newspaper, was the state Republican Party chairman—a compromise choice between Cook County Republicans and the rest of the state. He was one of nearly seventy-five club members, all men, who met Kerner and Harrison for lunch before the ribbon-cutting ceremony on the number-one tee. The two were going to play Dick Heath and club pro Earl Greenwell the first eighteen-hole round on the course. That evening, 125 couples were scheduled for dinner and more festivities.

The opening round was played in ninety-two-degree heat, but it didn't bother the governor. He was all sun-tanned and accustomed to being out on the golf course in the heat. Not wanting the governor to get beat or hustled, Dick made sure he got plenty of strokes. But by the time they reached the eleventh hole, the governor and Harrison were down a few strokes. To bring them back up, Dutch tried to trick Dick.

Both had hit their tee shots the same distance off the tee. Harrison was slightly back. He said it was a seven-iron shot and feathered the ball twelve feet from the cup, forgetting that Dick had built the course and knew the distance to the pin. He hit a soft nine about the same distance from the hole.

"Dutch hit a seven iron, and you hit a nine iron," the governor said.

"Yeah, the old pro tried to trick me," Dick said. "He didn't want me to go home busted."

They both laughed.

"Lay off a little," Dick said to Greenwell as they watched the governor lift his ball toward the pin. "You're playing too well. I don't want them to lose."

"They won't," Greenwell said.

"Good. I might want them to come back again."

At the end, Kerner and Harrison beat the local pair one up on their best ball. Dick had given the governor too many strokes, and he got them on the eighteenth hole. Everybody enjoyed the round.

The governor went to Vernon's home after the match to shower and change for the evening dinner at the club. At the reception line before dinner, the governor stood to Dick's right and Betty to his left. As each couple came in, Dick whispered to him who the people were and if the man had been to lunch at noon. Out of the seventy-five men who had been at the luncheon, he remembered forty-four by name. He nudged Dick if he didn't remember the name. Dick stood quietly by and counted, to his amazement, the forty-four names the governor spoke accurately with no nudges. When Dick's mother came by, he told the governor who she was. As he shook her hand, he leaned over and kissed her on the cheek.

"This is for having a nice son," he said.

Madeline and Skiv Heath, before his death, had always been strong Republicans. But Otto Kerner disarmed Madeline and many other strong Republicans that night. Before it was over, Vic Smith cornered Dick and said, laughing, "Can you get Kerner out of here? I won't have a Republican left in this town, if you don't."

After dinner, much fun and many stories, the governor was about to leave. His aides were trying to get him back to the airport to fly back to Springfield. Dick was walking with him to the door. Suddenly, he stopped and asked, "Where's the kitchen?"

"Follow me," Dick said.

Plates, glasses, silverware and cookware from 250 meals literally covered the small kitchen, the dirty remains of dinner stacked in every available place. Two older women, specially hired as extra help to wash dishes, worked side by side and didn't notice the governor and Dick walk through the kitchen door.

"Excuse me, ladies," Kerner said as he walked up to them, extending his hand. "I'd like to thank you for the effort you've made for this wonderful dinner tonight. I appreciate it very much."

Both women began searching for something to dry their hands. They never found it. The governor grabbed their hands, one after the other, holding their hands between his and looking them directly in the eyes as he thanked them again.

Dick had seen a lot of politicians in his time, but he thought Otto Kerner was the smoothest and most polished one he had ever seen. That included presidents and future presidents, senators and a host of other politicians who came through town and were supported by the Heath family and company.

With the full eighteen holes open for the 1967 Robinson Open, the tournament prize money was doubled to ten thousand dollars. The tournament was still played on the weekend in two rounds but got a good field, including professionals like former PGA tour player Al Bessilink, who won the tournament that year.

Because Robinson had nothing much in the way of hotels and motels, and the Old Lake Village, which had been expanded by four rooms, was filled during tournament time, players either had to use what was available in Robinson or drive forty or fifty miles to Terre Haute or Vincennes just across the state line in Indiana.

But other things moved ahead at the club. The new back nine was still pretty rough but playable. A tournament organization with six years of experience was in place and functioning efficiently. Maxine Zwermann directed some seventy-five women; Jack Chamblin handled the field marshals. Most of the club members were involved in some way or another. The tournament was well directed and made money.

Other decisions outside the tournament had been made to make money, too. Private golf carts were abolished, for one thing. Because the club pro Earl Greenwell owned his own carts and the club bought them from him, the decision caused hard feelings. Greenwell, with support from some club members, wasn't in favor of giving up the carts.

But Dick and Keith Correll worked long and hard to persuade everybody that because the carts were the biggest money-maker the club had on the golf end of the business, it would be in the best interest of the club to own them. They estimated golf carts would bring the club another twenty thousand dollars annually and got what they wanted. Even though Greenwell was compensated in other ways, he soon left the club.

At tournament time in 1967, Dick thought everyone should have been happy with the way things were going at both the club and the Heath company. That wasn't the case as he found out. He knew his relationship with Bob was continuing to change and had deteriorated farther than anyone realized. But an incident just before the tournament made it obvious to Dick that it was his success at the club that Bob resented.

Every year since 1962, a Calcutta was held on the Saturday night of the Robinson Open. People would buy the pros by bidding on them. Dick auctioned off each player to the highest bidder. The proceeds went into a pot, less 10 percent for the club. The winner of the Sunday round took the pot. It had nothing to do with the two rounds of the tournament or which player won.

Each year the pot got larger. In 1967, it reached nearly five thousand dollars. The Calcutta added an extra bit of excitement to the tournament, and everybody, especially Bob, looked forward to the event. He had always headed up a syndicate of several people to get a large amount of money together. If you were in Bob's syndicate, for example, you could put up whatever amount you wanted. If he had a thousand dollars in his pot to bet and you had put in a hundred dollars, you had 10 percent of the winnings.

Even though Bob had boycotted the tournament since it had started, he still loved to participate in the Calcutta as he had liked the ritual on New Year's Day of playing everybody's best ball. Dick always believed that Bob's jealousy about the prospects of the new nine holes Dick had engineered had killed, in some strange way, the New Year's Day game that Bob would no longer play.

"Are you ready for the Calcutta?" Dick asked Bob on the Friday morning before the tournament. "I saw some of the guys, and they said to tell you they've saved up some cash. They expect the pot to go to eight thousand dollars tomorrow night."

"I'm not going to be there," Bob said flatly.

"You're not going to be there?" Dick said, echoing his cousin. "You're kidding me."

"We're going to St. Louis to a sing-a-long."

"You're going to a what?" Dick said.

"We're going to St. Louis to a sing-a-long."

"A what?"

"To a sing-a-long. Jean made the arrangements some time ago."

"You're kidding me."

"No, I'm serious."

Dick looked at him, speechless, and walked out. It had been evident to everybody that Bob had changed. But it was particularly evident to the ones Dick had to tell that Bob wasn't going to be there for the Calcutta. It went on without him.

23

A monumental decision was in the works at the company just before the new plant was completed. Inflation and rising costs had shrunk candy profits to zero. Bayard Jr. had come up with a substitute for butter, and the board of directors decided to go along with it. Because of the profit situation, it had no choice but to make the first change in the Heath English Toffee Bar in fifty-three years.

Instead of using butter as one of the four ingredients of the candy, a high-grade corn oil margarine would be used. Bayard Jr. had done many tests. This particular blend changed the normal taste only slightly. The Nestle company's flavored chocolate was still one of the ingredients. And choice almonds and sugar were still used in the same quantity and of the same quality as always. Only on the wrapper where the ingredients were listed could the change be detected, the Heath family believed.

Shortly after the decision was made, the new plant was finished. Initial tests showed that everything was running as expected. The new plant would cut manufacturing costs considerably. Those savings and the savings from substituting the margarine for butter would insure the profits necessary for the company to grow and prosper.

"With the candy plant and the ice cream bar, it would be almost impossible now for anyone to screw up this company,"

Dick said to Bayard Jr. one day while the two cousins stood in the new plant, admiring it and reflecting on how far the company had come in the more than fifty years since their fathers had opened the confectionery on the west side of the Robinson Square. "Nobody could figure out a way to do it if they stayed up all night."

"Don't be too sure, Dick," Bayard Jr. said. "This family might find a way."

Bayard Jr. got the bugs worked out of the new plant very quickly and made the transition from the old plant very smoothly. His employees worked extremely hard and well under his supervision and praise. He could turn out whatever amount of candy that was required whenever it was needed. Things were going well throughout the company.

Ross Fife came into Dick's office one day and said he needed help with a huge ice cream company in Dallas. It was Cabell's Dairy, headed by Earl Cabell who had been the mayor of Dallas at the time President John F. Kennedy had been assassinated.

"He's a tough account," Fife said. "It'll be difficult to get him signed up."

"I'll give it a shot," Dick said. It had been awhile since he had hit the road, and he loved the prospect of tackling a good, tough account.

When Dick called Cabell, he said he was on his way to Chicago but would see him there. They agreed to meet at Trader Vic's and have lunch. Dick thought he could nail him there just as easily as he could in Texas. Besides, it was closer.

"Want me to come along, Dick?" Fife asked.

"No. I wouldn't have needed any help with him back in the old days. I don't think I will now. I hope not anyway."

Woody Blaha flew Dick to Chicago in the company plane and landed at Meigs Field. Dick told Blaha to wait for him and took a cab to the restaurant.

"I may need your help at the finishing line," Dick said before the cab pulled out. "I want to get back to Robinson tonight."

Dick and Cabell met at Trader Vic's at noon, started talking and drinking rum drinks Dick called Episka Punch. At the time, he wondered how to spell it. Later, he hoped he never found out.

"This punch drink will help you explain why a candy man got into the dairy business," Cabell said.

"We got into the business because we got in the habit of eating. My grandfather got us into the dairy business."

"How good is that Heath ice cream bar, Dick?"

"As good as they come, Earl. It is a quality ice cream bar, the kind we would make if we still had our dairy."

"I like to deal with dairy people."

"You've got one with me."

After a few drinks, they ordered lunch and ate it in an alcoholic haze. They were still drinking the rum drinks at three p.m. Dick thought he had Cabell sold on fifty or sixty units, but he wasn't sure. Both of them realized that Cabell didn't have a purchase order.

"Don't worry about it, Earl," Dick said. "I'll draw one up on this paper napkin."

"Fine. Go ahead, if you can do it."

They decided they would go for fifty units—twenty-five single-pack units and twenty-five multi-pack units. Dick had been so involved at the country club and away from the daily running of the ice cream-bar franchise that he hadn't kept in touch with increases in prices. He just knew there had been an increase.

"Hell, Earl," Dick said, "it just occurred to me that I don't know the newest price schedule."

"I'm not worried about that. Just order it."

Dick drew up the order on the napkin and gave it to Cabell for his okay. He glanced at it briefly, put it on the table and signed it.

"Are you sure this is all right this way, Earl?" Dick asked, wanting to be sure they were both in agreement.

"Sure. I've made many deals the same way."

"So have I, but I just wanted to make sure," Dick said. Ross will flip over this one, he thought.

"Let's have one more before you go," Cabell said and offered his hand to seal the deal.

The first rule of selling Dick followed was to be polite. So he felt he had no choice and agreed. By the end of the drink and after four hours of drinking, Dick was feeling no pain. He got hold of the bill and paid it. As he handed the waiter money for the bill, Dick started laughing.

"What's so funny?" Cabell asked.

"You wouldn't understand. I've got an aunt on our board who wouldn't understand our lunch. She'll probably bitch about it until she dies."

He gave the waiter an extra five dollars above the bill and the tip and asked him to call a cab and help him get in it. When he got to the airport, Blaha was waiting at the door.

"Home, James," Dick said, smiled and wobbled to the plane.

No sooner than he settled in the seat and fastened his seat belt, Dick fell asleep. He thought he had slept all the way to

Robinson anyway and was sober when they landed.

"Hell no, you didn't sleep all the way," Blaha told him as they walked to the car. "You wanted to try landing again."

"Really?" Dick said, laughing a bit. "I must have been still sulking because you told me I couldn't hit the county if I'd have tried to land the plane."

"You couldn't have hit the state of Illinois if you'd have tried to land the plane tonight. You were in the bag."

"I guess I'd better not take on these tough jobs more than once a year," Dick said, laughing again. "But Ross wanted a job done, and I did it."

Dick again turned his attention to the country club and the golf tournament. After a highly successful tournament the previous fall, club officials announced a purse of fifteen thousand dollars for the 1968 Robinson Open. To do it, Dick knew he was going to have to do some things differently.

Then in late May, he received a phone call from George Walsh, a PGA tour official from Belleville, Illinois. He wanted to know if Dick would like the Robinson Open to be a satellite of the Kemper Open on the PGA tour to be played the second week of September.

"Absolutely," Dick said without hesitation and without talking to anyone about it. He was thrilled. "We've already decided to raise the purse to fifteen thousand dollars this year. We might even be able to go higher."

"You'll have to go higher," Walsh said. "It'd have to be twenty-five thousand dollars. Can you do that?"

"How can we say no?"

"Make sure, and I'll call you back in a couple of days."

Dick knew this was a new challenge for the Robinson Open. He wondered how the club could raise the funds. That night, John and Jo Gwin were at the Heaths to play poker. But they mainly sat around talking about Walsh's call.

"I've got an idea to raise the money by selling five hundred dollar Gold Sponsors," Dick said. "For five hundred dollars the sponsor would get a spot in the ProAm round on Wednesday, a gold jacket for the man and a gold sweater for the wife. We would put on a free cocktail party for them on Saturday night, give them tickets, preferred bleacher seats and a prime parking spot."

The only thing Dick would have to do was sell the Gold Sponsors. With 150 amateur spots in the ProAm, that would allow him to sell as many as 150 Gold Sponsors or many more than would be necessary for the twenty-five thousand dollar purse.

Early the next day, he saw Maxine Zwermann, who had been assisting him with the tournament since its inception, and told her about his idea of the Gold Sponsors.

"Who do you expect to sell?" she asked.

"Well, Mort Imlay will buy one."

"I'd bet you that you couldn't sell Mort."

Imlay was a golf nut and loved the club. Dick knew he could sell him. Before he had a chance to approach Imlay, however, Walsh called back and said that there had been some changes in tour scheduling.

"If you can come up with the money and move the tournament to the third week of September," Walsh said, "you'll be alone and be a major tour stop on the PGA."

"We accept," Dick said. "Send us the contract."

At that moment, as far as Dick was concerned, the Robinson Open was the PGA Robinson Open, the most unlikely spot ever on the PGA tour. As the tournament had grown, so had the press coverage. Now Dick's wildest dreams had been realized. The impossible had happened. He knew the media would give more coverage and began to make plans for the tournament.

PGA officials would have to inspect the club and course before the contract could be signed and the PGA Robinson Open was official. But Dick knew there would be no problems after the six years' worth of work club members had done. The officials were impressed with all the facilities. They found fault with nothing, including the condition of the new back nine holes.

Dick met with Maxine again and asked her to be the tournament chair. She agreed, and they decided they needed a tournament headquarters. To finance it, they went to the People's Bank in Newton, Illinois, and borrowed twenty thousand dollars to remodel the old pro shop into a first-class tournament headquarters. Maxine, with Joy Reese's help, designed a beautiful and functional building.

With these steps in motion and a signed contract for the event on the table, momentum began picking up. The PGA sent a tournament manual outlining every detail necessary to be followed. It would require almost the entire membership to do the job. The club was the sponsor on the agreement with the PGA and had to raise the funds, host the tournament and pay the prize money. Nearly 350 volunteers were rounded up and twenty-six chairmen for various committees were appointed to take care of everything.

Soon after things were rolling, Dick called George Walsh to ask him who would be doing the telecast.

"Robinson isn't on the TV schedule," he said. "But you will get some television money out of the PGA TV proceeds."

"Can I do my own TV?" Dick asked.

"Sure. If you want to."

Dick told him that he wanted to do a six-station network. Walsh laughed and was a bit amazed but told Dick to contact Herb Kaplan or Joe O'Rourk of Hughes Sports Network who hired out on a free-lance basis.

O'Rourk thought it was a wild idea but agreed to supply a producer and a director for five thousand dollars each. The technical engineer was another twenty-five hundred dollars. With O'Rourk as the producer, the Hughes company would send the necessary equipment, including the large van, for twenty thousand dollars, hire the cameramen at the company prices, would send the lines from AT&T for eight thousand dollars and produce the show. Four television towers had to be built for the coverage, a job delegated to the Reese Lumber Company. The plans called for the last four holes to be covered for an hour on Saturday and an hour and a half on Sunday.

All the costs of the network created for the tournament would be borne by the Robinson Open Television Network. Dick planned to televise the tournament in markets in Terre Haute, Indianapolis and Evansville in Indiana, Champaign and Harrisburg in Illinois and St. Louis in Missouri. He purchased time from the television stations in those cities and planned the advertising campaign. Among the stations, he had some ABC, some CBS and some NBC affiliates.

As soon as he had all the costs figured, Dick asked O'Rourk the number of advertising spots that could be run in two days and divided the total cost by the number of spots. The result was $786 per thirty-second spot and included the cost of hiring John Derr of Hughes as chief announcer and Bob

Forbes of WTHI-TV, the CBS affiliate in Terre Haute. With the costs all in, all that was left was to find a color announcer and sell the advertising.

The senior senator from Illinois and the majority leader of the United States Senate, Everett McKinley Dirksen, was running for the Senate again in November 1968. Since he would be campaigning for reelection and the Heath family was a big financial supporter of Republican politicians and Vic Smith, the Robinson newspaper publisher, was still state Republican Party chairman, Dick decided to have Smith ask Senator Dirksen to be the color announcer. He accepted. Dick was more elated than ever. The country club was staging a PGA golf tournament, putting together a television network to televise it and having a U.S. senator as color announcer. He didn't know what else he could have wanted.

To raise money for the tournament itself besides selling tickets, programs, pairing sheets and concessions, the Gold Sponsor program Dick had originated was developed. For five hundred dollars, the sponsor got a spot in the Wednesday ProAm round, a gold blazer with a crest for the man, a sweater with a crest for the woman, four season badges, two bleacher tickets, preferred parking in the main lot, an invitation to the Gold Sponsors' cocktail party, mention in the tournament program and on a plaque hanging in the clubhouse.

Additionally, a Silver Sponsor program was offered. It sold for one hundred dollars and included the same things as the Gold Sponsor less the jacket, sweater, ProAm round and invitation to the cocktail party.

Maxine Zwermann was in charge of the PGA tournament program. Advertising had to be sold to pay for it. A raffle for a gold Cadillac to be given away on Sunday was added to the list of money-making activities. Thirty committees made up of four hundred volunteers were formed. And bleachers, ropes, stakes, leader boards, placards and all kinds of supplies were needed. Press conferences and outings to attact the press were scheduled regularly.

Dick and Bob Jones went to the Kemper Open in Sutton, Massachusetts, and met with Cuz Mindolla, the owner of the club and his own PGA tournament, to check out his operation. The men from Robinson were there also to attract the best field of pros they could get to play in the Robinson Open.

With everything going so well, the entire club membership and much of the community were elated and supportive in one way or another. That was not true at the Heath company, however. Not one single Silver or Gold Sponsor was purchased by the Heath company or a member of the Heath family. In the tournament program, which included ten full-page colored ads, the Heath company had purchased a half-page black-and-white spot. A marketing tool that could have been the company's was totally ignored by the Heath company management. The club was used by members of the family, key employees and the company more than any company in town, including Marathon Oil. And Old Lake Village was used more by the Heath company than anybody. This tournament was the vehicle to pay off the last capital debt to provide a great facility key to social, recreational and business needs of the Heath company and was supported hardly at all by the company.

But that wasn't something anyone could change. Other things had to be done. It was decided to seek Illinois Governor Richard Oglivie to be honorary tournament chairman and to play in the ProAm round on Wednesday. Again, Dick went through Vic Smith. The governor accepted both invitations. One of the side benefits, but a most important one, was that the Illinois Tourism Council bought 25 percent of the television spots to promote events being held throughout Illinois in the next year.

One of Dick's biggest problems had been the short notice he had to sell the television advertising, even though his costs were excellent on the cost-per-exposure. The tourism council was his first sale and was a big boost to the sales campaign. Since the Heath company had a Pepsi Cola bottling franchise, Dick contacted company headquarters in New York and sold another 25 percent of the spots.

Feeling good from the successes, he tried a move that had always worked well for him with the ice cream-bar franchise. He made a cold call to Anheuser-Busch brewery headquarters in St. Louis. When the operator answered, Dick asked who the brand managers were for Michelob and Budweiser.

"John Watson for Michelob," the operator said, "and John Higgenbotham for Budweiser."

"I'm Dick Heath, vice president and treasurer of the Heath candy company. May I speak with either of them?"

"Just a moment, please," the operator said and shortly came back on the line. "They're both in the same office. Just a moment, please, I'll ring."

John Watson answered and listened quietly while Dick told him all about what he'd done so far and why he was calling Anheuser-Busch. After a while he said, "Hold it, Dick, let me put this on conference so John Higgenbotham can hear this. Anybody who will put on a PGA tournament in Robinson, Illinois, and do their own television show has got to be nuts. But I want him to hear this."

Dick laughed, then spent the next ten minutes telling the men how the club got on the tour, about the television coverage and that he wanted Anheuser-Busch to buy 25 percent of the television advertising.

"Count us in," Watson said. "How could we turn anybody down who could pull off getting on the PGA tour and had the guts to put the TV package together?"

"Do you have the back page on your program sold?" Higgenbotham asked. "And what are your gold spots selling for?"

"The back page is gone," Dick said. "But I've got the inside front page open. And the gold sponsorships are five hundred dollars each."

"Okay. Bill us for the $16,675 for the TV spots, one thousand dollars for the inside cover and two thousand dollars for four gold spots."

It was Dick's turn to be quiet for a minute. This whole event was the culmination of a dream. The club was beautiful in all aspects. A PGA tournament was being held in Robinson. For a fleeting moment in time, the Crawford County Country Club was going to be the toast of the golf world. And Dick was the driving force behind it all.

"And Dick," Higgenbotham said, "will you sell our beer at the course?"

"You've got an exclusive on the beer. Which brand?"

This time there was silence on the other end. Dick could hear them talking in the background. Finally, Watson came on and said, "Make it Michelob. Gray Distributing in Lawrenceville will service you. And we'll be there for the tournament."

The whole conversation hadn't lasted more than twenty

minutes. Dick now had 75 percent of what he needed for television. The last 25 percent was going to be harder. He had contacted several companies and beat the bushes in Chicago trying to sell the last six spots. Everybody was interested, but the time was too short to fit the costs into depleted advertising budgets. Normally, what Dick was selling was done a year in advance.

It was getting late as far as selling the television spots were concerned. Things didn't look good. Dick mentioned this to Bayard Jr. when the two were talking in Dick's office one day.

"Why don't you try Milton Harrington of Liggett & Meyers?" Bayard Jr. asked. "Don't you remember we met him at the candy convention? He's into golf and might buy your remaining spots."

"I hadn't thought of him. I'll try him. He's got Arnold Palmer doing TV commercials for L&M cigarettes. Good idea."

After Bayard Jr. left the office, Dick put in another call as he had to Anheuser-Busch and as he had so many times before. Another operator, another secretary and finally Milton Harrington, the president of Liggett & Meyers, was on the phone talking with him. A few minutes of small talk later, Dick told him just what he had told them at Anheuser-Busch.

Harrington listened patiently. Then in a slow Southern drawl that belied his North Carolina upbringing, he said, "I'll tell you what, Dick. I'll buy the rest of your spots—that's no problem—if you'll let me play in the ProAm. I want to bring Andy Anderson, my executive vice president, with me, too. We'll buy the gold sponsorships."

"You've got it. We'd be pleased to have you and Mr. Anderson."

"Do you have the back page of your program sold?"

"Yes, but we have color inside ads."

"I'll take a page. Bill me for it all."

"You've got it."

"I have a couple of other things to ask you then. Can we land our Saberliner?"

"No, not in Robinson. You can land it in Terre Haute, though. That's an hour away. I can pick you up."

"Okay. Now another thing. I'm going to the Country Club of North Carolina this next week. Would you and some of your people like to meet me there for a day of golf?"

"Sounds good, but I'll have to get back to you on that," Dick said, knowing that he and his cousins would be there. "My two cousins might be interested."

Dick didn't remember a nicer telephone conversation than he had had with Milton Harrington. He had been more than cordial and his manners were impeccable. More importantly, Dick had his television network project together and paid for and was as thrilled as he could be. Most people had thought he was out of his mind to even attempt it. That had been part of the fun of it for him. And now he had pulled it off and would soon be off for a day of golf with one of America's richest men.

Earlier in the year, Dick had met on the golf course with the head of another company. Victor Gasket Company of Chicago had been looking for a site to build a new plant. The company had looked at Bloomington, Illinois, some place in Iowa and three other places and had Robinson on the list. Dick had found out that George Victor was a great amateur golfer with a one handicap and was due in Robinson the next morning.

"Bob," Dick said after he got Bob Machtley, the industrial

development manager for the area, on the phone, "when George Victor gets through with the people you want him to see, bring him to me and I'll sell him on coming to Robinson."

Machtley said okay, and Dick had a golf cart waiting for Victor the next morning at eleven a.m. and showed him around the club and Old Lake Village before teeing off.

"Everybody has basically got the same thing to offer you," Dick said out on the course as the two men headed down the first fairway after teeing off. "But they don't have a club like this for your people and accommodations for your out-of-town people. This is the place to be."

Victor agreed and later announced plans to build a five hundred-employee plant in Robinson. U.S. Senator Charles Percy later confirmed Dick's role in the Victor decision publicly at a rally in town. When Dick had someone in a golf cart where he had the person's undivided attention, he usually sold whatever it was he was selling.)

The Country Club of North Carolina, located near Durham and Liggett & Meyers' headquarters, was one of America's premier country clubs and had a challenging golf course. For a golfer, it was a treat to play there. Dick and Bob had gone to Bob-O-Link, a private men's club, as guests and played there several times in the early sixties. They thought the course was beautiful. But they thought this one in North Carolina was even more beautiful. Bayard Jr. agreed.

After finishing the round of golf with Harrington, a six handicapper in his early sixties, the three Heath cousins were sitting with their host in a guest house he had rented. They were still in golf attire and were drinking J&B scotch. That's all Harrington had brought. Bayard Jr. drank it anyway, but Bob usually drank Canadian Club and Dick drank vodka.

"Guess what I bought last week," Harrington said, sipping on his scotch and water.

"What did you buy, Milton?" Dick asked, expecting him to tell them about a car or something like that.

"I bought Paddington," he said as the three men looked at him, puzzled looks on their faces. "Got it for only a hundred and six."

They didn't know what Paddington was, but he had their attention when he said $106 million.

"Wrote a check out of our bank account."

"What's worth $106 million?" Bob asked.

"You're drinking it. We also own Alpo, Austin Nickols and Three-Minute Oats."

"They must love you spending all their money," Dick said.

"Yes, they really like that," Harrington said, putting his hand to his head and smoothing his white hair a bit.

24

With the new candy plant completed and fully operational, Jesse Texiera was busy trying various promotions for candy bars. Just before the Robinson Open and still thinking about the missed opportunity for company advertising in the tournament, Dick had joked with Texiera about "not promoting all the savings away" that the new plant would bring to the company.

"We need the sales to fill up the capacity of the plant," Texiera said.

"You're right about that," Dick said, thinking about mentioning the tournament advertising and deciding not to do it. No use in bringing something up that was over and done with. Anything said or done should be for the best interest of the company, he thought.

Handling of personnel was a case in point. People were constantly being moved around for the best interest of both the company and the people regardless of whether the department head favored the move. One of Dick's past secretaries, Patti Roads, had left the company to join his wife in a dress-shop venture called "The Barn" that the two women had started. Elizabeth Smith had replaced Patti. Then the job of office manager became available, and Bob wanted her for the job. She was a jewel, and Dick hated to lose her. But he shrugged his shoulders and let her go.

"I appreciate you letting me have Elizabeth," Bob said after the move was completed. "I know she'll do a great job."

Jim Hanlon, on the other hand, looked a bit frustrated in his position as marketing manager. A Notre Dame graduate, Hanlon had been hired in 1966 at Bob's insistence to be in charge of all marketing programs of all divisions. Dick thought the frustration was a result of Bob and Jesse Texiera being so dominating in their approach to management. Hanlon was a technician and more solid in his ideas than the men who were his bosses. It had always amused Dick how Hanlon, probably the most talented of the three in marketing strategy, ideas and implementation, wasn't being used to his fullest potential. But since Hanlon wasn't working for Dick, he wasn't about to cause problems by saying anything and went about his business.

Employees asked Dick about the tournament whenever they saw him at the plant. So did Bayard Jr. However, the rest of the family hardly said a word, even though all of them who were members of the club were on the committees. That didn't mean they would be much help.

But selling the family anything over the years had been difficult, much more difficult than selling friends. And selling anything to friends wasn't easy for Dick. He knew the membership pretty well now, though, and had been selling it something since 1962. Mort Imlay had been Dick's first and easiest sale of the gold sponsorships, buying one as soon as Dick had asked him to.

The whole Gold Sponsor package was a great promotional event and was key to raising the funds for the tournament. Dick was so busy with the whole package that he and Betty were eating dinner at the club almost seven days a week. After dinner, he sold Gold Sponsors and met with people vital to the success of the tournament. Maxine's husband, Carl Zwermann, donated eight thousand dollars to the club to pay for blacktopping the gravel parking lots. With these two major changes, the club was now ready for the PGA tournament in 1968. Later, other physical outside plans included a new swimming pool and a deck next to the 19th Hole. But for now, everything needed for the tournament was in place and ready. There wasn't a foot on the 150-acre complex, both inside and outside, that hadn't been touched to improve. And plans for the next six years included planting both large and small trees in appropriate places to make the club truly a showcase for Robinson and the Midwest.

It seemed that the more Dick did and wanted to do, the more Bob Heath fumed. Those who knew them both saw it clearly. Dick didn't know exactly why, but he knew the man he must have played two thousand rounds of golf with in their lifetimes and he were in competition off the course, too. The upcoming tournament brought the emotions more to the surface than ever before. But Dick was too busy to think much about them. It was tournament time.

The tournament was scheduled according to PGA requirements; the events were scheduled and ready after only four months of preparation. The course was staked and roped off, and the bleachers were up surrounding the eighteenth hole on three sides. Four television towers, including a special stairway to the anchor tower behind the seventeenth green for Senator Everett Dirksen to get to the TV platform, were up, and the circle drive in front of the clubhouse had the huge scoreboard in place. The press tent, the scoring tent and the registration were up and in operation. General Telephone had buried telephone cable around the entire course for the scorers to phone in each score on each hole to the communications trailer sitting north of tournament headquarters.

A TV van was parked below the new pro shop. Television cables ran to all the cameras now sitting on the towers, covered and ready for the final day. A large banner with the Robinson Open Television Network, Crawford County's newest and only network, displayed in foot-high letters was draped across the eighteenth hole tower that held the camera behind the eighteenth green.

Jack Chamblin's small farm opposite the third fairway was headquarters for the eighty tournament marshals. The 350 volunteers who had all paid for their red, white and blue uniforms had been prepared and knew what to do. A big gold Cadillac to be raffled off set in the circle of the driveway. And the club's slot machines were at the ready in the clubhouse to add to the revenue.

Robinson was about to become the toast of the golf world. The press would have to spend much time telling both national and international golfers where Robinson was located and where they would have to go to find lodging. Old Lake Village was needed for key tournament people, and Robinson only had a twenty-four-unit motel.

"I've never stayed in one state and played in another," one tour pro said about playing in Robinson and driving to Terre Haute, Indiana, to his motel.

With pros scattered everywhere, transportation was a major task. Volunteer drivers and cars were lined up to shuttle players back and forth. With all the trouble that would entail and hastily formed television coverage that would only break even, most people wouldn't have bothered.

But to Dick Heath, the tournament and the television coverage were symbols and proved something to him—that he could pull off something of this magnitude. And he wanted to show a large area of the club and let people see how great the community of Robinson, home of the Heath candy company, and its residents were.

That's the way it all looked on Tuesday afternoon, the day of the practice round for the pros, when Milton Harrington and Andy Anderson of Liggett & Meyers arrived from Terre Haute, where they had arrived in the company jet, along with the driver Dick had sent for them. The two men walked into tournament headquarters where Joe O'Rourk, producer of the TV coverage; Herb Kaplan, director; George Walsh, PGA field staff man; Maxine Zwermann; and Dick were holding a meeting.

"Good afternoon, gentlemen, and welcome to the Robinson Open," Dick said and introduced everybody.

Harrington wanted to play golf. The PGA officials permitted them to play an eighteen-hole practice round that afternoon, realizing the Liggett & Meyers was their second largest TV advertiser behind Anheuser-Busch. Both companies had long recognized the value of supporting professional golf with their advertising and were given special consideration by tournament and tour officials.

That night Dick and Betty hosted a cocktail party to introduce the Liggett & Meyers executives to the rest of the Heath family. Later, some of the family would accompany them to dinner at the club. Both men were gracious and charming. Harrington, however, was a bit too complimentary of Dick in front of the rest of the family to suit him.

"I don't think anyone in America," Harrington said to

Pete, Vernon, Bayard, Bob, Jack Morris and their wives, "has the talent anywhere to do what Dick has done with this tournament and club. It is a feat incomparable."

Dick appreciated the compliment but knew it was not what he needed. That was the last thing some of these Heaths wanted to hear. Harrington believed they were a family and were one for all and all for one. After tonight, Dick thought he would see that he had that wrong.

Bayard Jr. and Pat went to the club for dinner. Besides Dick and Betty, they were the only other family members to go. By the time the party of six got there, the club was jammed with professional golfers, press people and club members. After dinner, Harrington and Anderson joined the festivities and stayed long after the two Heath couples left. Dick had to meet Maxine at the club at five a.m. the next morning.

The next day the two Liggett & Meyers executives told Dick the night was the most fun they had had for a long time. They were staying at Old Lake Village with a few of the pros and other key tournament people and had stayed at the club partying until after one a.m. The two men had met many of the club members and were impressed, they said.

Harrington had originally planned to leave after Wednesday's ProAm round and fly back to New York for a board of director's meeting on Friday. On Wednesday morning, he cancelled the meeting and told Dick they now planned to stay until Friday morning. For the ProAm round, Harrington shot a seventy-five with his own ball, even though the tournament was a best-ball event.

Dick played the ProAm round with Illinois Governor Richard Ogilvie, PGA pro Bob Goably and Marathon Oil Company executive vice president Grant Young. The governor hit his ball left into the spectators on the first tee and got the round off to a good start. He stayed through dinner, enjoying himself and letting everyone know what a great event the Robinson Open had turned out to be.

While the governor was there, the slot machines had been put back in storage. With him present, there was no choice about what to do with them. The big party that night went on without them, and the ProAm prizes were presented.

Normally the pros leave the club when they complete their rounds and go back to their motel rooms to keep their concentration. This time they stayed around, to the surprise of the PGA officials, and mingled with the people. Many of them understood how difficult it was to stage a tournament at a small site like Robinson and wanted to help make it a success.

Dick's friends helped keep Harrington and Anderson happy at the 19th Hole Lounge throughout the evening. Since Liggett & Meyers owned Paddington, everybody was drinking J&B scotch. Dick even switched from smoking Viceroys to Larks.

The tournament got underway on Thursday morning. On Friday morning, Dick took Harrington and Anderson on a tour of the new candy plant. It was the world's most automated candy plant. Bayard had done a tremendous job completing it and getting it into operation. Both L&M men were greatly impressed.

On the way back to the country club, Harrington asked Dick if he was going to be in New York in the near future.

"I'll be there soon to meet with PGA officials to talk about next year's tournament," Dick said. "I don't know exactly when. Maybe a couple of weeks."

"Why don't you give me a call and let me know when you're coming?" he asked. "Let's get together."

"Sounds good to me. I'll give you a call when I find out for sure when I'm coming."

"Why don't you bring the company's financial statement with you, too?"

Dick looked quickly over at Harrington. In the past, many companies had wanted to talk to the Heath family about a merger. Vernon didn't want to talk to any of them. Bob, on the other hand, had been in Chicago and met with Bill Karnes, president of Beatrice, to explore the possibilities. Bob hadn't told anyone, but Dick heard about it, knew it as a fact and cared less. If anybody wanted to talk to them, he had no objections . He didn't think it hurt to talk to anybody.

By the same token, Dick knew that he would be criticized for meeting with Harrington and particularly for showing him the company financial statement. He also knew that he represented one of the three major interests in the company, equal to any other, that he was a director, elected in his own right, and that he was a vice president and treasurer of the company. Only Pete and Vernon equalled his status by the facts. And he knew further that he had the legal right and the moral obligation to do anything he considered to be in the best interest of the company. Bayard and Bob Heath weren't in the same position. Nor was Ruby Dowling or Mary Morris.

"I'll give you a call, Milton," Dick said, fully aware of the implications of Harrington's request, knowing Vernon's response but never thinking that anyone else, particularly the minor stockholders, would question his motives or actions. The latter would have irritated him.

On Saturday, the third round and the first day of the telecast, Senator Everett Dirksen arrived early in the afternoon. Dick took him to a room at Old Lake Village to brief him on what to say and what not to say when he was on the air. At his request, a bottle of gin was available in the room. While Dick and O'Rourk were briefing the senator, he was drinking gin and becoming highly entertaining. His flowery language was liberally sprinkled with expletives as he talked about President Lyndon Johnson, Chicago Mayor Richard Daley, Barry Goldwater and a variety of other current people and topics.

The minutes ticked off as anecdote after anecdote and comment after comment rolled off of his tongue. "The American people have been pissed on enough," Dirksen said after a tirade about how Congress handled its role with the war in Vietnam and the financial problems of New York City, "and one of these days they'll start kicking these assholes out of Congress."

"We're going to have to go," Dick finally said at 3:40 p.m. when the senator paused for breath. Senator Dirksen had to be in place by four p.m. for the one-hour telecast from the seventeenth hole tower. Dick had a golf cart for the two-minute ride around the lake, past the eighteenth hole and on to the tower where special steps had been built for the senator.

"Okay," Dirksen said, taking the last drink from the bottle of gin. "I don't want to stop and sign any autographs."

"That's fine because we have a time problem."

But when they reached the crowd, the spectators immediately spotted him in a Robinson Open cap and white hair flying. Everybody wanted to shake his hand. He complied as Dick slowed the golf cart to a crawl. It wasn't long before the senator was signing autographs, too.

Concerned about the time, Dick finally said, "I thought you weren't going to sign any autographs?"

"I wasn't," he said, "but I always make an exception for people who have loved ones in Vietnam."

It appeared to Dick that everybody must have had someone in Vietnam. Finally at 3:55 p.m., he got the senator to the top of the tower. He was loose and funny, doing it his way. In his distinctive voice and colorful language, he talked when the players were about to putt and then criticized their shots.

"That guy looks like he's never hit it off the beach before," Dirksen said gleefully as a golfer hit out of a sand trap. "He hit the sand farther than he did the ball."

Only the senator could get away with that, especially with the players. Even leader Dean Refram smiled when he was about to putt and Senator Dirksen was talking.

"How could anyone miss a putt that is only twenty feet from the cup?" Dirksen said, whispering in a voice that rasped but sounded like a fog horn as Refram sank a five-foot putt.

It was an unusual golf telecast. But it was a success. In fact, the whole tournament was a success in all respects. Dick didn't see how it could have gone off smoother. George Walsh, the PGA tournament supervisor, said the Robinson Open was as well done as any he had ever seen on the tour. Robinson and the country club had done themselves proud. Dean Refram had gone on to win the tournament and became the first Robinson Open winner with a course record nineteen under par, including a blazing sixty-five on the final round.

The morning after the tournament was over, Dick and Maxine were sitting in the tournament headquarters drinking coffee before starting to clean up. Everybody was gone. The course was empty. It was quiet.

"Finally, it's over," Maxine said. "I feel tired and let down."

"That's natural after what we've been through," Dick said.

"I guess. How much money did we make for the club? Do you know?"

"A whole lot. But I'm not sure yet. The prize money was thirty thousand dollars with the ProAm. I imagine we spent between ten thousand and fifteen thousand dollars for expenses. We probably got paid for a hundred Gold Sponsors. I had a lot of trade-offs for trees for the course, extra fertilizer and other things to help the club. That would give us seventy thousand dollars. We've got the Silver Sponsors' money, program profit, parking, ticket sales, concessions, which all our people ran with chits, and television money coming from the PGA. It's a big chunk to apply to that loan at American National on the club addition."

"I hope so with what everybody went through. Where do we go from here?"

"I don't know until I get back from New York."

"Did your friends from New York enjoy it?"

"Very much so. They wouldn't have stayed until Friday if they hadn't."

"I didn't see much of your family."

"No, but I didn't expect it."

"Don't they see the potential value for the Heath company in all this?"

"No, because they don't want to."

"That's sad."

While it was sad for the Heath company, many other companies in corporate America had realized the potential value of sponsoring golf tournaments quickly. These companies found the value to be one of the best promotional and advertising vehicles available. Practically every PGA tournament on the tour was grabbed up and sponsored by a company. The media gave these companies untold free advertising, public relations, customer relations, sales opportunities and general exposure.

All anyone had to do was look at the Kempers, Firestones, Kaisers, air lines, banks and other companies using the tournaments as marketing tools to realize the inherent value. No one knew it better than Milton Harrington and his advertising and marketing people.

Dick thought the golf tournament in Robinson could be the greatest marketing tool the Heath company could ever have. But Bob was in charge of sales, and he had gone to St. Louis for a sing-along. Dick was in charge of administration, and he knew the jealousies in the Heath family would prevent most family members from ever realizing the potential value of the tournament to the company because he had put it together.

After the tournament, little was said about it by any of the older members of the family with the exception of Bayard Sr. and Jack Morris Sr. Bernard Dowling, who had followed the tournament in the papers and watched it on television, said, "Congratulations, Dick. That was quite a feat." The younger Heaths, John and Allan, and Jack Jr. were also complimentary. Company people like Texiera, Fife and Hanlon knew the potential value of the tournament for the company. They just didn't say anything.

Bob didn't say anything, either. But it was obvious how he felt about the tournament and about Dick. Whenever the two happened to be together, on or off the course, Dick could see the same look on Bob's face that he had on the golf course when he was throwing clubs. Whatever negative things had happened between the two in the past had grown out of proportion. The spotlight on Dick from the tournament hadn't helped the relationship.

25

Two weeks after the 1968 Robinson Open, the Heath company pilot dropped Dick off early in the morning in Indianapolis. From there, he flew commercially to New York City to meet with PGA commissioner Joe Dey. The players were squabbling and nobody knew where the tour was headed. Arnold Palmer was heading a group to form another association. Before that happened, however, the problems were resolved and the tour went on under the auspices of the PGA.

Dick's schedule was tight. In addition to meeting with PGA officials, he had made an appointment with Milton Harrington at Liggett & Meyers at 1:30 p.m. After that, Dick was scheduled to catch a plane for Indianapolis at 6:30 p.m. and meet Woody Blaha for the return trip to Robinson to complete the fifteen-hour trip.

Just before noon, Dick walked into the national PGA headquarters and met with Dey and his people. The same date for the Robinson Open was available for next year, but the prize money would have to be at least seventy-five thousand dollars to remain a PGA tournament. That wasn't an insurmountable obstacle. Dick knew there had to be ways to raise the money. He had some ideas about how to solve the problem, save the tournament and benefit the club in a big way. Before making any commitments, however, he wanted to talk things over with Maxine and see how she would feel about his plan.

He thought she would like the idea, but he'd have to see.

After the meeting, Dick walked over to the Liggett & Meyers national headquarters at 630 Fifth Avenue for his 1:30 p.m. appointment with Milton Harrington. When the elevator stopped at the sixth floor, Dick walked directly into a large reception area with a lone receptionist seated behind a curved desk. She looked up from a paper she was reading.

"I'm Dick Heath," Dick said, flashing a grin and taking in the area in a sweeping glance. "I'm here to see Mr. Harrington."

"Just a minute, Mr. Heath," the woman said as she flipped a switch on the board to her right. "He's expecting you. I'll get his secretary."

Thirty seconds later, another woman walked through a wide, double door into the area. Dick had just lit a Lark cigarette and taken two drags from it. He looked around for an ashtray and put it out before the woman reached him. He was glad he switched from Viceroys, thinking it would have been rude of him to smoke any other brand here besides Chesterfield, L&M or Lark.

"Please come with me, Mr. Heath," the woman said and took him into a large suite located several feet behind her.

When he walked into the spacious office, his breath was almost taken away, he was so staggered by the size and decor of the office. He thought he had seen some outstanding offices while selling the ice cream bar to H.P. Hood Dairy, Sealtest, Borden, Foremost, Carnation, Meadow Gold and others. But he decided he hadn't seen anything that would ever come close in comparison.

It was like he was walking into someone's living room, not an office. He could see an executive desk near the window with New York skyscrapers as a backdrop and a view of

Central Park. Near the desk was a conference table with cushioned chairs around it. In the middle of the room was a living room suite, complete with a couch, coffee table and six plush, velvet-covered, soft-backed chairs.

The living room furniture was sitting on a large Oriental rug. Behind it to the left was a small bar and a door leading to a restroom. To the right were two doors, one leading to the board room, the other to a block of executive suites. Harrington's secretary's office was off through another door. Dick took a seat on the couch while the secretary knocked on the door of the board room and disappeared inside.

A few seconds later, the door opened and Harrington, Anderson and some other men walked out. "Hi, Dick," Harrington said, smiling and making the introductions. "I'm glad to see you again. You remember Andy. And this is Jim Moran, our financial officer."

"Glad to see you and Andy again, too," Dick said, nodded and shook hands with each man as Harrington introduced him. "Nice to meet you all. I like your home, Milton."

"We like it, too, Dick," Harrington said. "Let's go have a seat, relax a bit and have a drink. Tell me what you've been up to."

Dick told about his meeting with PGA officials. Everyone listened intently and asked questions. After the conversation turned to the Robinson tournament and what a good time it was, Harrington asked Dick if he had the company's financial statement. He handed him a copy of the latest one prepared by Heath's Indianapolis CPA firm. The statement showed a net worth of four million dollars and last year's earnings of $420,000.

Harrington glanced through it for a minute or two as they

continued to talk. Then he handed it to Moran, who started reading it in detail. Even though he was pouring over the statement, Dick didn't think the statement was very important to Harrington and his intentions. He'd made up his mind after he'd seen the candy plant in Robinson.

"We'd like to join hands with you, Dick," he said.

For the last year or two, the Heath company had been receiving letters and inquiries from Lipton tea, Quaker Oats, Beatrice Foods and other companies about merging. About a dozen large companies had expressed interest. None of the family had been interested.

"Like I told you in Robinson, Milton, I don't think the family would be interested. The family isn't willing to sell the company."

"I know, Dick, but it never hurts to listen to what someone has to offer you. Besides, how do you know what my offer is?"

With that, he started telling Dick about his company and its structure. Dick already knew quite a bit about the company, but he listened as Harrington spoke.

"This is the corporate office for all of the divisions," he said and ticked them off: "Cigarettes, liquor, dog food, rice and a couple of others."

The liquor division included J&B scotch, Wild Turkey bourbon and Austin Nichol wines; the dog food division included Alpo; and the rice division's main product was Three-Minute rice.

"Each division has its own board of directors, mans its own offices and runs its own show," Harrington said. "We support them with capital just like a bank. We have a mammoth computer in Durham, where our cigarette manufacturing operation is located, that handles the accounting for each division. Corporate headquarters just takes care of administration, advertising and financing."

By that time, Moran was over at the desk working with a spreadsheet. Harrington continued talking about the company and its marketing methods, explaining that he had a sales force of eight hundred company tobacco salesmen calling on the same buyers who purchase candy. With that kind of effort, Liggett & Meyers was 100 percent in the New York and New Jersey markets. The Heath company wasn't even in those markets because it wouldn't pay off two big jobbers.

After a while, Dick warmed up to the subject and began talking about the Heath company, its people and how it worked. Both Bayard Jr. and Dick had finished automating their respective divisions. The candy plant was running so smoothly that Bayard Jr. actually had little to do. The administration kept the company running well. Products were manufactured at the lowest possible cost. Jack Morris Sr. had always done a great job in buying and shipping. Even Bayard Sr., who would be critical of most anything, had always had high praise for Jack Sr.'s work.

Bayard Jr., Bob, Dick and Jack Sr. were paid a modest salary of twenty-seven thousand dollars annually. Pete and Vernon were paid thirty-six thousand dollars annually. So the executives weren't being overpaid for running the company. Of course, there were perks, but that went with the job. Individual family members had been using the company plane for their personal use from the day it was purchased. Everybody agreed that that was what it was for and included employees' use of the plane.

In the past, Dick had flown Jim Reedy to see Dr. Charles at Barnes Hospital in St. Louis. One of the candy plant employees, Naomi Cox, had also been flown to see him. The next time it was Joe Boker, one of the administrative people. He had been to a doctor in Robinson with a severe intestinal problem and was getting no better.

When Dick talked with Boker's wife, she told him her husband was lying on the couch and was too weak to do much else. Dick made arrangements for him to be flown to St. Louis on the company plane and went to the home to tell them to be at the plane by seven a.m. the next morning.

"We've always taken care of ourselves and our employees," Dick said. "They're like family."

"Nothing would change," Harrington said and spent the next hour telling Dick what Liggett & Meyers would do for everybody and what he would pay.

Dick kept saying the family wasn't interested. He could hardly believe that such a large corporation would be so interested in a small regional company that had 85 percent of its sales in five-cent toffee bars, ten-cent ice cream bars and Pepsi Colas. The volume of individual unit sales were at the peak of the company history, but the unit price was so low.

After all the talking, Harrington asked Dick to look at Liggett & Meyers' financial statement. Fabulous was the only word he could think of to describe it as he scanned the pages. He could see nothing but a tremendous growth of earnings in a corporation that was solidly capitalized and still very liquid. There was little debt. The company was paying good dividends, the stock was stable at a moderate price and the price-to-earnings ratio was above average. Liggett & Meyers couldn't be more stable.

"We could just exchange our Liggett & Meyers stock in our safety deposit box for Heath stock," Harrington said. "It would be a tax-free exchange."

While Dick was digesting all the information he had heard in the last hour, Harrington asked to be excused while he and Jim Moran went into the board room. Anderson fixed them each another J&B scotch. Dick and he continued talking and sipping their drinks. After about fifteen minutes, Harrington and Moran came back in, sat down and handed Dick the Heath company financial statement.

At this point, Harrington began shooting figures at Dick and telling him what Liggett & Meyers would do for Heath. Dick kept saying no, not to be coy or to drive a hard bargain, but because he truly didn't think the family would be interested. Harrington kept talking and upping the ante, telling Dick what a tough negotiator he was in this case.

"That really has nothing to do with it, Milton," Dick said, taking another sip of the scotch as what Harrington was saying was sinking in. "The family really doesn't want to sell. My father and my uncle started a little store on the Square in Robinson that has grown into something we're all proud of and want to keep."

"Your family can stay with the company," Harrington said, explaining that he wanted the Heath company to be the flagship company of Liggett & Meyers' confectionery division and thought it would be the largest single division of the company. It would be headquartered in Robinson and headed by a congenial Heath family.

What Harrington and the Liggett & Meyers people were concerned about was the long-range growth and earnings potential in the tobacco industry brought about by the surgeon general's warning about the health hazards of smoking. The company wanted to continue to diversify with hugh cash reserves and had plans to expand into the confectionery field.

Dick understood that Harrington wanted to buy the Heath company and build a huge office complex east of the new candy plant to get those plans in operation.

All the other manufacturing facilities would be built on the ground south of the present Heath property across the railroad tracks. In the first year, Harrington wanted to buy at least three other candy companies. As these and other companies were purchased and their manufacturing plants became obsolete, new plants would be built in Robinson. Then as soon as the new office complex was finished, all of the companies' sales, marketing and administrative functions would be moved to Robinson.

"How much of an investment do you want to make?" Dick asked, trying to get a handle on the magnitude of what he was hearing.

"It's unlimited. As long as you can justify the price with the return, there is no limit of funds."

"Even a billion dollars?" Dick asked, jokingly.

"Even a billion dollars, Dick," Harrington said.

Dick was stunned. He could barely believe the figures he had been hearing for the company. In fact, even though he'd heard it, he didn't believe it. Now he didn't know what to think.

"We could be talking about four thousand blue-collar jobs," Dick said hoarsely, "and many white-collar jobs."

"At least," Harrington said, smiling. "I want you to buy at least ten companies in the next few years. But it's not limited to just that. We can buy Marzetti salad dressing and Scribner Kent now. They are like Nabisco in England, only smaller. It's you and your family's ballgame, too."

Looking at Liggett & Meyers' financial statement, Dick

could see that it could borrow all the cash it would ever need. He knew people had no idea about how much money the tobacco companies had. But Harrington wanted to take Liggett & Meyers in another direction: He wanted the Heath company to be a part of it, too, and money was no object.

"Dick," Harrington said, taking a sip of his scotch and looking over his glass, "I'm going to give you my final offer. If you take it, it might get me fired."

"Don't get fired," Dick said weakly, thinking about the company's value while he waited for the offer. Net earnings in 1967 were a little more than $400,000 after taxes. The net worth of the balance sheet was $4.2 million. Compared to Liggett & Meyers on the New York Stock Exchange, the Heath company was worth, tops, six million dollars. Noel Cord of the company's Indianapolis CPA firm had valued it at seven million dollars.

"I'll exchange 900,000 shares of L&M stock, which is selling on the New York Stock Exchange at $27 a share, for the 10,675 of Heath stock," Harrington said evenly. "Our stock is paying dividends of $1.25 a share. For each share of Heath stock, we'll give you about 85 shares of L&M stock. On a comparative basis, our stock would be paying a dividend of $105.39 a share compared to $6 per share for Heath stock.

That was so astronomical Dick couldn't believe it. It was between seventeen and eighteen times more return on dividends and a little more than twenty-four million dollars of marketable Liggett & Meyers stock.

"That would be a tax-free exchange of $24,300,000 worth of Liggett & Meyers stock," Harrington said, "or about sixty times your annual earnings."

"What if they don't want the stock?" Dick asked.

"Okay, here's what I will do on a cash deal: Liggett & Meyers will buy the stock for $16.4 million, give your stockholders the first five years of Heath company earnings and give them two-thirds of the earnings the first five years for any company you acquire for us."

The more Harrington talked, the more Dick just sat there hardly saying a word. He didn't know what to say. But Harrington wasn't through yet. The two elder Heaths, Pete and Vernon, would get lifetime contracts for fifty thousand dollars a year.

"You name the contract time and amount of salary for you and the rest of your officers."

"That $50,000 sounds good," Dick said, thinking that it would nearly double the salary they were now receiving. "What about Jack Morris Jr. and Allan? They're making $10,000 now. Can they go to $25,000?"

"No problem. And you can all have employment contracts guaranteeing it."

"Okay, Milton," Dick said, still considering the whole offer absolutely unbelievable but warming to the idea. "Could I have your word that you'd throw in a million dollars worth of stock for our key employees or a half a million cash if the deal goes through?"

"You have it."

"Let's have another drink then," Dick said, thinking he really needed one. Hell, I would fire Harrington if I owned his company, he thought.

But Dick began thinking about the complete picture. What Moran had done was take the Heath figures and make the savings that made the offer not only possible but feasible. For example, the Heath company was paying 5 percent commission on candy sales. Liggett & Meyers had eight hundred salesmen, all on salary, out in the market place calling on many of the same accounts buying Heath products. The Heath products could be added, saving the 5 percent and increasing sales dramatically at the same time.

On freight, Liggett & Meyers owned its own warehouses and could combine Heath sales with cigarettes. The company's freight cost about 8.8 percent of the sales dollar the way it had to ship. By confining orders and using the Liggett & Meyers warehouses, the freight cost would drop to about 3.8 percent or a savings of another 5 percent.

Another 2 percent or 3 percent of the sales dollar could be added from computer savings. All together the initial savings amounted to some 12 percent of the sales dollar right off the top and immediately.

And those figures didn't include what Liggett & Meyers could do for Heath sales by getting the product into the New York-New Jersey markets. Nor did it include the effects Harrington had mentioned of cutting the company's one-minute TV spots for cigarettes to thirty-second spots and advertising the Heath English Toffee Bar on thirty-second spots at no increase in expense.

Dick was amazed at the possibilities and thought the offer was "a marriage made in heaven." Harrington still thought Dick was negotiating, although he never had been. The proposal was so far out of sight, that he thought even the Heaths would be staggered. How was anybody going to turn down the offer? People enter into business to make money, and this was the ultimate way to do it.

Dick told Harrington he'd be back in touch.

The next morning when Dick got to the office, he was still

stunned. A few minutes after he got there, Bayard Jr. came in and sat down.

"How're Uncle Milton and Andy?"

"They've lost their minds."

Dick told Bayard Jr. that he was going to drop in and see them when he was in New York. And Dick had asked him, as a lawyer, if he could show them the Heath company financial statement. Bayard Jr. had assured him he could.

"He offered us everything but his golf clubs," Dick said, "and I think he'd have thrown those in, too, if we want them."

Bayard Jr. went around the corner and told Jack Morris Sr. to come in. They both sat there for nearly a half an hour as Dick related the entire conversation. Both were skeptical and didn't seem to believe him.

"How the hell could I make something like this up?" Dick asked.

"Was he drunk?" Bayard Jr. asked.

"No. He was sober, and that's what he said."

"My God, Dick, I just can't believe that," Jack Sr. said, obviously bewildered. "Can you really believe it?"

"I don't know. But I'll be talking to him. I must have it all wrong, or there is something I've been missing."

"He would double the size of Robinson," Bayard Jr. said. "It would be like Hershey, Pennsylvania. The governor would go nuts."

"I'm about to that point," Dick said. "Right now I would believe it only in writing. I can't tell the rest of the family something I've had a hard time believing myself. They wouldn't believe me anyway. So I'll only tell them if I see it in writing."

"What are you going to do now?" Bayard Jr. asked.

"Let's go play golf. Maybe I'll wake up tomorrow."

"I can't today. You'll have to play by yourself."

After they left his office, Dick called Noel Cord, the company's accountant in Indianapolis, and asked what he thought the company was worth at the very top price.

"It hasn't changed since I told you a few days ago," Cord said. "Still seven million dollars. Why? That guy in New York want to buy it?"

"Yeah, he wants to buy it, and he's willing to pay a lot more than you say it's worth."

"It'd take a lot of nickel Heath bars to pay for it, even if he pays what it's worth."

"That's what I told him. I told him he'd better think about all this. Oh, well. Thanks."

Dick put the phone back in the cradle and sat quietly for a few minutes before heading out to the country club. He found Maxine in the tournament headquarters. By now, most everything had been cleaned up.

"How was your trip?" she asked.

"Fine," he said, and began explaining his meeting with PGA officials, the prize money, the guarantee—everything.

"That would do the club in," she said when he was finished. "It couldn't do that, could it?"

"Probably not. But you and I could," Dick said and explained his plan. "We would form a corporation and be the sponsor. We would give the club so much out of each ticket, sponsor, concessions, etc., for the volunteers who work on the tournament. That would go to pay off the American National Bank. I haven't got it all worked out yet. Possibly, I'll bring Mother into it. Whatever, I'd like to see the club get thirty to thirty-five thousand dollars out of it—which is more than fair. We may even have to get a sponsor. But we've got to do the tournament. I wouldn't want to do a TV show again, though. It's just too much work. So how does that sound?"

"Sounds interesting to me," she said. "And I think the club would like to insure a profit at no risk. Let me know when you get the details worked out and what it will take. I'm certainly interested in being a part of it. Right now let's get this year's tournament wrapped up. Look at all the mail we've been getting."

Dick grinned. He knew Maxine liked putting on the tournament as much as he did. And he knew he was fortunate to have somebody like her to depend on. She could turn out more work and get more done than anybody he'd ever seen.

26

The three oldest major Heath family interests, besides L.S., were the Bayard E. Heath Sr., the Everett E.Heath and the Virgil D. Heath families. Bayard Sr. and Skiv, of course, started the Heath Brothers store where the Heath candy bar was born. They were there in two businesses when L.S. bought the Model Ice Cream plant in 1915 and brought Pete into the business.

Because of their father's wishes and only in acquiescing to his paternal wishes were Vernon, Ruby and Mary even in the business—Vernon twenty years later and the two women more than thirty years later. L.S. was the kind of father who would normally divide his interest evenly among all his children. But when the company incorporated in 1946, he was given an extra eight hundred shares of company stock, with the approval of Bayard Sr., Skiv and Pete, so he in turn could give it to his daughters. When he realized the inequity, he gave half of the shares back to his four sons' children as a "gift" from him. The gifts, however, were really out of the shares the sons had given him in exchange from the partnership to the corporation.

Even with the Bayard Sr. and Pat Keisling buy-back in the early sixties, Bayard Jr., the Skiv Heath family and the Pete Heath family had 5,375 shares of company stock against the Vernon Heath family, the Ruby Dowling family and the Mary

Morris family 5,300-share interest. The control of the company, therefore, was with Bayard Jr., Bob and Dick.

That was the reason why the three cousins could develop the ice cream bar and the fund-raising division, and that was the reason why they could get rid of the yoke of the dairy, build the plant, put in the accounting system and direct the company to where it was, even though they had Vernon and John and Allan Heath, Jack Morris Jr. and Bernard and Ruby Dowling (all of whom had either little education beyond high school, experience, capability or business knowledge but were family) with which to contend.

But as Dick saw it, as long as the three cousins stayed together, all the families would remain in business, and the company would prosper with growth and earnings. The ice cream bar and the automated new candy plant would insure that.

Then when Bob and Dick's relationship had changed, Dick thought the family being together in the business was ultimately going to be history. He knew how much the other three branches of the family disliked Bob. Although it wasn't his intention when starting a family business, L.S. had created a monster, and his sons had allowed him to do it.

Dick saw in the Liggett & Meyers offer the only way the family could survive in its own company and salvage the business. Not only would each family have a great deal of wealth, he believed, but the entire family would have many things which were as important:

First, the Liggett & Meyers offer would pay back the key people in the company to whom so much was owed. The company would not have been successful without them;

Second, the people of Robinson and the friends with

whom family members had lived among for years would prosper as jobs were created and the community grew;

Third, and the most important thing to L.S.'s legacy, the family members who wanted them would have positions available to them for generations;

Fourth, a market for the stock would be established so when someone within the family died, the heirs could pay the huge inheritance taxes by selling some stock at true market value;

And fifth, everybody would share in the success.

So Dick had no doubt that the Liggett & Meyers offer could give the Heath family everything it had now and much more. Liggett & Meyers was a unique company, providing banking and assistance to its divisions. The company didn't have the personnel to run its companies and was buying management.

And Dick wanted his family members to see the offer in writing. He was working to get it all wrapped up so he could show it to them. It was to be finished and available after the first of the year. As Christmas approached, the offer and its ramifications were on his mind.

He knew Jack Jr. was unhappy and frustrated with his job and ten thousand-dollar annual salary. At the time, Jack Jr. was supposed to be working for Jesse Texiera, Bob's sales manager, but wasn't doing much.

On Monday morning, December 23, Jack Jr. went to Dick's office and said he was thinking about leaving the company. Dick felt he was serious and had been close enough to him to take him into his confidence.

"Look," Dick said, concerned enough about him to tell him a little about the upcoming Liggett & Meyers deal and what it would do for him, "just take it easy. Sit tight. There is something coming down that will really help you."

"What is it?"

Dick hesitated. He didn't want to tell Jack Jr. about the offer and the twenty-five thousand-dollar salary in it for him. But he thought it would keep his younger cousin around for better times.

"Well, I guess I can tell you," Dick said. "Liggett & Meyers is going to make the family a fabulous offer, so just cool it for a while. You'll be taken care of pretty well."

At this point, Dick just wanted him to hang on and wait for the written offer from Liggett & Meyers to legitimize and support Harrington's verbal offer before he up and left the company. The last thing Dick thought about was that Jack Jr. would tell Texiera. He wasn't even family. But Jack Jr. went directly to his sales manager and told him what was in the works. Obviously, Dick was going to tell everyone after all the specifics had been worked out and he had a written offer.

Texiera obviously knew this, too. Yet he also knew Bob Heath almost as well as Dick did and knew Bob's temper and how he would react to the information. Further, Texiera knew exactly how the stock set because he and Dick had talked about it. And even though Texiera was closer to Bayard Jr. than he was to Bob, he undoubtedly could see what might happen. If Texiera could break the relationship between Bob and Dick once and for all, interesting possibilities existed for Jesse Texiera and the future of the company.

"I'd tell Bob about this if I were you, Jack," Texiera said after listening quietly to the story. "It's something he'd want to know. And he should know."

Jack Jr. went directly to Bob's office and told him what

Dick had said about the Liggett & Meyers offer. Because of Bob's talks with Beatrice Foods or for whatever reason, he was enraged with what his young cousin told him. To say that Bob had a temper tantrum wouldn't do justice to his actions.

"Why, that son-of-a-bitch," Bob said, yelling and storming out of his office. "I'll show him he can't run this fucking company."

The first person he ran into was Don Roads, the comptroller of the company and hired by the authority of the board of directors. Bob, a vice president in charge of sales with 375 shares of the company who couldn't elect himself to the board, was ranting and raving about the Liggett & Meyers deal and something about improprieties found in an audit. Roads didn't have a clue as to what was causing the rage.

"You're fired," Bob said, shouting loudly as his face reddened deeply. "Get your office cleared out and be out of here by noon."

When Roads came to Dick and told him what had happened, Dick told him to ignore the firing because Bob had no more authority to fire him than Dick would to go over to the sales division and fire Jesse Texiera or Ross Fife, both of whom also had been hired by the authority of the board. As a lawyer and the secretary of the board, Bayard Jr. confirmed that position with Dick.

"Robert has fired his putter down the fairway again," Dick said, "this time hitting a stranger not even involved in the game."

Dick's first impulse was to go in and knock him right out of his chair, thinking it was what Pete should have done long ago. His second impulse was to fire Texiera. His third impulse was to do neither. He knew the company and the employees had had enough of Bob's running around like a spoiled kid and didn't intend to act that way himself.

His next impulse, one he decided to act upon, was to immediately call Milton Harrington and simply tell him what had happened. After doing that quickly, Dick told him that if he was serious about the offer and wanted to make one to get it out before the end of the day and to send it to everybody's post office box because Christmas was just two days away.

It was 10:30 a.m. Central Standard Time and 11:30 a.m. in New York. Harrington was sorry to hear about Bob's reaction but said he would call a meeting of the executive committee of the board of directors immediately and get the offer out by nightfall.

Dick decided to wait until the offer was in everybody's hands before saying anything else. He told Don Roads to go ahead and do his work. Roads refused.

"I've had enough of him," he said. "I want out of this place."

Shrugging, Dick told him he knew how he felt. So all Dick could do was wait for the offer to arrive and see what happened. He couldn't even guess about that but knew everything would come to a head soon. Vernon was leaving on December 26 for the Rose Bowl game in southern California and would be gone until the first week in January. Dick would see him Thursday after the offer arrived.

The cash offer that Dick had asked Harrington to prepare arrived on Christmas Day. On Thursday morning, Bayard Jr. and Dick found letters on their desk from Pete, who was now chairman of the board, advising them that they had been put on a leave of absence from the company until further notice by the board of directors of L.S. Heath & Sons, Inc.

Bayard Jr. started laughing and called Jack Morris Sr. from the office next door. "Come and read this stupid letter."

"What board put the executive vice president and secretary and the vice president and treasurer on a leave of absence?" Jack Sr. asked after he had finished reading the letter.

Bayard Jr. asked Jack Sr. if he'd been to a meeting. Jack Sr. said he hadn't even heard of one, let alone attended one. Both men asked Dick. He shook his head and laughed. Ruby had been in Mexico at the time. Out of the eight directors, the three men knew that four definitely weren't at the meeting and had received no notice of a meeting.

"I'm going to play golf," Bayard Jr. said, laughed and shook his head. "I guess Bob, Pete, Vernon and John decided to have their own board meeting."

Which is exactly what had happened. After hearing about the Liggett & Meyers offer, Bob called a meeting of his father, uncle, cousin and himself without proper notice and conducted business with four directors who represented less than 50 percent of the outstanding stock and without a quorum. Bob was angry. He wanted Bayard Jr. and Dick out of the way, so he put them on leaves of absence. As was often the case with Bob, his temper overruled his logic.

In that frame of mind, he got his father to sign papers he didn't want to sign to put Bayard Jr. and Dick on leaves and to take part in decisions he didn't want to make. Then after Vernon went to California, ignoring his legal and fiduciary responsibilities to the stockholders, Pete hit the bottle, ignoring his responsibilities, too.

While Pete, Vernon and John weren't highly educated on corporate affairs, Bob knew what a board could and couldn't do and how to go about doing things. He also knew what he was doing and knew that it would never stand up in a legal sense.

So Dick wondered why he did it. Obviously he was having a temper tantrum, but he had to know something else. He knew Bayard Jr.'s and Dick's reaction to what he had done. With that insane move, Dick believed his cousin thought he had the chance to grab the power he wanted. He knew Bayard Jr. and Jack Morris Sr. knew about the Liggett & Meyers offer. And although he knew neither was involved, he put Bayard Jr. on a leave of absence but not Jack Sr. because he didn't want to offend Mary right then. Bob got Pete to sign something Vernon wouldn't. But then Bob could make Pete jump out the window if he wanted him to.

What an incredible family, what an incredible letter, Dick thought as he picked it up and read aloud: "'The Board of Directors of L.S. Heath & Sons, Inc., hereby puts Bayard E. Heath Jr. and Richard J. Heath on a leave of absence until January 3, 1969.' Signed, 'Virgil D. Heath, Chairman of the Board.' Old Santa Claus was busy last night, Hogan. He must not have missed the meeting by much when he brought these letters by."

"It's a joke, Dick," Bayard Jr. said. "It's not legal for another thing. It specifically states in our bylaws exactly what the board of directors has to do to place an officer on leave of absence. This is garbage."

"The silly son-of-a-bitch," Dick said, "using his drunken dad to sign this and putting us on leaves of absence is the stupidest thing he's done yet. He could lose the house on this one."

"Great," Bayard Jr. said. "Let's go play golf. The weather is great."

And the weather was great. It was a balmy sixty degrees on a sunny day. But Dick couldn't keep his mind on the game and went back to his office. What had been on his mind and started him thinking was that he and Vernon were the only two officers authorized to sign checks. Vernon would be gone. With himself on a leave of absence, Dick wondered who was going to sign the payroll and accounts payable checks.

He decided to sign the payroll checks because he didn't want Heath employees to be inconvenienced while "Bob was acting like a kid." As for the accounts payable, Dick knew they could wait.

Bob decided they couldn't wait. He called Verdi Mitchell, Dick's cashier, the day after Christmas and told her he wanted to sign the accounts payable checks. That was more than $500,000 worth of checks that Dick normally signed.

Mitchell had been with the Heath company longer than just about anybody. She had worked for Bayard Sr. and Skiv before they had moved out to the Jackson Street address. She couldn't believe what Bob was doing but knew his temper and way of doing things. She put the stack of checks in front of Dick that Bob had asked her to bring to him.

"Bob wants me to bring these to him to sign," Mitchell said. "You usually sign them."

Dick automatically started to sign the first check but stopped. The checks were made out on the Second National Bank account in Robinson. If Bob signed the checks, Dick thought there could be about six charges against his cousin. And perhaps the bank would honor the checks. If that happened, Dick knew he could have some fun with the people around there—$521,000 worth of fun.

"Verdi," Dick said, thinking that Bob still would be angry

enough to sign the checks, "take them to him like he told you. I want him to sign them. I also want you to know I've had enough of our employees being put in the middle by him. I'm sorry for that. I don't want you in the middle of a building family cat fight."

"He's not on the signature card," Mitchell said.

"I know that. Just put them on his desk."

Mitchell wanted to hold them. But Dick wanted Bob to sign the checks and told her they'd also lose all of the 2 percent discounts on accounts paid in ten days and thirty days to pay the full invoice if the bills weren't paid.

To let things cool down and not make things worse than they already were, Bayard Jr. and Dick decided not to do anything until Vernon got back from the Rose Bowl on Monday, January 3, 1969, more than a week away.

Meanwhile, Bob signed the checks and the Second National Bank of Robinson honored them. The whole town knew what was taking place. The board room was now the country club and the Square in Robinson. Every employee in the building was aware of every move that was made.

Bob was burning bridges all over the place with the employees and knew that Bayard and Dick wouldn't tolerate that. If the company wasn't sold to Liggett & Meyers, then they wouldn't want to put up with the family any longer. Texiera was just sitting back, watching everything unfold. Dick learned that Jack Jr. had told Texiera and Bob about the Liggett & Meyers offer and went looking for Jack Jr. Dick was irritated about what had happened as a result, but he knew Jack Jr. was young and was being used by Texiera. Dick doubted that his young cousin knew what he had done. And while it wasn't something that Dick could prove, he thought that somehow Mary was involved and had something in mind. He knew she could always add and was conniving enough.

When Vernon got back to Robinson after the Rose Bowl, Dick went to see him in his office and took the letter from Bob that put him on the leave of absence.

"I didn't sign that," Vernon said. "Pete did."

"I'm not here to talk about that. I want to talk about this fabulous offer. When are we going to have a meeting to discuss it?"

"The family is against it."

"Oh, you've had another meeting?"

"Mary said she is against it," Vernon said. "So is Ruby and Pete and Bob. I'm against it, too."

"Why? How can you be against something like this?"

"Because I could never go into the First Methodist Church," Vernon said, trembling slightly and looking under the desk at his shoes. "What would my friends at the church think of us getting involved with a cigarette and liquor company? Knowing that we're a part of something like that, they would never let me in the door."

"That's your reason?"

"Yes."

"Give the church a million dollars and see what they say."

Before Vernon could say anything, Dick picked up the phone from his uncle's desk and dialed Milton Harrington's private number. After saying hello and telling him that he was in Vernon's office, Dick said, "Milton, would you throw a million dollars in the deal for Vernon to give the Methodist church here in Robinson? He thinks he'll be kicked out of the church for selling out to a company that sells cigarettes and liquor. So I wanted to ask you straight out."

"Sure, Dick," Harrington said and chuckled, "we could do that."

"You will? Okay, you tell him directly."

"Sure."

Dick handed Vernon the phone. Harrington told him the money could come from Liggett & Meyers on behalf of Vernon, or he would just give the money to him and he could give it to the church or whomever he wanted. Vernon was visably shaken by the offer but was still saying no when he hung up the phone.

"Look at all the good that million dollars could do for any charity," Dick said. "Just give the money to the church and see what your friends say. It would pay for their retirement home in Lawrenceville."

Vernon still said no, mumbling more about the money coming from a cigarette and liquor company. But Dick thought he knew the real reason. Vernon didn't want to expose John and Allan to the world, and it was as simple as that. They weren't the only ones in his family Vernon was concerned about, either. Dick knew you could put Vernon at the top of the list.

Back in his office, Dick rolled the situation around in his mind. He knew Vernon and Bob didn't want the family together at a board or stockholders meeting because they were afraid he might persuade them to take the offer. Another thing he knew was that Vernon and Bob probably had forgotten Bayard Jr. had given Heath stock to his two minor sons.

That there were minor stockholders would make a differ-ence because a corporation is an entity created under the watchful eyes of the state, Dick thought as the situation churned through his mind. And a corporation has rules and laws about how it is to operate. The owners of a corporation are the stockholders who own shares of stock and represent a portion of the ownership. The purpose of the corporation is to make the most money for the stockholders, whether they have large or small amounts of stock.

The stockholders elect a board of directors who have the responsibilities to them to make decisions in their best interests. Their best interests are for the company to make the best return on their investment. And the directors elect the officers who are paid to fulfill that aim. A corporation is not for the whims or personal ambitions of anyone. Jealousy, self-serving and personal interests are only for the people who own their own businesses.

And when corporate officers turn down good, sound, legitimate offers based on personal whims and ambitions while committing illegal acts, all sorts of legal problems arise. Dick felt there was no justification for refusing the offer, but he also knew that approaching the problem from that angle would be a long, drawn-out and messy affair. If he could avoid that route, he would. It wasn't his style.

His style was to go for the kill. And looking at it from that perspective, Dick knew the Liggett & Meyers offer could be made so the family would go for it. He picked up the phone and dialed New York City again. Harrington was somewhat surprised and shocked by what was happening within the family.

"Milton," Dick said, "if you want to buy the Heath company, bring a Brinks truck with twenty million dollars in one hundred-dollar bills and unload it in the board room."

"Do what? I don't think I heard you right."

"You heard right."

"You're not serious, Dick."

"Yes, I'm serious. If you stacked these bills on the board room table, the family couldn't see each other across it. Bring a small piece of paper that reads, 'I will sell my shares of stock in L.S. Heath & Sons, 'Inc., to Liggett & Meyers for my percentage of the cut on the table.' Leave a space for their signatures. You bring that, and I'll supply the pens and the family."

"You are serious, aren't you?"

"Yes, I'm serious. I know this family. You'll own the family if you'll do this."

As it was, Ruby was going to do as Mary wanted her to do. Ruby said her bank advised her not to sell. Dick didn't know about that. But he did know that if the Continental Illinois Bank officials did say it, it would have to be because they were afraid that the Chase Bank in New York would get her trust account. He saw no way they could look at it any other way with the magnitude of the offer and especially if the Liggett & Meyers stock was involved.

Dick thought Pete would have taken the offer in a second if he could have voted his convictions and later told Dick as much. Pete's vote was controlled or greatly influenced by his son's long-held ambition to be president of the company. Because of his ambitions, Bob had the most to lose by rejecting the offer. But his temper and bad judgment blinded him regarding the possibilities of what could happen either way and what Dick considered the ulterior motives of Texiera and Mary Morris.

With the kind of money or stock involved in the offer, Mary was a baffling case for Dick to figure out. In cash, she would be getting $1.5 million plus the five-year percentages;

in L&M stock, she would be getting $3.3 million and $125,000 in dividends. And since he couldn't figure it out, Dick thought there was something wrong that wasn't discernible.

Bayard Jr. and Jack Morris Sr. couldn't believe the offer was being rejected either. The three of them examined each person's motives and waited. They didn't think Pete, Vernon, Bob and John realized how vulnerable they had left themselves with their methods. Neither a shareholders meeting nor a board of directors meeting had yet been called to legally decide upon the offer. Bayard Jr. and Dick both knew that and watched closely. Bayard Jr. was astounded at Bob's lack of corporate know-how. The rest of the family was easy to understand in that regard. But not Bob.

So while the offer remained on the table, a couple of months passed with no one doing anything. Vernon simply thought it was just another family squabble, and everything would be back to normal before long.

While the situation dragged on, Dick attended to and finished other company business. Prior to the Liggett & Meyers offer, the company had been negotiating with Harry L. Crisp of Marion, Illinois, for the sale of the Heath Pepsi Cola franchise. The company needed the building for extra candy storage and had been working on the deal for some time. Dick had gone to Marion and closed the sale of $700,000 cash for the franchise, vendors, trucks, cases and bottles before Christmas. Final details were concluded, and the bottling division went the way of the dairy division.

27

While the Heath family was involved in the turmoil brought on by the Liggett & Meyers offer, the city of Robinson had another problem. A HUD grant of $300,000 was available to build a community center in Robinson. Community leaders thought the center was badly needed. To qualify for the grant, the city of Robinson would have to put up one-third of the funds needed and then HUD would put up two-thirds. Twice a referendum to raise the money from the taxpayers had been brought to a vote, and twice the referendum was narrowly defeated.

With a week left before the city would lose the grant, the city fathers called a meeting at the courthouse for Friday afternoon and asked Vernon and Dick Heath to attend. One of the community leaders who had insisted on calling the meeting was Kent Lewis, editor and publisher of the *Robinson Daily News*. He wanted to make a final stab at raising the funds rather than losing them without making an effort.

Lewis had called the various business leaders to the meeting in the courthouse at one p.m. and had personally asked Dick to attend. The room was packed. Vernon was there. So was Bayard Sr. After Lewis called the meeting to order, he looked quietly out over the crowd for a few seconds.

"You all know the tax referendum was voted down twice," he said. "However, there are many citizens of this community who want the community center. And we need it. But one week from today the HUD grant of nearly $300,000 will go to Effingham. If we don't come up with $150,000 in a week, it's gone. I know of only one man who can possibly raise $150,000 in a week. And he's in this room right now. I've asked him to try."

Everybody looked around the room as Lewis paused. He waited until the audience looked back at him.

"That man is Dick Heath," Lewis said and heads swung around to look at Dick. "How about it, Dick?"

"Well, I've got a little time on my hands," Dick said, a bit surprised because Lewis hadn't said a word to him about raising money when he'd invited him to the meeting.

Quite a few people laughed because everybody in town knew what was going on at the Heath company. Dick got up and walked to the front of the room, thinking of what he was going to say and how to raise the money as he went. By the time he reached Lewis, Dick had a pretty good idea of how he was going to get the job done.

"With your help, I'll do it," Dick said. "The money will be raised. So plan to have a bonfire on the site Thursday afternoon to celebrate."

That brought a nervous sort of laughter from the audience. Several people gave him an are-you-crazy look. Lewis chuckled and asked him how many volunteers he wanted.

"Five ought to do it," Dick said and selected five members of the audience. "I'd like for you all to meet me at Frank's lumber yard at nine o'clock in the morning. And I'd like Joe King and Wayne Morrow to wait and see me after the meeting today."

King and Morrow were, respectively, presidents of the

two Robinson banks, the Second National Bank of Robinson and the Crawford County State Bank. Both men nodded, acknowledging that they would wait.

"Isn't the short amount of time going to work against you, Dick?" somebody asked. "That's an awful short time to raise $150,000."

"I'm really glad we only have six days," Dick said. "We'll get the job done. And don't worry, you'll all hear from us."

He didn't know what they expected him to say; he'd taken the job and had figured out how to do it. All he needed now was their help and their money. They left, some of them shaking their heads, not knowing what Dick was going to do.

After the room cleared, Dick met with the two bank presidents, explained his plan of having each contributor sign a note for a contribution rather than give cash and persuaded them to give him a stack of promissory notes. As each bank's contribution, Dick wanted a 6 percent interest rate and a five-year payoff period on all signed notes. That figured out to $11.20 a month to pay off a five hundred-dollar contribution and $22.40 for a one thousand-dollar contribution. Other than than, he wanted the notes discounted to par. When both men agreed, Dick knew he had just gotten the job done right there.

His next move that afternoon was to chase down Ray Luton, a good friend who was a retired vice president for Marathon Oil Company. The Marathon refinery and field production were significant parts of the local economy and supplied many jobs to area residents. The company had been good at contributing to community projects.

When he found Luton, Dick explained the crisis and told him he'd like to have half the amount from Marathon. Luton said that was quite a bit but would call corporate headquarters in Findlay, Ohio, and get back to him. With Luton making the call, Dick counted the seventy-five thousand dollars in the till.

The next step was to contact the Heath family members and company. Both the family and the company had always contributed significantly to all civic projects. But it was Dick Heath raising the money this time, and he wasn't sure how they would respond. Bayard Sr. gave Dick a check for himself and Bayard Jr. And although Dick asked each member of the family personally, no one else contributed. They all said they couldn't afford a contribution. The company, however, in the midst of the turmoil with Dick brought on by the Liggett & Meyers offer, voted to contribute five thousand dollars.

"You're the only member of the family who contributed anything, personally, Bayard," Dick told his uncle after everyone had turned him down. "If L.S. Heath were around, he would get his old teacher's switch and start using it."

Dick knew that was blunt but true. His uncle merely nodded his head. But Dick knew there was no use to worry about the Heath family now and continued working. He knew the secret was the notes and the financing. They could never have raised the needed cash in a week. Organizations like the Elks, Moose, American Legion, VFW, Women's Club and Junior Women's Club all came through with big donations. Many volunteers were out collecting what they could.

When Dick saw Ray Luton early Thursday, he had a pleasant smile on his face and acknowledged that Marathon Oil had come through with the seventy-five thousand dollars. He was there as Robinson Mayor Carl Zwermann lit a huge bonfire later that day.

As he watched the smoke sail into the sky, Dick thought how he was really happy about how the community had reacted and wished the Heath family could work together that way. More than $150,000 had been raised.

"The extra money will furnish the civic center very nicely and make it even better," Zwermann said. "We owe a lot to Dick Heath and all of you who have made this center possible. Your contributions will be remembered on a plaque in the building listing all the donors to this drive."

An old friend was standing near Dick and asked, as others were to ask later, "Why did you consider it was advantageous to have such a short time?"

"Because the time was so short," Dick said, a sparkle in his eyes, "and everyone knew it. They couldn't say, 'I'll think about it and let you know.' They knew it was either yes or no. The notes allowed them to spread their contributions out. The short time forced a decision."

Maxine Zwermann was at the bonfire with her husband. When she saw Dick, she said, "I hope this doesn't hurt us in trying to raise money for the tournament."

"Maxine, the tournament isn't until September. This is only February. It should help us, if anything."

And Dick felt it would help. People had responded to the project because it was good for the community. Many saw that the Robinson Open was good for the community, too. In calling on so many people in the past week, however, Dick had heard from many of them about their concern regarding what was going on within the Heath company. At the time, he had refused to talk about it. But he knew the problem wasn't going to go away. Before long, he would have to do something about the situation.

During the weeks just before and after Christmas, Dick believed Bob had caused, directed or allowed seven illegal acts to be committed:

1) He fired Don Roads, Dick's comptroller, who was a corporate officer hired by the company treasurer (Dick) with the consent of the board of directors;

2) No notice had been given for a board of directors meeting, let alone a legally called meeting that required a ten-day notice;

3) To conduct legal business, a quorum of five directors must be present. Only four directors were present at the illegally called meeting. And the four directors who were there represented less than 50 percent of the outstanding stock;

4) Legal procedures were not followed according to the bylaws of the corporation to put a corporate officer on a leave of absence;

5) Vernon went to California for ten days to see a football game and take a vacation, totally ignoring his legal and fiduciary responsibilities to the company and its stockholders, particularly the minor ones who are protected by law more stringently than adult stockholders;

6) Vernon and Dick were the only two officers who could sign corporate checks. The company had a corporate resolution and signature cards at the Second National Bank of Robinson. Bob had illegally signed more than $500,000 of accounts payable checks, which Dick had told his cashier could wait until the following week; and

7) Bob's actions involved many key employees being placed in a position of taking sides. His acts jeopardized the stability of the company and were clearly against the best interests of the stockholders.

But regardless of how it looked to Dick, the situation at the company was still legally unresolved since the offer still existed and a stockholders meeting hadn't been held. Something had to be done.

Bob Douglas, a local attorney who was a friend of both Bayard Jr. and Dick, had worked for the law firm of Wildman, Harold, Allen and Dixon in Chicago, one of the top litigation firms in the country. For a handsome fee that enabled him to establish his own practice, Douglas introduced Bayard Jr. and Dick to the law firm and encouraged the firm to take their case. The two Heath men went to Chicago and detailed the bizarre affair.

Harold Huff, one of the firm's top lawyers, was assigned the case. After he had heard all the particulars and reviewed the situation, he prepared a suit with sixteen counts against Pete, Vernon, Bob and John. Before the suit was filed, however, Huff wanted Harrington to withdraw the Liggett & Meyers offer to snap the jaws shut on them and rack up huge damages.

Dick called Harrington, who agreed to immediately withdraw the offer because of a lack of action and did so in a letter dated March 1, 1969. This added another count to the lawsuit and damages were set at twenty million dollars for the complaint, which would be filed as soon as the offer had been withdrawn.

When the family members saw the withdrawal of the offer, they knew they had made another mistake. Vernon immediately sent a letter to the stockholders asking them whether they were in favor of the Liggett & Meyers offer. It was the funniest thing Dick had ever seen Vernon do yet. Dick laughed when he saw the letter.

"What offer do we have?" he wrote on the letter and sent it back to Vernon. It was too late to vote on the offer at that point.

The complaint was drafted with seventeen counts against the corporation and the responsible individuals. Dick thought the proof was overwhelmingly against them. As far as he was concerned, they were all history. What Bob had done and Vernon hadn't done were responsible for damages that were more by far than any of their assets. This was one suit where Dick thought the paper trail was complete. Bob wouldn't have a golf club to throw again after this was over.

That would be true of everyone named in the suit, Dick thought. With that in mind, he and Bayard Jr. agreed to leave Joyce off the complaint. She had had nothing to do with any of it. But they were prepared to proceed with the lawsuit.

Then Madeline, Dick's mother, read the complaint. She refused to go along with it and begged Dick not to do it. She wanted to keep peace in the family.

"You'll destroy the company," she said. "I've been too close to Thelma for that. And besides, no matter what they did, Skiv wouldn't want you to do it. Please don't go ahead with it, Dick. If not for me, then for your father."

After some discussion, both Bayard Jr. and Dick agreed to abide by her wishes. Before they were able to decide on another course of action, charges were being put together to terminate Dick's employment at the company. The corporate bylaws were being followed. Bob, in Vernon's absence, handed Dick a notice on Saturday, March 22, that told him of the meeting and its purpose. The notice said, "Notice is hereby given that at the meeting of the Board of Directors of L.S. Heath & Sons, Incorporated, to be held on March 28, 1969, at ten a.m. at 206 South Jackson Street, Robinson, Illinois, the Board will consider and take action upon a proposal to remove Richard J. Heath as an officer of the corporation, and to terminate his employment with the corporation."

Dick had been aware of the charges for some time but knew he had done nothing to warrant dismissal. He had put everything he had into the company and what he thought was best for it. After consulting with Harold Huff, Dick sent a written request to the company secretary that the charges be put in writing and signed by the officers and directors bringing the charges.

The first charge was that Dick, "while employed as treasurer of the corporation, did from time to time during the period April 2, 1968, to December 26, 1968, without the knowledge or authorization of the Board of Directors, draw upon or cause to be drawn upon the corporation's special account at the Indiana National Bank of Indianapolis, certain checks in an aggregate amount in excess of his authorized salary, which checks were negotiated for his presumed benefit."

Dick understood the charge but not the reason it was made. He had been trying to help secure Kenneth Hocking, a contractor who was involved with the Motel Corporation, financing for some contracts in Peru that would return more than enough money in commission to take care of the Fountain Lodge or Motel Corporation of Illinois obligations. After the corporation sent an attorney to South America to check out the potential and the risk of the venture, Dick had put nearly $160,000 of his own money on the line for the deal.

Until everything came together and the money came in, Dick tried to carry the thing personally. It became an almost impossible situation financially, and he had taken some cash advances on his salary. But that had been an accepted practice in the Heath company since the early days for an officer who found it necessary. The second charge was related and made it sound as if Dick were negligent.

It said that Dick, "while employed as treasurer of the corporation, did from time to time during the period of April 2, 1968, to December 26, 1968, fail to keep a correct and complete record of account showing accurately at all times the financial condition of the corporation, in violation of his duty as treasurer under the bylaws of the corporation."

To Dick's way of thinking, he had taken care of the accounting and financial records in a responsible manner. At the time a balance sheet was prepared, he knew there was a fixed point and the business of the corporation went on before and after that period. Any balance sheet, then, might not accurately reflect every detailed transaction. When he took the advance and picked it up in the next period, that corrected the imbalance. That's the way it had always been done in the company with that system.

Bob read the resolution that Dick be removed from the company at the board meeting. The meeting was then opened up for discussion. Bayard Jr. and Jack Morris Sr. were absent among the board members. But the room was filled with attorneys for both sides, company employees and Mary Morris.

After establishing that Dick had been authorized a salary of $2,585 per month for the 1968 fiscal year, Bob presented the board with a list of checks drawn on the executive payroll account at the Indiana National Bank. All the checks except one during the April-through-December period were signed by Don Roads and made payable to Dick.

"They total $55,978.36," Bill Hancock, corporate controller, said when Bob asked him to explain the situation, "and cleared the bank during that time."

Hancock continued, pointing to the paper he held in his hand. "Then in the middle column," he said, "we indicate the checks that went through the regular payroll system through the computer, and were the authorized amount of checks that was recorded in the company books, totaling $23,223.36."

The difference, Bob pointed out, represented "an amount which exceeded Dick's authorized salary by $32,755." Then Bob went to a statement he said showed "the accumulative amount in the amount per month by which said checks exceed Dick's authorized salary."

On the second charge, Hancock indicated that Dick failed to show the accurate financial record of the company by overstating the cash on the balance sheet.

"We determined the book balance was the figures from/the special account at the Indiana National Bank and reconciled these book accounts for each month through the bank statements for the period April 1968 through October 1968 and found after completing our bank reconciliation that cash was overstated in the following accounts: April 1968, cash was overstated $19,816.64; May 1968, cash was overstated $21,843.06; June 1968, cash was overstated $19,808.06; July 1968, cash was overstated $32,858.68; August 1968, cash was overstated $40,672.68; September 1968, cash was overstated $43,587.68; and October 1968, cash was overstated $41,002.68."

Before concluding his presentation of information, Bob told the directors that Dick had deposited a check in the special account on January 14, 1969. That check was in the amount of $33,089.98.

"The books of the company show outstanding cash advances to Dick," Bob said, "at this date of $13,089.98."

Harold Huff, Dick's attorney, established that Dick had used the advances to try and prevent default of the Motel Corporation, that other officers had taken cash advances and that balance sheets were only a reflection of conditions at a fixed point. There wasn't much else to do unless lawsuits were filed.

Dick explained the company's role in the Fountain Lodge venture and how he felt a responsibility to the people who had invested because the Heaths had and two of them were directors. That promoted a lengthy discussion that led to Dick's involvement with Kenneth Hocking.

After both sides had had their say, everybody was excused except the board of directors and the secretary. A motion was made by Bob and seconded by John to remove Dick "from the office of vice president and from the office of treasurer of the corporation for cause, effective as of the close of business March 28, 1969." In a roll call vote, Pete, Vernon, Ruby, Bob and John voted in favor of the resolution; Dick voted against it.

The board went on to other business. Like Bayard Jr., Dick had already decided to leave the company. Neither of them wanted to be around the company or the family anymore. But Dick hated to leave like this.

Vernon never thought Dick would leave without a fight. When he had gone to tell Vernon they were leaving and talk about the salary advances in January, he was sick in bed.

"I can explain the advances," Dick said. "But we're leaving. Bayard is going to practice law, which is what he's always wanted to do anyway. I'm just leaving. You'll have to live with your decisions. I can't. And you can have Bob. I don't want any part of him."

Vernon had just looked at him, and Dick walked out. He had nothing else to say.

After Madeline had so strongly rejected the suit and it was withdrawn and the directors had voted to terminate Dick's employment, the attorneys representing the Heath company and Bayard Jr. and Dick began negotiating a settlement for the stock. Dick knew it would not even be close to what Liggett & Meyers had offered.

To begin with, the company owed quite a bit on the new candy plant. But to avoid the suit, the value was substantially higher than Noel Cord had valued the stock before Dick had gone to New York. The company agreed to pay Bayard Jr., Dick and their immediate families eight hundred dollars a share, plus their legal fees, including the Douglas fee. The company had to borrow the money and reached its limit with the bank.

What was ironic to Dick was that Bayard Sr. and Skiv had started the main and only lasting part of the company. Pete was around and became part of the company. Vernon came back only because Skiv insisted strongly enough. Ruby and Mary were given their shares because of their father. And Skiv insisted his sisters have an income, even though they never worked in the company. Now the two sons of the two brothers who had started the candy company were no longer involved with the company.

When Bayard Jr. and Dick left the company, and ultimately Jack Morris Sr., Bob was left in a minority position with the family. Bob knew as weak as Vernon was he wouldn't live long and thought the presidency would be available. While they were with the company, neither Bayard nor Dick cared who was president as long as family didn't lose the opportunity. Dick knew that opportunity might now be lost.

The closing was in the board room. After the papers had all been signed and everybody had left, Bob and Dick were alone. Dick started to leave but stopped at the door before walking down the stairs for the last time.

He looked at Bob and said, "It's over, but I'll give you one piece of advice before I leave. Before the sun goes down today, for your own benefit, go down and fire Jesse Texiera."

Bob just looked at him with the same cold look he had had for a long time and said nothing.

Dick shrugged and walked out. He'd watched Jesse Texiera. He was a shrewd, talented man. When Texiera had turned against Bayard Jr., whom he was close to, on the Liggett & Meyers offer, Dick knew he was ambitious. There was that "lean and hungry" look Caesar saw in Cassius. If Texiera would turn on Bayard Jr., Dick knew he would certainly turn on Bob. And Texiera saw an opportunity to benefit by a split in the family. He'd see, or make, opportunities in the future, Dick thought. At the time, the remaining stock ownership in the family and percentages were as follows:

Virgil L. Heath Family - 2,500 shares - 32 percent
Vernon D. Heath Family - 2,500 shares - 32 percent
Ruby Dowling Family - 1,325 shares - 17.1 percent
Mary Morris Family - 1,475 shares - 18.9 percent
TOTAL - 7,800 shares - 100 percent

Knowing that it was only a matter of time before something else happened to change the ownership percentage, Dick wondered what it would be and who would set it off.

28

Soon after Dick sold his stock to the company, he had to pay off the Indiana National Bank for the $300,000 he had borrowed to try to clean up the company's mess over the Fountain Lodge fiasco. No one else gave him much money for his or her share of the obligation, so the entire amount was Dick's loss. People wondered where his money had disappeared so quickly. He found some satisfaction in telling them. The Fountain Lodge deal also helped collapse the Reese Lumber yard in which Dick was a partner.

But probably the most angry Dick got over the whole thing was some time later when Chuck Correll, still cashier at the Second National Bank, called and wanted to talk about another financial obligation.

"Pete and Vernon cancelled that ten thousand-dollar company check on the loan for the company you got for Bus Stevens' defense, Dick," Correll said. "I hate to bother you with it, but you signed the check."

Dick just shook his head. He knew the arrangements but was angry that the collateral was summarily cancelled, leaving him responsible.

"The Heaths who had principles and integrity have long since died or are gone, Chuck," Dick said later when he wrote out a new check from his personal account. "You're only dealing with the remnants of a once-great family."

When Bayard Jr. and Dick left the company, Jim Hanlon, the marketing manager, left, too. He apparently also had had enough of the Heath family.

One negative aspect of the situation was that it spilled out into the country club. Everybody talked about it and took sides. It got so bad that Dr. Keith Correll went to Bob and asked him to get Texiera and Ed Core to lay off the club with company business. Bob assured him he would take care of it.

Not long after they had sold their stock, Bayard Jr. and Dick were at the club, talking and having a drink. The end of the Heath family they had grown up with was at hand. After thirty-three years of living in Robinson, Dick knew eventually he would leave and go somewhere else.

Bayard Jr. had his law degree and loved to practice law Miami was his logical choice since it was his wife's hometown, and he had first practiced law there. And Bayard Jr. didn't feel as deeply as Dick did about Robinson.

Dick loved Robinson and the people he grew up with. Nobody's roots, particularly in the Heath family, could be any deeper than his. But the events that had just taken place were so traumatic to him, like a nightmare of dealing with something he couldn't keep from happening. Money wasn't what he wanted, even though he knew it took money to live and accomplish things in life. And he wanted to accomplish things.

Society uses money as a standard of success. He knew that, for some reason, a person with money receives a certain respect no matter what kind of person he is. Unfortunately, money is power, and power changes people. Most people don't know how to act when they get money. They forget how they got there. Some get there by luck without having anything to do with it. Society, however, looks at the end, not the means. Real success lies in accomplishments that go on long after the individual is gone.

The Heath family, Dick thought, had an opportunity to accomplish things only a few people have. It wasn't just the money the family could have received—it lost an opportunity to have really accomplished something that would have lasted far beyond any member of the family. It could have created thousands of jobs in Robinson for the people who had been kind to the family. With millions of dollars it could never spend, the Heath family could have formed a Heath Foundation to educate young people and really do something in the world that only a few families have done.

When it's all over, Dick wondered, what would the world finally say about the Heath family? What would the world say about Pete, Vernon, Ruby and Mary and their accomplishments? For some reason, as long as he could remember, Dick had a burning desire to accomplish things. It had started when he was in grade school playing basketball. He wanted to win the game, whatever the game was.

"I've got a home purchased in Key Biscayne," Bayard Jr. said, "and a position with a good law firm. I hate to start practice in a new career at fifty years old. But I don't know what else to do. What are you going to do, Dick?"

"I don't know. I'll probably run the golf tournament for a while. I really don't care what I do as long as I'm away from that bunch."

"Would you have believed this?"

"No, I wouldn't. I wish I were back in that red chair with L.S. I'd tell him that what he was creating would blow up. But I have to admit I would have never believed that Bob would change."

"But he did."

"Yes, he sure did. His environment changed him. He got carried away with this president stuff. He knew you would probably be the president after Vernon. He figured with your age and how much you love to play golf you wouldn't want to stay and work that hard or that long."

"That's for sure. There's more to life than putting up with all those family problems."

"Then when he found out about Liggett & Meyers, it was like missing a ten-foot putt in a tight game. He probably felt Milton would want me to lead the division after you. Do you remember what Milton said about me at the cocktail party at my home that Tuesday night?"

"Yeah. That's true. He really believed you were something special."

"You know, Bayard, his son was a West Point graduate and captain in the Special Forces in Vietnam. He was about my age. In New York, just before I left, we had a drink in a little bar before I caught a cab to the airport. He told me I reminded him of his son. He liked me."

"It really couldn't be that much of a surprise being with him at the Country Club of North Carolina and then at the tournament. Hell, he made no secret of the expansion he wanted when we were all with him down in North Carolina."

"Yes, but what hit Bob was that he felt his world being blown up when he knew the offer was actually coming. Nobody goes that beserk without even seeing the offer."

"You're right about that. He knew he was wrong doing what he did, though. He should have been left busted along with Pete and Vernon. I never saw such an open-and-shut case."

"Look what he did. You had nothing to do with it at all, yet he gave you that stupid letter, too. He decided to kill two birds with one stone."

"I guess. He knew what we would do. He wanted to bring it out in the open, so there would be no return."

"And Pete and Vernon never even knew what it was all about. Joyce never did either. I wanted to talk to her about the real motive, but I guess that will come some day."

"I'm not sure he'll even get what he wants."

"If he only knew what was in store for him. I told him about Texiera when I left the board room. He doesn't know what Tex is going to do. I told him to fire him that day."

"What did he say?"

"Nothing. His ass was still in the clouds. It's like Dode Douglas said the other day when I was talking to him about what happened. 'I knew that temper would finally explode and really hurt someone,' he said, 'but I didn't know it would affect so many.' What Bob did affected the people of Robinson. They're the real losers in this mess."

"Bigger than the family?" Bayard Jr. asked.

"Maybe just in a different way. But I think you'll eventually see that."

29

With no obligations to the company and no full-time job after leaving the company, Dick told Maxine Zwermann he now had the time to really work on the tournament. And he did work. The experience of the past seven years, particularly that of the 1968 tournament, had been extremely helpful in preparing for the larger purse and bigger gate now possible and necessary. *Sports Illustrated* contacted tournament officials and wanted to do a story on what it called "the Cinderella tournament of the PGA tour."

After the '69 tournament was over and everything was cleared up, Maxine handed Dick a stack of letters three inches high. People who had once lived in Robinson had sent newspaper clippings of the tournament from all over the country, including the *Sports Illustrated* article in the October issue headlined, "Here's to you, Mr. Robinson—the pros love you. ..." The picture with the article showed Dick in his tournament blazer leaning against the tournament headquarters door with a drink in his hand.

"There is no golf course on the PGA tour quite like the Crawford County Country Club (the 4Cs) in Robinson, Ill.," the article began. "Where else can you get to the locker room 30 minutes before you leave your hotel room? Where else can you find a clubhouse doorman wearing an Episcopal minister's collar? Where else can you find slot machines in the clubhouse? And where else can you three-putt to the accompaniment of a high school pep band practicing for a football game?"

The part about the slot machines irritated Dick. Mark Mulvoy, the reporter, had promised there would be no mention of them in the article. Dick didn't care that he mentioned the band practicing a half a mile away through the woods for Friday night's football game. He wouldn't even have cared if the article had mentioned a couple of pros prancing around the fourth green like drum majors, keeping time with their putters.

But the slot machine reference did bother him. Mulvoy's word had meant nothing. Either he had promised whatever he was asked to get his story, Dick thought, or his editor had vetoed the promise. Regardless, there was nothing Dick could do about it. And he had a great deal more to worry about anyway.

Now each tournament had to show financial responsibility at the time of the signing of the agreement. That resulted because the Michigan Golf Classic had not had the prize money to pay the players three weeks earlier. They ended up getting about fifty cents on the dollar. At the time, Dick had called Jack Tuthill, field director of the PGA staff in New York, and offered five thousand dollars out of the profits from the Robinson Open already in the bank to help cover the deficit. Of course, Tuthill had refused. But it hadn't hurt. Dick had told Maxine that they "would get great mileage" out of offering something he knew wouldn't be taken.

Later, PGA Commissioner Joe Dey thanked Dick for the offer and emphasized that by showing financial responsibility, situations like the Michigan Classic could be avoided in the future. Dick knew it was a wise business decision. He also knew that the requirement to show financial responsibility and the increase in prize money would prevent the club from sponsoring the tournament. Up to this point, the tournaments were run for the benefit of the club. The club, however, could not take the risk any longer. It was time to implement the plan he had been considering for a year or more.

Dick had mentioned his idea to Maxine after learning that the PGA would require proof of financial responsibility of all tournament promoters. She had told him she was interested. Now he told her he wanted to form a company called Golf Management Services, Inc. (GMS), with her, his mother and him as primary stockholders.

Both Maxine and Madeline agreed, and the corporation was formed. GMS would sign the agreement with the PGA for the 1970 Robinson Open Golf Classic hosted by the Crawford County Country Club and offer a $100,000 purse. With that arrangement, the Indiana National Bank agreed to guarantee financial responsibility to the PGA.

Dick and Maxine worked out a plan to give the club a percentage of the proceeds. As soon as they had the particulars detailed and an agreement drawn up, Dick called a membership meeting to present the plan which would give the club between thirty thousand and thirty-five thousand dollars for the use of the facilities and the volunteer help. It didn't make any difference to the members who owned the tournament. The club was guaranteed a profit no matter what happened.

It had been a long time since Dick didn't feel any responsibility to complete or sell something. Leaving the Heath company had lifted some of that responsibility from him. But he was still chairman of the board and president of the country club, president of Old Lake Village, Inc., and was involved with the local cable company, a small shop and office complex on the west edge of Robinson, the lumber yard, a computer service started by Don Roads after Bob fired him, and community activities. The largest share of his time, though, was available to develop and promote the tournament.

Besides losing the Liggett & Meyers offer, the Heath company lost the opportunity to use the golf tournament as a major marketing vehicle. Milton Harrington had realized the potential. The company would have been the permanent sponsor of the event had the offer been accepted. Even though it hadn't and the company never sponsored anything, out-of-towners for years afterwards thought the Heath company had always been behind the tournament.

Both the company and the tournament survived and continued in separate paths. Jack Morris Jr. had been made treasurer of the company to fill the position vacated by Dick. Ron Bailey, a local man who had come to Heath's from Marathon Oil Company's corporate office in Findlay, Ohio, just before the blowup over the Liggett & Meyer's offer and had completed the audit that discovered the amount of Dick's salary advances, was appointed comptroller when Roads was fired. Bailey had been hired by Dick as Roads' assistant.

As Jack Jr. was moving up in the company, Jack Morris Sr. had been moved out. He had aligned himself with Bayard Jr. and Dick on the Liggett & Meyers offer, believing it was the only salvation of the family in the business. His wife, Mary, was on the other side. It wasn't long before Jack Sr., who had twenty-four years with the company, was fired. Mary filed for divorce.

His drinking increased, and he became ill. Although Dick knew Jack Sr. had a drinking problem, Dick had always liked him and thought he was a good man who knew his job and did it well. Jack Sr. had made the company a lot of money in the years he was there. Bayard Jr. agreed with Dick.

"Jack had the knack of buying," Bayard Jr. told Dick. "He could buy better drunk than most people could buy sober. Sure, his drinking became terrible, especially after all the problems. But he wasn't alone in that regard."

Shortly afterwards, Jack Sr. went to Dick and asked him if he would be the executor of his will. Dick told him he would be honored if that's what he wanted. The company had bought the fifty shares of stock L.S. had given him, but Jack Sr. had little else to his name.

Dick had always considered Jack Sr. a close friend and offered to help him in the divorce. After the divorce was filed, Dick called Harold Huff, the Chicago attorney who had represented Bayard Jr. and him against the family earlier in the year. Huff agreed to take the case and agreed that because of the circumstances Jack Sr. should receive alimony.

The case was tried in the circuit court at the Robinson courthouse in front of a judge. Huff put Dick on the stand, after John Heath had testified on Mary's behalf, to tell why Jack Sr. qualified for alimony.

Testifying that he was the Heath company treasurer from 1960 to 1969, Dick said he signed Jack Sr.'s monthly check, and out of a twenty-three hundred dollar monthly salary, his net check was only three hundred dollars. Bayard Sr., who was treasurer of the company from 1946 to 1960, had told Dick that Jack Sr. had always taken a small check, too.

It had been Dick's understanding that Jack Sr. had taken his salary in that way because he wanted to pay the income taxes on his salary and Mary's dividends both out of his check.

The small amount left over gave Jack Sr. enough money for personal expenses and pocket change. With everything else paid, that was all he cared about.

No cross examination followed. Huff then explained that Jack Sr. was now quite ill, unable to work, with a wife who was quite wealthy and had a tremendous income. Further, he said they had been married for thirty years.

"If you took the funds for the taxes he had withheld," Huff said, "and they were reinvested in a retirement fund, funds that were his, that he earned but paid for his wife's taxes, we wouldn't be here today."

Jack Sr. wasn't able to be in the courtroom, but he won an alimony settlement of a five thousand-dollar annual payment. To Huff's knowledge, it was the first case in Illinois where a woman was ordered to pay alimony to a man in a divorce court. But Mary was not going to have to pay for long. Jack Sr.'s illness worsened, and he was soon in the hospital in Robinson. He was only fifty-six years old, a weak and broken man at the last.

After he entered the hospital, Dick called Jack Sr.'s two sisters from Minneapolis to come down. Dick and Betty met the two women, who were staying at Old Lake Village, for dinner at the country club. About 6:30 that evening, Dick got a call from the hospital asking him to come there at once. He told Jack Sr.'s sisters that he would call if there was any need to.

Not long after Dick arrived and was with him a few minutes, Jack Morris Sr. died. On the way out of the room, Dick met Jack Jr. They stared at each other briefly before speaking.

"He's dead, Jackie," Dick said coldly and walked away.

Later he overheard him on the phone talking to Mary.

"The ball game's over," Jack Jr. said.

You got that right, Dick thought, irritated that Jack Jr. would refer to his father's death in such a way.

Before his illness, Jack Sr. had always told Dick he wanted to be buried at the Veteran's Hospital Cemetery in Danville, Illinois. The funeral was held in Robinson. His family, many of his friends and former employees paid their last respects to a man Dick thought was a good man who had always done his job at the Heath company.

But Bayard Sr. and Dick were the only two who accompanied the body for burial at the cemetery in Danville ninety miles north of Robinson. Dick had made arrangements for an Honor Guard there. The ceremony was delayed while they waited for Jack Jr.

"He said he'll be here," Bayard Sr. said. "He'll be here any time."

"He ain't coming," Dick said.

After standing in the cold, snowy March wind for forty-five minutes, even Bayard Sr. was ready to go on. The Honor Guard paid the government's final salute to the veteran of the European Campaign in World War II. While the shots rang out and echoed across the cemetery through the spitting snow, Bayard Sr. turned to Dick and said, "At least he's with the kinds of men who were like him."

"Yes," Dick said softly as a tear rolled quietly, slowly down his cheek, for once at a loss for words. "Yes, he is."

After the ceremony, Bayard Sr. accepted the American flag on behalf of the family.

Shortly after Jack Sr.'s death and more than a year after he had left the company, Dick was at the 19th Hole Lounge when

Pete walked into the club. Other than at Jack Sr.'s funeral, this was the first time Dick had seen Pete for some time. They had never talked about what had happened the year before.

"Would you have a drink with me, Dick?" Pete asked after the two exchanged cordial greetings. "I'd like to talk."

Dick said he'd have a drink, and they walked to a corner table and ordered. Pete had already been drinking and started talking about the past, going back to when Skiv was still living and different years in the business. It was a rambling, disjointed, but pleasantly nostalgic conversation. For the most part, Dick listened.

Then, growing somber and tears welling in his eyes, Pete said, "One of these days when I see Skiv, I don't know what I'm going to say to him. How am I going to explain what happened?"

Dick said nothing.

"You know Bob made me sign that letter to you and Bayard?" Pete said after a few seconds of silence. "Vernon wouldn't sign it. So Bob told me I had to. I didn't want to do it, and I know it was wrong."

By this time, tears were rolling slowly down his cheeks. Still, Dick said nothing but sat and listened.

"Will you forgive me for what I did?" Pete asked, pleading. "I doubt whether Skiv will."

"Yes, Pete," Dick finally said, "I'll forgive you. There's nothing to be gained from it anymore. However, I'll never forget what you and Vernon did on the ten thousand dollars for Bus Stevens."

"That was Vernon's doing. I had nothing to do with it."

"No, Pete, you have to take the responsibility for that, too."

"Well, I'm glad it's over."

"It's not over, Pete. Yes, it's over with Bayard and me. But you haven't seen anything yet."

It was Pete's turn to say nothing. Dick put a dollar on the table and walked out. He knew he had better leave the tip because Pete, like his son, Bob, never carried any money.

30

At the next annual meeting of the club, Dick was again running for trustee with Friday Chapman and Mort Imlay. Both were close friends of Dick's and had been excellent board members. The term for director was three years. Much of the secret of the success of the club was the continuity of management.

This was the first time Dick had come up for reelection since leaving the Heath company. The three current trustees were nominated from the floor. A small group led by Jesse Texiera and Monty Maples, a local physician, put his name in nomination. Each member could vote for three trustees. The group backing Maples voted only for him, figuring that would get him elected. Dick's friends saw what was happening and voted only for him.

By this political turn of events, it turned out that Maples, Chapman and Dick were elected trustees. Dick was infuriated but accepted the results. After a lot of persuading with Imlay, Dick appointed him as his replacement and resigned. The Heath affair had been brought out in the open and into the club.

After nearly ten years, Dick was no longer the president and chairman of the board. His era was finished, but the Crawford County Country Club was much improved and there for everyone to enjoy. He would continue handling the Robinson Open Golf Classic through the company he and

Maxine had formed. Club members continued to help with the tournament and in every way necessary.

But while everybody else was contributing, the Heath company was doing nothing to help. Key employees were still disagreeing over company direction and policy. In one dispute, Ross Fife, the ice cream-bar franchise division manager, decked Ed Core and soon left the company for Houston to join a firm selling Heath Ice Cream Bars.

Dick didn't know the circumstances and didn't want to know. Whatever it was, he didn't think Texiera would want Fife around. Like Jim Hanlon, he was an extremely talented man who was a true professional and knew how to run the ice cream-bar division. When Fife left, Don White, who had been with the company since 1948, took Fife's job.

With everything else going on and the company still in turmoil, Vernon became ill again. He'd always been a weak, frail man. This time it was his liver, and he died early in 1971. He was buried in the Heath family plot in the Robinson Cemetery next to his father and mother, Skiv and L.S.'s two aunts. The plot was large enough to take care of the first and second generations of Heaths and their wives.

Vernon's death opened up more problems for the company, problems that Dick had seen coming for some time. But he was still getting blamed for many of the negative things that had happened to the family. Shortly after the funeral, he saw Vernon's widow, Bea, in the post office one morning.

"Good morning, Bea," Dick said. "How are you today?"

"You killed Vernon, Dick," she said without acknowledging his greeting or question. "You killed him."

Dick just looked at her, shaking his head, ignoring her comment but thinking perhaps she thought he had breathed on him at a party. Dick didn't think she knew how lucky she was with what Vernon had been a part of not long ago and what would happen now. With his death, Dick knew the door was open for what Texiera had been waiting for—a more active role in the company decision-making process. As long as Vernon was alive, Dick and everybody knew Texiera wouldn't have the guts or wouldn't connive against Pete. It would have been too risky for him to even try.

At the time the Liggett & Meyers offer had come down, most of the family had known that Vernon wasn't a healthy man. Dick had tried to tell him then that if something happened to him, it would be hard to tell what would happen in his immediate family or in the Heath family in general. But things would change. That was undeniable.

Immediately after Vernon's death, Bob finally achieved the goal he'd had since about 1958. He was elected president of L.S. Heath and Sons, Inc., a position he could have assured for himself through Bayard Jr. and Dick. What Bob had never realized was that being president was never important to either of his cousins. If he had wanted it that badly, all he would have had to do was tell them. Bayard Jr. never believed in titles anyway. He liked life too much and wanted to play golf with Pat. To that end, he had even joined the Terre Haute Country Club and loved to go over there to play golf with his friends.

As for Dick having the idea of being president, he never cared either. He enjoyed building the club and the golf tournament too much to want to be president. And if Liggett & Meyers had acquired the company, he would have been doing the basic thing that Milton Harrington wanted him to do. And that was going out and acquiring those companies to bring them under the Heath banner as part of the Heath

Division of Liggett & Meyers. Selling those companies to join them would have been his job. He had no doubt, either, that he would have emptied Harrington's bank account and acquired several good companies. Selling, not leading a company, was his forte. Harrington knew that, and that's the reason he wanted the company.

Liggett & Meyers wasn't interested in just buying a single candy company. Harrington thought he was buying a nice, congenial, close-knit family. Dick had bragged to him how nice everyone was. Harrington would never have paid what he offered for the flagship company if he had known the truth. Only until he saw the family in its truest light did he realize what a mistake he had made.

If he had really wanted the Heath company and at the price he was offering, Dick thought Milton Harrington would have flown that Saberliner into Terre Haute one more time. But the actions of Pete, Vernon, Bob and John were so tacky and so underhanded that the entire board of directors at Liggett & Meyers must have been in shock, Dick thought. The board had permitted Harrington to offer so much more than the company was worth to begin with.

And to see or hear about the kinds of behavior by the rest of the family told them this wasn't the kind of people they wanted to lead that division of Liggett & Meyers and wasn't what they thought they were getting. To Dick, it was totally bush league and bad manners. Yet Harrington had made the deal with Dick and had put it in writing.

When he called Harrington from Chicago asking him to withdraw the offer to establish damages and cement the case, he had seemed greatly relieved and did it quickly. Never, Dick felt, was a major successful company so misled for what it thought it was buying. Dick had tried to tell Harrington that afternoon in his New York office why the family didn't want to sell, but he wouldn't listen. The problem was that he was sold on a small, country candy company that had wide name recognition and Dick and his abilities that he never realized what the rest of the family was like. When he saw how the family really was, he left his Saberliner in New York.

Liggett & Meyers' cash reserves and credit could have built a confectionery and food empire in Robinson. The company already had twenty-five acres where the candy plant set and all the land needed across the railroad. Dick had no doubt that Robinson lost four thousand future jobs when the offer wasn't accepted.

And Bob, now president of the company, had been the key to the entire deal. He was smart enough to know how great an opportunity it was and yet, because he was angry and had thrown a temper tantrum and acted so illogically, he felt he couldn't back down. His jealousy and burning desire to become president led him to destroy the one outstanding chance for the family to become extremely successful and wealthy and bring many new jobs to Robinson.

The biggest miscalculation Bob made from the beginning of the Liggett & Meyers episode was in thinking that the rest of the family was for him and against Dick. They voted against the offer for reasons different than his. Vernon was worried about his image in the church and town and also about the status of John and Allan in a new, larger and more public company. Ruby was listening to the Illinois Continental Bank, which didn't want to see the merger take place because it might lose her trust account. This was terrible advice and exposed the bank to a lawsuit. The bank knew that the Chase

Manhattan Bank was Liggett & Meyers' bank. Pete would have grabbed the deal in a second if it weren't for Bob. Mary decided against it after wanting something like it to happen all her life. She was getting ready to divorce Morris and might have thought she would have to give him too much money.

Yet Bob thought the family liked him because they were in his corner on the issue. Rather, their hatred or dislike of him increased over the way he handled the situation from the beginning. His actions had totally jeopardized their personal fortunes and their interests in the company. Only Madeline had prevented a total disaster was the way Dick saw it.

31

For more than a year, Bob Heath lived out his dream of being the president of L.S. Heath & Sons, Inc. But with Vernon dead, Texiera had an open field. Although Vernon had not been well, no one had thought he would die so quickly. When he did, Bob began living in a false paradise. While he was savoring his great triumph, Texiera was busy back in the wings. He knew he could manipulate Jack Jr. as he had before. Pete was still alive, but Ruby and Mary apparently could care less about him. He was pretty much alone and helpless, even though he was chairman of the board. His father was gone, two brothers were dead and Bayard Sr. was out of the business.

The most important part from Texiera's perspective had been neatly taken care of by Bob's own greed. When it came down to it, the only two who could have saved him were Bayard Jr. and Dick. And Bayard Jr. was practicing law in Florida, and Dick was running a golf tournament. With his two cousins' families' stock, Bob would have had slightly more than 50 percent—enough to retain control of the company. Just as Bayard Jr. and Dick had been in a minority position, Pete's family, with 32 percent of the stock, was in the same position.

All the while, Dick figured, Jesse Texiera, Jack Morris Jr. and John Heath apparently had plotted Bob's overthrow. Only Texiera would have had the guts, the leadership and the ability to go up against the strong personality of Bob Heath, Dick knew. Texiera knew straight out that after persuading Jack Jr. to go along in the Liggett & Meyers' fiasco it was easy to get Mary.

In fact, while Dick assumed Texiera spearheaded the move to get rid of Bob, he also considered that Mary may have been behind it. She hated Bob with a passion. Only she could have persuaded Ruby to oust Bob and do that to her brother Pete. No one else could have gotten Ruby to go along with the plan. Her husband, Bernard, would not have been a party to it on his own volition. But still someone would have masterminded it. And that left Jesse Texiera.

Getting John and Allan to go along would not have been that difficult since the plan was to move John from the print shop to president of the company. That would have appealed to him in a second. His mother would have been elated. And Allan would have loved to be the chairman of the board. His rise to the top would be considered spectacular.

So it was Dick's belief that Texiera called the shots with help from Jack Jr. and John. It was pretty quiet, though. Dick hadn't heard a word of it. Had he heard, he thought he would have undoubtedly tried to head it off with Ruby, Mary and Vernon's widow, Bea. But there was never an opportunity and was probably wishful thinking on Dick's part, anyway.

When it came time for the annual meeting in 1972, the seeds had been sown and word hadn't leaked out. To get the job done quietly and effectively created a problem. If everybody went to the annual meeting, anything could happen with Pete and Bob there.

Pete might persuade Ruby or any of them to back out of the coup. He believed the old saying, "Blood's thicker 'n water."

And those people on the other side were not the kinds of people to do battle with Bob.

Any one of them could lose his or her nerve in the heat of battle. It had been Dick's experience in dealing with this board and company that you never knew. But Texiera would bet his last dollar that none of them wanted to face Bob one-on-one. With his temper, he might do anything. So they hired two attorneys to do the job for them.

Dick had no emotions except anger when he heard about the situation. Bob and he had had their differences, but Dick didn't like the way his ouster had been handled. Obviously, the other side didn't want any compromise or one could have been worked out. Regardless, Dick didn't think it was all a great shock to Bob.

The moment Dick heard about what he later called the June Massacre, he made up his mind that he'd never say, "I told you so," to Pete or Bob. Had Bayard Jr. and Dick still been with the company, it wouldn't have happened. And Dick could only imagine what would have happened had Bob been aware of the coup plans, been prepared for it and handled it the way Dick himself would have.

The meeting would have been in the board room at nine a.m. When Bob walked into the room that morning in June, he would have seen only two lawyers representing the balance of the shareholders not in attendance. No family members would have been present. It wouldn't have been too difficult for them to use outside attorneys to do the dirty work because they could care less, had no emotional involvement and would vote how they were paid to vote. That would have been to explode Bob's dream right in his face.

And had he known that earlier, when he walked into the

room, he could have strode confidently to the head of the long conference table, set his briefcase beside him and took a few papers from it. Getting angry would have been to no avail.

"Gentlemen, I'm calling the meeting to order of the annual shareholders of L.S. Heath & Sons, Inc.," Bob would have said, as his steely eyes looked around the table at the empty chairs and the two lawyers. "Since the secretary of the corporation is not here, I'll dispense with the reading of the minutes of the last shareholders meeting."

Seeing Bob's calm, confident manner, the two attroneys might have been a bit nervous and uneasy. But they would also be chomping at the bit to unleash their clients' surprise to Bob.

He would have adjusted his glasses, gave them an icy stare as he would have given Dick if they were playing the last hole for the club championship, tied. It had been twenty years since that June 1952 night in Korea when Bob led his company up the hill in darkness and walked into an ambush from the Chinese battalion waiting at the top of the hill. But he was still a tough, worthy adversary.

"I will now have the election of the directors," Bob would have said.

At this point, the two attorneys would have handed Bob the proxies they were carrying, signed by Mary Heath Morris, John R. Morris Jr., Robert Morris, Bernard Dowling, Ruby Dowling, John L. Heath, Allan Heath and Beatrice K. Heath.

Bob would have looked at them for a few seconds and said, "I see there are a total of fifty-three hundred shares represented. There are seven directors to be elected. Therefore, gentlemen, you have seven times fifty-three hundred shares or 37,100 votes. I represent twenty-five hundred shares or 17,500 votes. And, as president and chief executive officer, I will exercise my right under Illinois law to vote the company's treasury stock, which is five thousand shares. This is treasury stock purchased by the company from the Bayard E. Heath and Everett E. Heath families. That five thousand shares represents thirty-five thousand votes. Let's see, the number of votes is 12,800 times seven directors or 89,600 votes. To elect a director, it takes 12,800 votes per director."

By this time, the attorneys would have had stunned looks on their faces. The treasury stock is owned by the company. Who votes it? Under the law, the president had the right. So their clients would have had only enough votes to elect three directors, provided Bob would give them a few votes. And he would have had enough votes to elect four directors, the majority. It wouldn't have taken long for the board to be named and elected. Obviously, Bob would have been re-elected.

"As president, with full support of the majority of the board of directors, I am immediately terminating the following employees: John Heath, Allan Heath, John R. Morris Jr. and Jesse Texiera," Bob would have said to the startled attorneys, closed the meeting and walked out.

When the word of what happened would have reached those in the family who were being fired, they would have gone into shock. What could they do? Their fifty-three hundred shares would have been available, and the company history would have been changed again as it could have been with the Liggett & Meyers offer.

So that is what could have happened. But Bob Heath was ambushed again, and it was him sitting in the chair this time instead of his cousin. Dick wondered while sitting in the same chair if Bob had remembered what Dick had told him about getting "rid of Texiera before the sun goes down."

Whatever he could have done, did do or didn't do no longer matter. It was too late. Everybody else had ganged up on him, and it was over as far as Pete and him being officers. The lawyers took charge as planned. Armed with the proxy votes and their instructions, it didn't take long for the directors to be elected and for these directors to elect John president to replace Bob. It was a slick way of doing the job. Nobody had to get emotional.

And Bob was out. He could still be on the board of directors. Under Illinois law, they couldn't stop that. But the stockholders control the directors, and the directors elect the officers.

Many people thought Bob was fired from the company, too. That wasn't the case. After the new president was hired, he simply did not hire Bob as an employee of L.S. Heath & Sons, Inc. Both he and Pete were essentially told to get out and, of course, had no choice.

Driving up to Bob's spacious, well-landscaped home after it was all over, Dick looked to his right to the ninth hole of the new half of the golf course. He couldn't see it, but it was only two hundred yards away through the trees.

Dick hardly recognized Bob. He was tired looking, and his spirits were low. But he was angry.

"These scabs of the family have had nothing to do in building the business," Bob said. "They are only there because someone felt sorry for the incompetent bastards and gave them a gift. You could add up the total IQs of John, Allan and Jack and it would be tough to get into any university.

"John and Allan are another Vernon Heath who never knew one damn thing about the business. And that silly-assed

Jackie Morris wants the whole world to think he's bright. He's not bright enough to run the Palestine milk route, and everyone knows it."

While Dick listened as they sat on the patio, Bob told about the meeting and his feelings. After he finished, Dick sat quietly for a minute longer before speaking.

"It reminds me of the story in *Gulliver's Travels* where the little people caught the giant sleeping," Dick said. "What now?"

Bob smiled weakly and said he didn't have any plans right now. Of course, his family had its stock, but it was a minority stock and lacking in strength. He and his father had decided to sell the family stock.

In the charter when the corporation was formed, it was decreed that the company had the first right of refusal for purchase of any stock. So Pete and Bob could get an offer, but the company had the right to match the offer and buy the stock.

Bob was fighting the company for a settlement, threatening to sell to an outsider for an outrageously high price. Bayard Sr. and his daughter had sold their stock for nearly four hundred dollars a share in 1962. The company had borrowed the necessary one million dollars plus to buy the stock.

Then when Bayard Jr. and Dick and their families had left the company in 1969, the company purchased the shares for about eight hundred dollars each. Again, the company borrowed the $2.3 million to make the purchase.

Now in 1972, Bob wanted fifteen hundred dollars a share for his family's stock. And he finally got it. The company went to the well again, so to speak, and borrowed $3.75 million for that purpose. That made about seven million dollars borrowed to keep the stock in the company and $3.5 million borrowed to build the new candy plant in 1967-68 and keep the company in business.

Were things through at the old cheese plant, as Dode Douglas used to call it? Dick wondered. Something was wrong with a company that borrowed seven million dollars to buy a quarter of the stock in a company that had only gotten its net worth up to four million dollars in 1969 at the time of the Liggett & Meyers offer and a $400,000 net profit.

At a nickel and a dime apiece, Dick knew it would take a lot of candy bars to pay back the money and keep things going. But everybody who was left put up all the Heath stock and all signed the note jointly and severally to keep the company afloat. Somehow it managed.

And Dick looked at the numbers game going on within the remaining family's shareholders. After retiring Pete's family's shares, the outstanding stock dropped from seventy-eight hundred shares to fifty-three hundred shares. John's family still had its twenty-five hundred shares, and it was still a minority position. Together, Ruby's and Mary's families could now have control with 51 percent of the stock.

Dick didn't know what to call it, but he thought it was rather ironic that the daughters, who were brought into the company as shareholders by L.S. because he wanted his daughters and his family gathered around him in the family business, now had controlling interest in the company.

Outside the company, the rest of the family members went their separate ways. Bob soon decided to open an office in Robinson and build HUD apartments and pursue other business interests. He bought the People's Bank in Newton, Illinois, and a large interest in the Crawford County State Bank in Robinson. Later, he became president of the board of directors of the University of Illinois Alumni Association.

Pete just retired. Eventually, Dick went by to see his uncle and aunt. Again, Dick promised himself that he wouldn't say anything about the past or the Liggett & Meyers deal. The last time Dick had been to their house, he'd tried to make them realize what could happen either way the deal went.

Joyce and her husband, Penn, had been there at the time. She had been caught in the middle between Bob and Dick. As always and which Dick understood, she said, "You know he's my brother, and I love him."

This time when Thelma opened the door, Dick stood quietly, looking into her eyes. He didn't have to say anything. Pete was sitting in his old recliner chair. He was pale and drawn, hands shaking slightly. He looked as if he were in shock. Thelma sat down next to Dick.

"Can you believe that bunch?" Thelma asked.

"Yes, I can. Don't you? You know them as well or better than I do."

"But I didn't think any of them would do this."

"Not by themselves anyway."

"Was it Texiera?"

"Certainly," Dick said, thinking that Bob had realized it and told Pete and Thelma. "No one else would have had the guts."

"You knew what would happen, didn't you?"

"I was pretty sure. I thought everything was going to come apart at the seams some day. I just didn't know when."

Bob had worked on selling the stock for quite a while. Not knowing for sure, Dick figured his strategy had been to get a major company interested in buying the stock that was a minority stock position by pointing out that 32 percent is a big minority block that would eventually have the opportunity to take over the company. With Ruby's age, the new stockholder could eventually get control. The company would have two seats (Bob's and Pete's), get to know the rest and have a chance to make a deal down the road.

Whatever happened, he was successful in getting his price. The third major sellout left the following outstanding stock:

	Shares	Percentage
John, Allan and Bea Heath	2,500	47.1
Mary Morris Family	1,475	27.8
Ruby Dowling Family	1,325	25.1
TOTAL	5,300	100

32

After the smoke cleared from the latest coup, Pete grew ill and died later in 1972. His life was sad at the end. Years of drinking had taken their toll on his body. After Dick's conversations with Pete at the club and in his home, Dick never saw his uncle alive again.

His life had started out on a sweet note but was ended on bitter ones. Except the money, he had lost all L.S. had tried to provide for: a family business to take care of all the family, a sense of family and a feeling of personal worth.

Bayard Sr. had now seen all of his younger brothers buried in front of him. He was seventy-eight years old and looked tired. But Dick thought he'd looked that way for a long time. Bayard Sr.'s wife died in 1973. The eldest son of L.S. lived quietly alone.

Early one morning, Dick saw his uncle at the country club. "Would you have time to come by my apartment, Dick?" Bayard Sr. asked. "I want to show you something."

"Sure, Bayard. I'll come by whenever you wish."

What the old man wanted to show his nephew was some sixty-five handwritten pages of a book about the history of the Heath company. Dick sat down to read it. Bayard Sr.'s penmanship was neat, stylish and easy to read.

"How come your son writes so bad, Bayard?" Dick asked.

"Kids don't take the time to learn anything the way Dad

taught Skiv and me. It's a different world today."

A half an hour later, Dick finished reading. "It's good, Bayard," he said, half-serious and half-kidding. He knew his uncle was opinionated and wouldn't normally give anyone else credit for anything. But he did give others credit in his version of the Heath story. "I might argue a little bit with it. But for you, it's not bad. Are you going to finish it?"

"Yes, I want to write the whole story. Dad only took it to where your dad died."

"I hope you finish it, Bayard, but I don't know if you'll live long enough to see the whole story finished about the family."

"Well, you can write that some day."

"Maybe I will."

They talked about other things. In the past, Bayard Sr. felt that Dick didn't understand him, and Dick felt Bayard Sr. didn't understand him. Most of the conversation was about the Heath family and how Bayard Sr. felt about the whole situation.

"Skiv and I developed the Heath candy bar, which was the company," Bayard Sr. said. "Dad always wanted everybody in the family in the company, no matter who they were or what ability they had. He wanted everyone treated equally. Ability didn't make any difference.

"I used to argue with Dad that some day it would tear up the business. He wouldn't listen. I was against bringing Vernon in. He wasn't a businessman in any sense. He was a journalist. Yet Dad and Skiv wanted him to come back as an equal partner in a business he had nothing to do with."

Bayard Sr. said he felt it was wrong to give his father thirty-two hundred shares, out of 12,800, in a business he didn't start to allow him to give it to his two daughters so they'd be a part of the company. Bayard Sr. had always believed that Ruby and Mary had husbands to provide for them.

"The only important part of the business was the candy operation Skiv and I created and developed," he said. "All Dad was interested in was the dairy. It lost money, and candy profits subsidized the huge dairy losses. But then he brings everybody into it. I didn't see any reason to bring family members into the company on an equal basis when they didn't have any part of the building of the business. Just being born into the family shouldn't give anybody the right to have a job created that contributes nothing to the success of the company."

Dick nodded in agreement. He was seeing his Uncle Bayard in a different light, bringing with it a new appreciation of him. They had needed this time together. It felt good to both of them.

"Oh, I wanted to tell you, Dick," Bayard Sr. said, a smile tugging at the corners of his mouth. "After Liggett & Meyers sent the offer to everybody, I looked into their stock. I liked it and bought several thousand shares. I've made a lot of money on it. And after the stock split, it's even higher than what I bought it for without the split."

Dick smiled and thought back to the Liggett & Meyers offer. He had been over and over it in his mind over the years. It was too late and unneccesary, but he wondered if anybody would ever understand that Liggett & Meyers was willing to pay so much for the Heath company and why they were so willing. It seemed so clear and simple to him.

In real dollars, the price wasn't really so high in either dollars or Liggett & Meyers stock. The Heath company would have saved the broker commission from the candy sales. The Liggett & Meyers salaried sales force would have eliminated the commission and increased sales.

Adding the Heath bar to its line of products would have added no expenses. With nearly four million in sales, this alone would have been a $200,000 annual savings or additional income with no more effort or increase in production.

The Heath company had high freight charges because it was selling one basic item, normally an average of six to eight cases per order. It was shipping truck and rail car loads to twenty public warehouses throughout the United States. Liggett & Meyers owned its warehouses. Heath items would have been shipped as part of a larger order where the cost would have been cheaper. The freight savings would have resulted in savings of about $450,000.

Administrative costs would have saved more money. Liggett & Meyers had a large IBM computer system in one of its tobacco plants in Durham, North Carolina. The Heath company computer work could be processed on those machines.

And finally, Liggett & Meyers was buying one-minute television spots on various products the company was selling. The plan had been to reduce its commercials to thirty-second spots, add a Heath thirty-second spot and not increase costs. This would have been the biggest boost to sales, and Liggett & Meyers would have automatically put the Heath products in the huge New York-New Jersey market where the company wasn't selling much of anything.

Liggett & Meyers, Dick figured, would have quadrupled Heath's earnings which it had no way to do on its own. It would have allowed Harrington to justify buying the company for far too much to the board of directors. From the cash offer terms, the Heath stockholders would have received those increased efficiency earnings of the Heath company for the first five years.

If the stockholders had taken 900,000 shares of Liggett & Meyers stock, the value of the stock would have gone up even more, reflecting the Heath increased earnings. And in accepting the stock exchange, the Heath stockholders would have benefited from the earnings of all the other divisions of the company. Two years after the offer, Liggett & Meyers increased its dividends to the point where the individual Heath stockholders would have been receiving twelve times the amount of dividends L.S. Heath & Sons, Inc., were paying. All that was in the past, Dick knew, but he was pleased his uncle had benefited from his smart investment in the stock.

They talked for more than an hour after Dick finished reading the manuscript. Not once was Dick even tempted to mention the ice cream bar. He was mellowing a bit, too.

In the process of mellowing, Dick had drifted away from the family and the company. He no longer had a financial interest in it, and business kept him on the road. In 1976, Dick and Betty were divorced after more than twenty years of marriage. He moved to Evansville, Indiana, to build and develop a golf course and private country club he and Maxine Zwermann owned. And although the Oak Meadows Country Club took much of his time, he was still active in the golf tournaments in Robinson and around the country.

Maxine and Carl Zwermann came to the club almost every weekend. One Saturday night they planned to have dinner with Dick at the club restaurant. He was looking forward to the evening.

Then an old girlfriend called. She was a beautiful blonde who had lived at Oak Meadows with her husband. When the husband found out about his wife's affair with Dick, the husband moved her to Florida where they had a second home.

"I've got to go to Lafayette," the woman told Dick in a telephone conversation one day. "I've got it figured where I can get into Evansville for a two-hour layover and be with you between eight and nine Saturday evening. Can you manage that?"

"Sure," Dick said and thought of his dinner date with the Zwermanns. He didn't want to tell them or anyone the reason he needed to be free that night. He liked to be with his partner and her husband, but he loved to be with the woman he'd promised he would meet at the north end of the parking lot in a golf cart ten days later.

By the time he'd gotten off the phone, he had a vague idea of what to do. He would call his old friend Jack Chamblin who was now chairman of the board of directors at the Crawford County Country Club.

"I need a favor, Jack," Dick said as soon as he reached Chamblin.

"What?"

"I need you to have a cocktail party and dinner party, and make sure all the trustees are there a week from Saturday."

"Why?"

Dick explained the circumstances.

Knowing Carl Zwermann was on the board, Chamblin laughed and said, "That's no problem. But what reason do I give everybody?"

"I don't care what you do," Dick said. "Tell 'em it's about changing the name of the club. After all the PGA tournaments and attention there, people still look at it as a little hick-town country club because of the name: Crawford County Country Club—the 4Cs, *Sports Illustrated* called it. Sounds like a singing group."

"Might work. We've talked about it before. But what would we call it?"

"I don't care what you call it. Call it Crooked Creek Country Club or Quail Creek Country Club or whatever. Maybe you ought to call it Charlie Clark Country Club, keeping the 4Cs. The membership won't go with it, anyway. And I need to get away that night."

"Okay. You've got it. Saturday evening. Have a good time."

"You got it. I appreciate you going to the trouble. You'll have fun with the trustees and their wives, though."

A few days later, Maxine called and told Dick that they would have to cancel out on dinner the following Saturday night.

"What's wrong?" Dick asked.

"Jack Chamblin called. He is inviting all the trustees and their wives to the club for a dinner party. He has something important to talk about, and he wants Carl there. I'll be down Monday, but we need to go."

"I understand," Dick said. "Enjoy the party."

Saturday evening at eight o'clock, he was parked in a golf cart at the north end of the parking lot. While waiting for his lover, Dick's mind drifted to the past.

He and Maxine had done six PGA tournaments in Robinson (1968-73) and two PGA tournaments in St. Louis back-to-back with Robinson in 1972 and 1973. Afterwards, he had become commissioner of Tournament Golf International.

It seemed like yesterday that Maxine and he and their Golf Management Services corporation had started the Oak Meadows Country Club real estate complex on D. Mead Johnson's property in Evansville. As he looked around in the fading evening light, he could see the forty-two room lodge, the old home, now a clubhouse doubled in size, the pro shop, the condominium to the west of the club and the $200,000-$400,000 homes built on some of the single-family lots.

He thought about the fifteen hundred-plus members he had gotten, making it the largest country club in Indiana. Looking back at the two million-dollar clubhouse, he could see the crowd and the magnificent structure spread before him like paint on canvas. The millions of dollars that the Zwermanns and his mother had put in Oak Meadows had made it one of the show places of the Midwest.

Standing there alone and enjoying what he had helped create gave him a sense of pride he felt with some of the things he had accomplished. It was a nice feeling. Not as nice as it would have been to be a part of what Liggett & Meyers and the Heath company could have done for the people and economy of Robinson and Crawford County, he thought, but nice.

The place was so full that he and the woman he was meeting had few places to meet in private. And they couldn't be seen in public at Oak Meadows. Most everyone would recognize them. Besides being beautiful, the woman was well-known and had been on the cover of a national magazine. So the only place Dick could find their privacy was on the golf course. The night was warm, and he'd brought a blanket with him.

When she arrived, she jumped in the cart, kicked off her high heels and slid her arms around Dick's neck. They started kissing and carressing each other.

"Let's get out of here," Dick said, pulling back.

"Where are we going?" she whispered. "Can't we go to your office or to a room upstairs? How about one of the lodge rooms?"

"It's too risky. Someone might see us. You stand out like a Christmas tree."

"I made it as fast as I could. I've got an hour."

He started the cart and headed down the left side of number one fairway, cut across both number one and number nine fairways to park under the spreading branches of the huge two hundred-year-old oak tree, the tree that gave him the idea for Oak Meadows.

From there they could see the dining room and the upstairs cocktail lounge overlooking the course. They could see the lights and the people down the hill through the darkness. Dick spread the blanket on the ground, and they spent the hour together.

At nine p.m., the woman was on her way out of Evansville and on to Layfayette. And Dick was back in the clubhouse, having a martini.

Maxine called the next day and told Dick about the party and about the presentation Chamblin made to the board. The board passed the proposal. Now it had to be taken to the full membership for a vote.

"I'll be damned," Dick said.

Not long afterwards, Bayard Sr. paid Dick a visit. The old man was in his early eighties and was not in good health.

He had gotten Wayne Morrow, president of the Crawford County State Bank, to drive him to Evansville. Bayard Sr. was still chairman of the board of the bank.

"Dick, you've got to get back up to Robinson and do something," Bayard Sr. said immediately.

"About what, Bayard?"

"They're trying to change the name of the club to Quail Creek. Skiv and I were founding members of the Crawford County Country Club. That was nineteen hundred and twenty-four. We worked hard for the club. And that name should remain."

Dick saw that he was serious and that the membership was apparently serious about changing the name. At this point, Dick didn't know what he could do. He didn't really want the name changed. He'd just wanted some time for love-making. But he promised his uncle he'd see what he could do to head off the name change.

At the next regular meeting, the membership voted to change the name of the Crawford County Country Club to the Quail Creek Country Club. Dick never for a minute thought that would happen when he mentioned the idea to Chamblin.

The next New Year's Eve, Carl and Maxine Zwermann and Curt and Francis Huber, the couple who got Dick and Maxine to start the project in Evansville, were at a table with Dick. Next to them sat the Jesse Texieras, the Ed Cores and Jack Morris Jr. who had all come to Oak Meadows for the night.

During dinner, Jack looked over at Dick, cocked one eyebrow up and said, "Well, Dick, they finally did something up at the country club that you didn't have anything to do with."

"What's that, Jackie?"

"They changed the name of the club," Jack said and explained what had happened in elaborate detail. When he finished, he said, "And you never had anything to do with it. How about that?"

"Oh, you never know," Dick said, smiling. "You never know when my ghost is floating around up there somewhere."

Maxine looked suspiciously at him. She never said anything but later asked him why he'd said that when he knew he didn't have anything to do with the name change.

"Well, you never know," he said and let it go at that.

Bayard Sr.'s health continued to fail. Finally, he fell into a coma and was hospitalized in Robinson. Bayard Jr. and his wife Pat came up from Miami. His sister Pat came back from California. And after Bayard Jr. called Dick in Evansville, Indiana, he rushed to the hospital.

For a few minutes after he arrived, Dick visited with Bayard Jr. and Pat, then looked at Bayard Sr. lying in the bed in a coma.

"It doesn't look good," Bayard Jr. said. "He's been unconscious for quite a while."

They stood around talking quietly for half an hour. Dick chuckled as he thought about his uncle's hostility toward the ice cream-bar franchise.

"I'll wake him up," Dick said to his two cousins and walked over to their father's bedside. Leaning down with his mouth close to his uncle's ear, Dick said, "Before you go, you had better tell me you were wrong about the ice cream bar."

At first, Bayard Sr.'s eyelids moved slightly and the lashes fluttered momentarily. Then he snapped out of it and came flying out of the coma.

"I wasn't wrong about that ice cream bar," he said weakly. "You know better than that."

Within minutes, Bayard Sr. was all right for the moment. Dick had hit him better than any adrenalin shot. Everybody was surprised, except Dick. He told them he could still get his uncle's attention.

By the next day, however, Bayard Sr. was gone. He was the last of L.S. and his four sons. After the funeral, he was buried in the family plot with his wife, Beth, his father and mother and his three brothers.

At the graveside, Dick stood while his uncle's coffin sat before the family and friends and words were being said. Dick thought about his father, buried a few feet away, and what might have been. With Skiv alive, the company would have turned out differently.

As it was, Dick had told many of his friends how the script would go after Bayard Jr. and he left. Anybody looking at the numbers of the stock who knew the players would have known the next step. It would only take a little time for that to happen, Dick thought.

33

In the mid-seventies, a tremendous shortage of sugar occurred and sugar prices soared. Any company using sugar had no choice but to raise prices. The nickel candy bars had already disappeared. But it took nearly forty years for the Heath English Toffee Bar to go from a nickel to a dime.

During the next few years, candy bars went from a dime to forty cents and higher. And there was inflation during this time, but not 400 percent. What happened was the effect of changing sugar prices. After buying Pete's stock and putting the company and directors deeply in debt, the sugar prices forced the price of candy bars up to a quarter at the peak of the sugar shortage.

This shortage lasted long enough for the consumer to get accustomed to paying the inflated prices. Then sugar prices suddenly plummeted to their preshortage, normal price, but neither the candy nor the bottling industries lowered their prices any significant or corresponding amount.

Without a doubt, the rise and fall of the sugar prices were a godsend to not only the Heath company but to all companies in the industry. It was a break unparalleled in the history of the industry. Because of the Heath company's tremendous debt, it benefited enough to get some of the load off its back and move ahead.

A windfall like the "sugar bonanza" is a once-in-a-lifetime

thing. Most people go through life without ever having one. The Heath family had had several. Now with the three buyouts and the new plant debt, another lucky break happened at the right time.

All through this period, market prices fluctuated wildly at times. To continue making a profit, the company had to always be on the lookout to cut costs. Because of the rising price of butter, the company had decided to change the toffee formula in 1967 from butter, almonds, sugar and chocolate by substituting margarine.

The public caught on right away. Andy Rooney brought it up on *60 Minutes* in a commentary about things not being the way they used to be years ago. As an example, he talked about how good the Heath English Toffee Bar used to be compared to the new version with margarine and read the labeled ingredients. That didn't help the company and candy image. Nearly ten years later, the company changed to a soybean oil and other additives.

In the early period that Dick was with the Heath company, the family never had a fear of another company getting in the toffee candy field. Everybody thought other companies wouldn't consider it worth the narrow percentage of toffee candy consumed relative to other types of candy.

Additionally, the margin of profit was small. And the one thing the Heath company didn't want to get into was a merchandising war. Not only did the company not have the huge advertising dollars but total distribution was weak and costs were high.

To further cut costs and increase profits, the Heath company decided to save some money on chocolate and get into the chocolate business. The company put in its own chocolate plant and quit buying coatings from Nestle.

Not long afterwards, Nestle came out with its own toffee ice cream bar, and Hershey came out with its own toffee candy bar called Skor. The ingredients of the toffee candy contained butter and almonds and tasted much like the original Heath bar.

Because of his poor leadership, John's presidency was in the way from the beginning. He loved the prestige but wasn't the one to lead the company. And since his stock was too big of a block for the company to acquire, he was kept happy and out of the everyday running of the business.

During this period, Jack Morris Jr. became the first chief executive officer (CEO) in a newly created position. While there had been no CEO in the past and the president, in principle, ran the company, Dick thought it was easy to see why the new rung in the corporate ladder had been added during John's presidency. The CEO, when there was one, voted the treasury stock. That was now seventy-five hundred shares, the shares that L.S.'s first three sons had gotten when the company incorporated in 1946.

With the title, Jack Jr. controlled the board and company decisions. The titles of president and chairman of the board meant nothing. It didn't matter who had those titles. And Mary's and Ruby's twenty-eight hundred shares and Vernon's family's twenty-five hundred shares added up to only fifty-three hundred shares. The CEO ran the company, no matter what his mother, his aunt or anyone else thought.

All the while, the company faced the possibility of the death of one of the stockholders and the resultant inheritance and capital gains taxes which would necessitate selling stock to outsiders because the company couldn't finance a buyout of the outstanding stock.

Nobody knew what was going to happen. And before anything did, Bob was killed in a car-truck accident, and everyone was reminded that it really wouldn't matter what happened to the Heath company in the grand scheme of life. By this time, Bob's eyes had failed him badly. He was getting tunnel vision and probably shouldn't have been driving.

In his capacity as president of the University of Illinois Alumni Association, he was on his way to Indiana University in Bloomington to arrange for a joint meeting between the two alumni associations. On U.S. Highway 41 near Sullivan, Indiana, he pulled out across the four-lane roadway in front of a large coal truck coming from his right. The truck was unable to stop and struck the car broadside. Bob was killed instantly.

Dick was in his Marion, Illinois, home waiting for a call from John Rooney, originally from Robinson and the chief financial officer of Guaranty Federal Savings and Loan of Galveston, Texas, to find out if a five million-dollar loan for Dick's latest project, a coal operation, had gone through. At 9:05 a.m. on September 14, 1981, Maxine Zwermann called to tell him of Bob's death. Dick was stunned. The two cousins hadn't been close for a long time. They hadn't played golf together since the summer of 1968 when Bob quit playing much golf and took up tennis.

Other than the time he had stopped by the house after Bob's ouster from the company, Dick only saw Bob a few times. He rarely came to the club when Dick was still around. And when he moved on to Evansville, there was no chance of running into Bob. Still, Dick was struck and hardly believed his cousin could be dead. They'd been through a lot together. And he was a survivor.

Two minutes later, Jack Chamblin called to tell Dick about

Bob. Then Thelma called. She asked Dick to be with her and Joyce at the funeral two days later. He agreed. No sooner had he hung up the phone than it rang again. It was John Rooney. He had told Dick he would call at exactly nine a.m. with the results of the loan application.

"I thought you'd be waiting for my call," Rooney said. "Your phone has been busy for half an hour."

"Bob just got killed this morning, John," Dick said. "I've been on the phone about that."

"Oh, I'm sorry to hear that. How'd it happen?"

Dick filled him in on the particulars, then asked about the loan.

"You got it, Dick. All five million."

Before the funeral, Jean caused a minor uproar by announcing that she absolutely would not allow her husband to be buried in the Heath plot at the old Robinson cemetery. She didn't want him buried with the other Heaths, even though the ones buried there had nothing to do with what had been done to Bob. Even Vernon was dead when the move on Bob was made.

But Jean wouldn't even bury Bob in the old cemetery, let alone in the Heath plot. She even insisted that Pete be moved to the new cemetery to be buried near his son.

"What the hell does she want to dig up old Pete for?" Dick asked nobody in particular when the situation occurred. Nobody answered. "This whole family is crazy."

He said nothing to Jean and Thelma, though. He had long stayed out of their business.

Everybody in the family was surprised at the turn of events. But Pete was dug up and moved to the new cemetery. Thelma, who was going to Cocoa Beach, Florida, where Madeline was living, went along with the move.

After Bob's funeral, Dick went to Bob and Jean's home for the last time and sat in the same chair on the patio that he had when he was there after the June Massacre. He sat there for a while, thinking about all those years, almost forty-five years, since Bob and he began their almost inseparable ways. It seemed so long ago.

Dick thought of the old saying that "you can win if you have the game in your hands." For a fleeting moment, he believed the game had been in their hands. They had had the opportunity to create something so rare that few other people ever had the opportunity to do. The heights to which Dick thought they could have taken the Heath company were virtually unending. It would have been something that made history, a memorial forever to the Heath family, there long after Bob and he were both gone.

As Dick left the house, he paused at his car and looked back one more time. "Oh," he said softly, "what a game we could have played, my old brother."

AFTERWORD

Jesse Texiera was elected president of L.S. Heath & Sons, Inc., in 1983, becoming the first non-family member to hold the title. He had started his climb to the top long ago and skillfully worked through the steps. He also had been the first non-family member elected to the board of directors, other than two bank directors who were needed for the money when the company was heavily in debt. Not bad for an old candy peddler, I thought, when I heard about Texiera's good fortune.

To elect him president, Ruby Dowling's vote was needed. She was eighty-five years old at the time and had her assets in a trust administered by the Continental Bank in Chicago. Although she had a vote on the board of directors, neither she nor her sister Mary Morris were ever involved in the family business and were given Heath company stock by their father and brothers. Ruby, who had no children, had always intended to give her assets, equally, back to the heirs of L.S. Heath.

She took the train to Chicago to meet with her trust officers periodically and was so proud the bank was her trustee and represented her so well. But that trusteeship was changed to her friend Herbert Kuebler just before Texiera became president, and the money apparently was left to Mary's family upon Ruby's death. John knew he was out as president and filed suit to have Ruby declared incompetent. That suit never reached the trial stage and was settled out of court.

John was bumped up to chairman of the board, with Allan as vice chairman — both with salaries of $250,000 annually to keep them from making a fuss about a change in Ruby's trust and will. As chief executive officer, Jack Jr. had control of the company. He was in charge. And essentially, considering John and Allan's empty titles, save for Jack Jr., all the Heaths were out of the business.

Neither Jack Jr. nor Texiera wanted John to be involved in it, anyway. So with his title and hefty salary, John moved to Phoenix and was only required to come back for board meetings four times a year. He was safe out there, and it was cheaper than buying out his family. As he had done in the past, John continued to fly around the country in the company plane and sit on committees and boards outside the company.

In Robinson, the company struggled to keep the family business intact, keeping one eye on the business and one eye on the age of the stockholders. When any one of them died, it would be virtually impossible to buy the stock and keep an outsider from getting a foothold in the company.

John knew the situation and began considering his options. I saw the story unfolding and sat helplessly by as it happened. The biggest loser in the Liggett & Meyers deal, to my way of thinking, was the company itself. Had the family sold the company for the 900,000 shares of Liggett & Meyers stock, as I had wanted it to, or even if everybody had agreed to the cash offer, none of the current problems would be of any concern. With the Liggett & Meyers two-for-one stock split in 1974, less than five years after the offer for the Heath company, the Heath family would have had 1.8 million shares and maintained dividends had the stock offer been accepted.

In 1983, the full implications of not having accepted the

Liggett & Meyers offer became apparent. Grand Metropolitian of England purchased Liggett & Meyers for sixty-nine dollars a share. Not counting any dividends throughout the fifteen years since the offer, the Heath company stock would have been worth $124,000,000, a figure 310 times the 1969 Heath company earnings.

I calculated one day that if all the dividends the Heath family would have received had been reinvested in Liggett & Meyers stock, the total stock the family later owned would have been in excess of $200,000,000. And while I was speculating, I thought, there was no telling what it could have led to or what the value would be if I would have had a crack at acquiring all those companies Harrington had wanted.

The reality of the situation was that the Heath family was practically out of the business. John's family could sell out or someone could die at any time. It was a game of chance. John had played one of his cards by trying to break Ruby's trust. That had been a move to neutralize the voting of her stock and give him more control by retaining the company presidency. When he accepted the money for not continuing with the suit and moved to Phoenix, Arizona, however, it virtually guaranteed that L.S.'s dream of a family-owned business would come to an end.

While that may not have been Ruby's intention, she was not overly sensitive to other people's concerns. Her husband, Bernard Dowling, had died in the mid-seventies. A few of the family members were in attendance at the small Catholic funeral. I had made a 160-mile drive on a rainy day to pay my respects. Ruby said she didn't like funerals and didn't attend.

At any rate, nothing more came of the issues of Ruby's competency and the change of her trust after the agreement was reached and the salaries and positions for John and Allan were set. That was the end of the tactic, but John was beginning to see that his fat salary as chairman of the board for backing off would be a paltry sum compared to what he could get for his shares of Heath stock. He liked his life in Phoenix. And it took money to keep living that way.

Later, when Jesse Texiera retired to Texas, Ron Bailey was elected president. Jack Morris Jr. remained as chief executive officer and the controlling force in the company. He had Ruby's and Mary's shares, given to them by L.S. so they would always have an income, behind him. That represented a 52.9 percent majority interest of outstanding stock, and he had the voting rights to the company treasury stock.

John had no say-so in the company. He carried very little weight. He did have some 47.1 percent of the outstanding Heath stock in his immediate family and started looking around for a buyer. That was his big card.

As usual, the company got the first crack at buying the stock. With the economic circumstances being what they were and the stock worth what it was, there was no way the company would be able to come up with the thirty million dollars John wanted for his family's stock. The company had several things working against it.

For openers, Ruby was in her late eighties, and Mary was in her early seventies. At their deaths, estate taxes would take 30 percent and inheritance taxes would take 25 percent for a total of 55 percent of the total stock value. An untimely death could virtually wipe out the company.

On the other hand, if John sold his 47.1 percent to an outsider, it would just be a matter of time before Ruby or Mary did die. Then a well-financed outsider could quickly gain control of the majority interest. It wouldn't be long before the entire company would be swallowed up.

That's where Jim Hanlon stepped back into the Heath picture. He had left the company about the same time as Bayard Jr. and I at the time of the Liggett & Meyers offer. All I knew was that Hanlon had gone to Peter Paul in some sort of sales capacity. It didn't surprise me when I heard that he became president of the company. Nor did it surprise me that Hanlon had later become president of Cadbury Frye, a large Canadian company. Then I lost track of him and what he was doing.

While I didn't know about him, Hanlon went to Leaf, Inc., to become president of its American operations. When I heard that Hanlon was president and had engineered the purchase of John's 47.1 percent of the outstanding company stock, I wasn't surprised, either. Obviously, the Morrises and Ruby's executor could not match the figure Hanlon had offered to John.

"The game is going to be history as far as the family in the Heath company," I told a friend when I heard about the sale. "It's only going to be a matter of time."

"Why?"

"When Ruby dies, and she is now in her late eighties, the price of her stock would be valued for inheritance tax purposes at the same price Leaf paid John. With Leaf owning 47.1 percent of the company, Hanlon and his people would never allow the company to buy her stock. The trust, whatever it is, could not raise the funds to pay the tax without selling even a little bit of the stock. After a $600,000 exemption, inheritance taxes take about 50 percent. And the stock sold goes to the highest bidder."

I was rather amused by the whole turn of events.

After John sold out in 1987, Jack Jr. and Bailey searched for ways to stave off the impending takeover or buyout. No solution could be found. Negotiations between Leaf, Inc., and L.S. Heath & Sons, Inc., for the remaining 52.9 percent of outstanding stock began in earnest in the fall of 1988. By Christmas, an agreement had been reached to purchase the stock for thirty-five million dollars.

I was happy for everybody in the family who shared in the Leaf buyout. What I didn't like was that many of the administrative and sales employees weren't taken care of. In a quick paring down of salaries and transfer of administrative duties, many of the old Heath employees were given severance pay and let go.

Jack Jr. and Bailey, the chief executive officer and president, were not retained in the agreement. The final stock went for the price it did because it was voting stock, and Leaf gained control of the company by getting the CEO position and the last family member out of the business. For all intents and purposes, that closed the door on the seventy-five-year history of the Heath company that started in a little store on the Robinson Square.

What remained on my mind, however, was how Ruby's money from the trust became a part of the Bay-Mor Investments, Inc., capital. When she died in May 1994, I filed an intent-to-sue notice in the circuit court in Robinson, charging fraud in the changing of Ruby's will. That suit was subsequently filed in federal court in Benton, Illinois, in November 1994, against the estates of Ruby Dowling and Mary Morris (who died just weeks after Ruby and left a large portion of her estate to a trust, administered by the First National Bank of

Oblong, Illinois, to supply funds for worthy organizations in Crawford County, Illinois), John R. Morris Jr., Robert R. Morris Sr., Herbert Kuebler, trustee of the Ruby Dowling trust, and Heath Investment Capital, Inc.

I knew the last battle within the family would take place after the Heath story was published. If Ruby's will had been changed, it would have had to have been when she was in her eighties and nearly or completely incompetent. By the time it would have been done, most of the family members still alive were far removed from the business.

I don't know how the final chapter of the Heath family will read. I only know there will be a final chapter, even though it may be dragged out in court for years. In 1969, Bayard Jr. and I did not fight. This time, I plan to fight through to the end. What started out as a nice, sweet story about a humble family building a successful business has turned quite bitter.

— RICHARD J. HEATH
DECEMBER 1994